History

(12)

PEASANTS REVOLT
and
Agrarian Reforms

By

Dr. Ashok Kumar Singh

Commonwealth

Peasants Revolt and Agrarian Reforms

Edition **2027**

ISBN 81-900046-6-2

Published by :
COMMONWEALTH PUBLISHERS (P) LTD.
4831/24, Govind Lane,
Ansari Road, Darya Ganj,
New Delhi - 110002
Ph. : 23272541, 23242541
e-mail : commonwealthpublishers2016@gmail.com

Distributed by :
ARJUN PUBLISHING HOUSE
4831/24, Govind Lane,
Ansari Road, Darya Ganj,
New Delhi - 110002
Ph. : 23272541, 23242541
e-mail : arjunbooks2001@gmail.com

Laser Typesetting by :
Dimple Computers
Delhi

Printed at :
Milan Enterprises
Delhi

PEASANTS REVOLT AND AGRARIAN REFORMS

CHAMBAL VALLEY DEVELOPMENT FOUNDATION

SERIES

5

DEDICATED
to my
RESPECTED PARENTS
Sri SHRI NARAIN SINGH
and
Smt. KAMALA SINGH

Preface

The plight of the peasants of Awadh was noted by Jawahar Lal Nehru, who had his first experience of rural conditions under the taluqdars when he visited some disturbed areas in the district of Pratapgarh. Their miserable conditions can best be described in his own words ; '... I listened to their innumerable tales of sorrow, their crushing and evergrowing burden of rent, illegal exactions, ejectments from land and mud-huts ...... toiling all day to find what they produced was not theirs ......' Such being the conditions, the 'Agrarian unrest in United Provinces with special reference to Awadh Region', though strictly regional and time-bound, deserved, it was felt, closer scrutiny.

There are only a few published works, which provide some useful information on this subject. Irwin's—*The Garden of India* presents a critical study of the taluqdari system in Awadh, while Sarvadhikari's work—*The Taluqdari Settlement in Oudh*, based on *Parliamentary Papers* and Government records, is an attempt to refute Irwin's view point and defend the taluqdari system. Jagdish Raj's *The Mutiny and British Land Policy in North India*, B.R. Misra's *Land Revenue Policy in the United Provinces* and T.R. Metcalf's *Land, Londlords and the British Raj*, and Dr. Virendra Deo Pandey's D. Litt. thesis *Land Revenue Administration of Awadh (1856-1921)*, form only a small part of the present study. The present study fills a gap of an important aspect of the history of United Provinces.

The study is based on original sources, both printed and unprinted. These are in the form of *Proceedings*, *Despatches* and published and unpublished *Administrative Reports*, *Settlement Reports*, *District*, *Pargana* and *Village* Papers. The information gathered from official sources has been checked and verified from other sources wherever these have been available. The author has endeavoured to submit a reliable and balanced account based on the study of original sources. So far as proper names and place names are concerned, these have been spelt according to the present usage, while the original spellings had, of necessity, to be preserved in quotations.

I am deeply indebted to Professor Virendra Deo Pandey under whose continued guidance and encouragement the work has been completed. I am also thankful to Professor S.N. Qanungo and all other staff members of the Department of History, Lucknow University, for their ready and ungrudging help.

It is, however, not possible to thank the very large number of persons by name to whom the author owes his debt of gratitude during all these toiling years. The co-operation of the Staff of the Library and Records Section of the National Archives of India, New Delhi, the Uttar Pradesh State Archives, Lucknow and Allahabad, Uttar Pradesh Secretariat Records Room, and the Nehru Memorial Museum and Library deserves special mention.

And, above all I honestly believe that this book could have never been completed without the blessings of my parents and also my brothers, Sri Anil Singh and Sri Ajai Singh, who have inspired and encouraged me throughout.

Ashok Kumar Singh

Contents

1

Geographical Features and Historical Background

Situated in the heartland of Indian subcontinent, the United Provinces has had a rich and glorious past. Presently nomenclatured as Uttar Pradesh, the state, all through the ages, has occupied a unique position in the social, cultural, religious and economic history of the country as a whole. Recent excavations leading to archaeological finds in several parts of this most populous State have carried its past history to perhaps man's earliest progress on the path of civilization.[1] It is worthy of note that whereas remains of palaeolithic and neolithic cultures have been unearthed in the south-eastern (Mirzapur) parts and the Bundelkhand regions, recent excavations at some places have linked its past with the famous Harappan culture.[2] Further, during the hazy phase of its early past, the land was the birth-place of *Rama* and *Krishna* who embody all that is the best and noblest in the Indian culture and philosophy. It was also the birth-place of the *Buddha* and the tradition of giving birth to pioneers in various fields of culture and polity has been carried on to this day, as shall be noted hereafter. Even during the medieval phase of its history, the earlier tradition was carried on by *Kabir*, *Surdas*, and *Tulsidas* who, as social reformers and trend-

---

1. *Archaeological Survey of India, Report, 1958-59.* pp. 17-18.
2. *Ibid.*, Report on the Excavations at Atranji-kher and Alamgirpur. 1963 and 1965.

setters of revivalism, have left deep imprints on the social and philosophical planes of the country.

The State of United Provinces has not only led in the religious and philosophical spheres but has distinguished in other fields as well. While philosopher kings like Pravahana Jaivali, Ajatasatru and the Brahmadattas of Kashi were able administrators, their traditions were carried on by Harshvardhana and other.[1] The city of Kanauj was, for sometime, the capital of India and, during the early medieval period the Chandelas, who were mighty builders, enriched the regions with monuments of lasting fame.[2] Later, the State was a bone of contention between the warring Muslim states with the Sharqis of Jaunpur gaining some prominence till it passed into the hands of the Surs and the mighty Mughals. During the twilight of the latter (Mughals), United Provinces again came into prominence under the illustrious Nawabs of Awadh till ultimately it succumbed to the might of the British.

The present State of Uttar Pradesh has passed through various nomenclatures during the period of its occupation by the British. It was formerly known as the North-Western Provinces and in 1877 the Lieutenant-Governorship of the N.W. Provinces and the Chief Commissionership of Awadh were amalgamated.[3] Its name was changed into the United Provinces of Agra and Oudh in 1902 which was shortened into mere United Provinces in 1921.[4] After the dawn of Independence, it has been named as Uttar Pradesh. Fortunately, during the reorganisation of the provinces into states the boundaries of several provinces underwent changes and

---

1. Mookerji, R.K., *Hindu Civilization*, p. 69.
2. Mitra, S.K., *Early Rulers of Khojuraho*, p. 73.
3. *Uttar Pradesh*, a U.P. Government Publication,
4. *Ibid.*, p. 8.

numerous states were formed out of them, the present state of Uttar Pradesh we spared and its geographical limits remained as before.

For administrative purposes, the former United Provinces was divided into ten (10) Commissionaries or Divisions and forty-eight districts at the beginning of the present review :

Divisions	*Districts*
1. Varanasi	Varanasi, Ghazipur, Jaunpur, Ballia and Mirzapur.
2. Gorakhpur	Gorakhpur, Basti, Azamgarh and Deoria.
3. Allahabad	Allahabad, Fatehpur, Kanpur, Etawah and Farrukhabad.
4. Agra	Agra, Mathura, Etah, Mainpuri and Aligarh.
5. Jhansi	Jhansi, Jalaun, Banda, Hamirpur and Lalitpur.
6. Rohilkhand	Bareilly, Badayun, Bijnor, Moradabad, Shahjahanpur Pilibhit and Rampur.
7. Meerut	Dehradun, Saharanpur, Meerut, Muzaffarnagar and Bulandshahr.
8. Garhwal	Chamoli, Garhwal, Tehri-Garhwal and Uttar Kashi.
9. Lucknow	Lucknow, Unnao, Rae Bareli, Sitapur, Hardoi and Kheri.
10. Faizabad	Faizabad, Gonda, Bahraich, Sultanpur, Pratapgarh and Barabanki.[1]

It would be noticed from the above that the districts have been grouped in the Divisions after taking into consideration their geographical features. The Northern hilly regions have

1. *Uttar Pradesh*, p. 14·

been grouped and named Garhwal Division. Similarly, the Tarai belt districts of the Divisions of Rohilkhand and Gorakhpur have been grouped on same considerations. Though these districts are partly rich in their forest wealth, yet these have been aligned with the agriculture-dominated districts of the plains. The Division of Jhansi comprises those districts that fall into the arid zone. Those of the plains have been grouped into Divisions according to the feasibility of approach to a central district and on considerations their importance as well. The three notable estates—those of Tehri, Rampur and Benares (Varanasi) have since either been a district or merged in the district adjoining them. The Division of Rohilkhand function with headquarter at Bareilly.

On the economic front, the United Provinces has led the way in all types of agricultural products and its richly fertile plains have, in the past been a bone of contention for possession between different dynasties and rulers. It may be mentioned in passing that during the period of study, the state had a surplus agricultural production. Alongside, it had numerous flourishing industries, particularly of cloth-goods, handicrafts and brass-ware which were in great demand in the outside world till the British smothered them through a policy of blanket-monopoly of all export-import trade in the interest of their own industries. In the past, the State was famous for its silk cloth-goods, kimkhwabs and embroidered chiken which were highly prized in Europe along with its brass-ware industry at Varanasi and Moradabad[1] But the emphasis has all along been on agriculture and some 80 per cent of its population has been involved in cultivation and allied works.[2]

British occupation of the State was a gradual process beginning from the days of Robert Clive and ending with the

1. Mukerjee, Radhakamal, *Economic History of India*, 1600—1800, pp. 23—41 (for details).
2. *Uttar Pradesh*, pp. 66 and 76—97.

annexation of Awadh in 1856. They (the British) had very early realised its produtive capacity and the process of its occupation as well as extension towards the Nepal borders took almost a full century and is too well-known to merit any detailed description. As is only natural, the Sate has all along been densely populated. The concentration of population is densest in its eastern districts and gradually recedes as one proceeds west and-north-westwards towards the hilly regions. In so far as the caste composition of the population of the State is concerned, it comprises of the two principal communities of Hindus and Muslims with their numerous castes and subcastes.

There is also a thinly scattered population of Christians particularly in the hill areas as revealed from the Census figures[1]. All *Varnas*, castes and sub-castes engage themselves in agriculture through the upper castes of the Brahmans and Kashatriyas did not formerly take to ploughing themselves. Thus numerous agriculturist communities labelled as agriculturists had come up with the passage of time. Quite a sizeable number of the society belong to the scheduled castes which, too, had developed numerous sub-castes among themselves.

There is, however, a certain anomaly in the Census figures about the caste-composition (both Hindu and Muslims) of the agriculturists. A few examples would make this clear. Many families belonging to the castes and sub-castes of these two communities have taken to industrial occupation. Carders (*dhunias*), painters (*rangrez*), banglessellers (*churihars*), tailors (*darzis*), etc., though partly subsisting on such industrial occupations, might have considerable landed property in their possession, that might be the main source of their large family's subsistence ; yet at the time the Census, these would be denoted as occupational castes, which, in reality, they are

---

1. *Census of India*, Part I, pp. 89 (1911) : *Ibid.* 1921, pp. 79—86.

not[1]. This peculiarity is common to both communities, Hindu and Muslim. A leather-worker (*chamar*) might have managed to acquire considerable land for cultivation, but at the time of Census he would get himself entered in the books as a leather-worker[2]. Such anomalies apart, almost all castes, high and low, depend largely on agricultural pursuits in the State.

The total area of the vast-extending State of United Provinces is some 2·94 lakh sq. Kms. and almost two-thirds of this has been under cultivation since very early times[3]. Barring the hilly terrain or the slopes of the Himalayas which comprise the division of Garhwal noted earlier, the arable land of the State can be divided into three zones from the agricultural point of view. The first is the *Tarai* area which stretches from the lower reaches of the Himalayas and extends eastwards comprising the northern fringes of the districts of Bareilly, Pilibhit, Kheri (Lakhimpur), Sitapur, Gonda, Basti and Gorakhpur. Though the area is noted for its forest-wealth, yet its soil is rich and eminently suited for the cultivation of sugarcane, wheat, rice and jute[4]. This area has almost a monopoly of sugar mills, as shall be related later.

The next or the second zone is the Gangetic Doab which is generally indicative of the land lying in between the rivers Ganga and Yamuna but also includes the land watered by the numerous tributaries of the Ganga that spring from the lower slopes of the Himalayas, Since the annual rains have perennially brought own alluvial contents and compost from the

---

1. Crooke, W., *Natives 6f Northern India*, p. 130.
2. Crooke, W,, *Natives of Northern India*, p. 124 (also the Chapter '*The Castes of the Plains*', pp. 85—105 and the next Chapter '*Industrial Castes*', p. 106 ff).
3. *Uttar Pradesh*, p. 12 ff.
4. *Ibid.*, pp. 76—120.

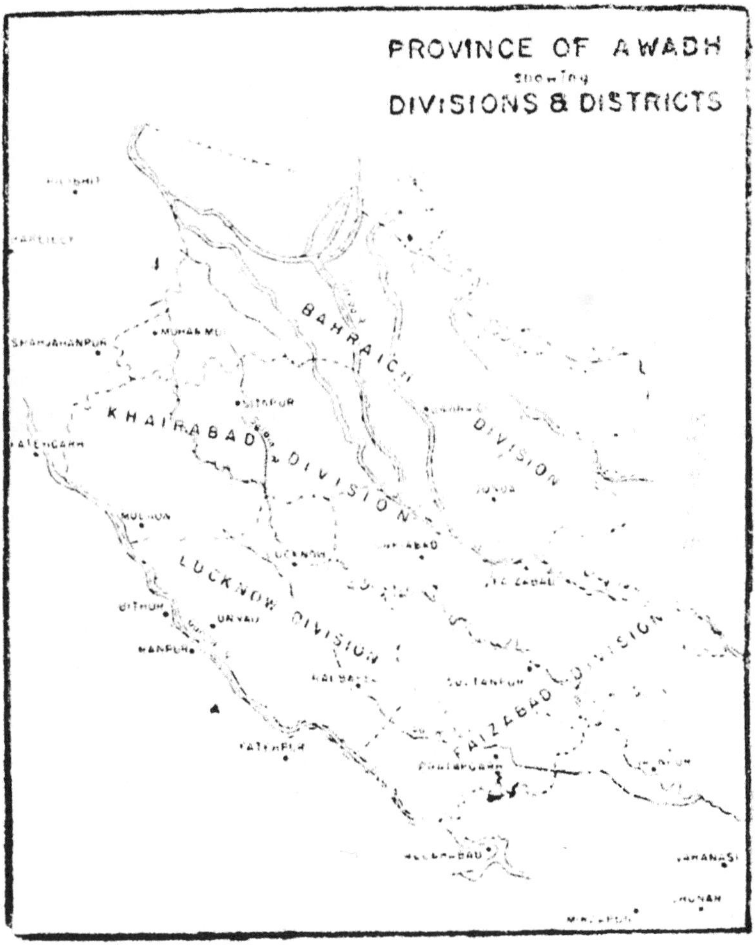
PROVINCE OF AWADH
showing
DIVISIONS & DISTRICTS
BAHRAICH DIVISION
KHAIRABAD DIVISION
LUCKNOW DIVISION
FAIZABAD DIVISION
SHAHJAHANPUR
SITAPUR
BITHUR
SULTANPUR
VARANASI

forests of the north, the whole tract is noted for its fertility. Beside the numerous minor streams, the notable rivers flowing through this region are the Yamuna (Jamuna), Ganga, Ramganga, Kali, Sharda, Gomti, Ghaghra and the Rapti the Sai and the Tons, (Now named Tamsa) not excepted. All these have contributed both to the affluence and misery of the people of the State[1].

The third zone comprises of the districts falling within the Division of Jhansi, southern parts of the districts of Allahabad and the Mirzapur district[2]. Since the Vindhyan plateau slopes northwards, this region is hilly and not favourable to the same degree of agricultural productivity as the Doab. Scarcity of water and rainfall (as shall be noted later) plague this region. This region has three rivers, the Cambal, the Betwa and the Ken that emanate from the Vindhyan Range and join the Yamuna while another river, the Tones, also having its source in the Vindhyas, joins the Ganga as that rivers meanders towards Varanasi (this Tons is not to be confused with the northern Tons noted earlier). The waters of these rivers had not been utilised fully during the period of the present review.

The three regions and the Garhwal tract receive differing amounts of rainfall during the year. Thus wile the hilly regions normally raceive in between 100 and 200 cms., of rainfall and the Terai area also receives more than 100 cms., the Gangetic plains receive 100 to 120 cms. in the eastern parts and 80 to 100 cms. in the western[3]. However, the extreme northern regions receive in between 260 and 300 cms.

---

1. Srivastava, H.S., *History of Indian Famines and Development of Famine Policy*, 1858—1918, p. 326, for floods as causing famines and misery to the people.
2. *Uttar Pradesh*, pp. 1—3.
3. *Uttar Pradesh*, pp. 4-5.

annually[1]. The arid regions of the Jhansi Divisions receive about 60 to 80 cms. annually, if the raingods are merciful[2]. Most of the rainfall is between the months of mid-June to September and only 7 per cent of the total rainfall is received in the winters[3]. The districts of Deoria and Gorakhpur receive the highest amount of rainfall (avrrage 184·7 cms.) in the plains while Mathura receives the least (average 54·4 cms).

While the Northern regions are rich in forest and mineral wealth, the fertility of the Doab has been almost legendary. During the Hindu period of its history several dynasties rose and fell vying for its possession.[4] Even during the period of Muslim occupation, its productivity was a byword and tempted Mohammed Bin Tughluq to impose heavier taxes on the agricultur ists of the Doab. It was left to Shershah and Akbar to bring about rationality of taxation on an equitable basis of production. So far as the arid regions of Jhansi division are concerned, several tanks and reservoirs were caused to be constructed by Hindu rulers, particularly the Chandellas, which however, fell into decay in later times and little attempt was made even during the British period to relieve the masses of this region from their sufferings[5].

There are two principal cropping seasons in the State, known as *Kharif* and *Rabi*, the former sown during the monsoon days and the latter during the onset of the winter. The principal crops raised are those of wheat, rice, barley, maize, millet, oilseeds, sugarcame and certain types of coarse grains, though hemp, jute and cotton are also grown mostly in the Tarai and north-western regions[6]. In earlier times, the peasantry had to depend on walls and tanks for irrigation and

1. *Ibid.*,
2. *Ibid.*
3. *Ibid.*
4. Smith. V.A., *Early History of India*, pp. 8—9.
5. Mitra, S.K, *Early Rulers of Khajuraho*, pp. 6, 33, etc..
6. *Uttar Pradesh*, p. 76.

the credit for constructing a major canal for the first time goes to Shah Jahan whose Jamuna Canal was renovated by the East India Company and named as the Eastern Jamuna Canal[1]. Just before the holocaust of 1856—57 the Upper Ganges Canal (1854) has been constructed ; subsequently the Agra Canal (1874), the Lower Ganges Canal (1878), Betwa Canal (1885), Ken Canal (1907), Dhasan Canal (1911), Garai Canal (1915), and the Ghaghra Canal (1916) were constructed before the period of the present review.

Section—II

It is generally agreed that the basic stanchion for the socio-economic development of all societies the world over both in the past and the present has been agriculture, and such progress, through agriculture and its allied industries involves many consideration, Of these latter, the factors of land, the people, their political constitution, and the administrative machinery (especially when the country is in bondage) are of prime importance. Natural conditions, environment, standard of civilization achieved and other circumstance in a country are a part thereof might differ leading the inhabitants to other vocations like hunting and fishing for subsistence, but the basis remains the same. This is very true in the case of the Indian sub-continent of which the State of United Provinces is an integral part. Earlier, a brief notice of the geographical features, climatic conditions, the people and the arability of the land of the State has been submitted ; the various systems of landownership and its (land's) distribution prior to the days of the present inquiry may be briefly outlines along with their relation to the other two factors, *viz.*, political constitution and the admistrative machinery.

It would be presumptuous on our part to detail an account of the various land-systems the peasantry and the people have enjoyed since long past, as these have arrested the attention

---

1. *Uttar Pradesh*, p. 76.

of eminent schloars and been authoritatively dealth with[1]. Yet a brief notice of the system and the conditions in which the peasantry lived and laboured prior to the beginning of the present inquiry would, it is felt, not be out of place. The first consideration is land itself and it "can be variously classified as cultivable, cultivated, fallow. barron, low, high, hilly, marshy, jungly... fit for becoming a house-site... reclaimed from river-bed, etc."[2] Since long past, there had been controversy regarding the ownership of the land—as to whether it belonged to the ruler or the actual tiller of the soil[3]. The consensus of opinion among the authorities during the Hindu period of Indian history was that the ruler's ownership of the land was "rather theoretical" than actual[4].

---

1. Cf. Sircar, D.C., *Landlordism and Tenancy in Ancient and Medieval India as revealed by Epigraphical records* ;
   Habib, Irfan, *Agrarian System of the Moghul Empire* ;
   Gupta, S.C., *Agrarian Relations and Early British Rule in India,*
   Baden-Powell, B.H., *Land System of British India,* 3 Volumes ;
   Ibid,, *Land Revenue Administration in British India,*
   Carnegy, Patrick, *Notes on the Lend Tenures and Revenue Assessments in Upper India* ;
   Siddiqi, M.H., *Agrarian Unrest in India. The United Provinces* ;
   Siddiqi, Asia, *Agrarian Change in a North Indian* State—Uttar Pradesh ;
2. Sircar, D.C., *Landlordism and Tenancy in Ancient and Medieval India,* p. 3.
3. *Ibid.*, pp. 1—3.
4. *Ibid.*, p. 2 ; Recently, Dr. V.D. Pande has also investigated the '*Land Revenue Administration of Awadh*' (1056—1921) and the supplicant is indebted to many of his suggestions regarding the actual conditions obtaining in the two Divisions of Awadh (Lucknow and Faizabad) towards the beginning of the present inquiry.

Ever since the tumultuous of 1857, the attention of the British had been focussed more towards tho mainfold problems concerning the safety of their vast possessions in India from some real and imaginary threats from the *North-West particularly from Russia*[1]. Convequently, only luke-warm efforts had been made towards pressing problems concerning the lot of the peasantry of the State, promotion of agriculture and uniform system of land tensure. There were different systems of the latter throughout the country ; the *Ryotwary* System neld sway in the southern provinces (states) ; Bengal and Bihar had the controversial Permanent System of Settlement along with a microscopic part of United Provinces (parts of Ghazipur and Varanasi districts) ; rest of the State of United Provinces had both *Zamindari* and *Taluqdari* systems while the Punjab had a different one[2]. Since United Provinces did not offer any Scope for taxation on the industrial side, the British were in favour of S" periodical settlements (of land tenure) for short terms"[3] with a view to augment their income from land-revenue. Apart from stabilising the hold of the landlords and *taluqdars on* the tenantry. After the first cedastral settlement two other settlements were made which have been noted and commented upon by various scholars[4]. Owing to the changed political conditions in the country, there was no fourth Settlement after the struggle for freedom gained momentum[5].

The primary consideration that exercised the minds of the

---

1. Cf. Majumdar, R.C. (ed.), *British Paramountcy Indian Renaissance*, Part I, p. 1000 ff.
2. Cf Majumdar, R.C., (ed.), *British Paramountcy and Indian Renaissance*, Part I, pp. 360 ff., 806 ff., 878 ff.
3. *Ibid.*, p. 360.
4. Driver, P.N., *Problems of Zamindari and Land-tenure Construction in India.*
5. Pandey, V.D., *Land Revenue Administration of Awadh*, pp. 175—267.

Settlement Officers was logically *,the merit or rate of assessment'* of revenue on the cultivators "whether they be in Oudh or the North-western Provinces" (or the whole of the U.P. State)[1]. Patrick Carnegy, who was one of the Settlement Officers, had thus summarised his mode of assessment.[2] According to him, "the gross produce per ordinary cultivator will be (could be) Rs. 20/- per annum." He further continues : "Of this sum, three-fifths or Rs. 12, will be absorbed as the cultivator's own share, and the remaining two-fifths, or Rs. 8, will go to the proprietor as gross rental, this being the proportion in which the produce is very generally, though by no means invariably divided, between landlord and tenant. Of this latter amount at 51¼ per cent, Rs. 4·3 will be paid to Government as revenue and cesses ; and Rs. 3·13 remain as the landlord's profit."[3] He considered this mode or the ratio as 'light'.[4]

Even assuming that the above mode of assessment and the calculated share of the landlord was justified, there was no check on the latter (landlord) to realise, and stick to, his stipulated share of profit amounting to Rs. 3·13, as conceived by Carnegy or the other Settlement Officers for obvious reasons. In the first place, there was no law to check the landlord from realising more than what had been in the minds of the Settlement Officers. Secondly, as pointed out by scholars often times, the Settlement Officers were, as per the Government's overt policy, not to antagonise the landlords who enjoyed "the blessing of either the British rule or of the oriental despotism" and "suffered in f ll measure from the glaring evils of both"[5].

1. Carnegy, Patrick, *Notes on the Land Tenures and Revenue Assessment in Upper India*, p. 125.
2. *Ibid.*
3. *Ibid.*
4. *Ibid.*
5. Majumdar, R.C., (ed.), *British Paramountcy and Indian Renaissancy*, pp. 295, 391.

Thirdly, as pointed out earlier, in the absence of industries, there was tremendous pressure on land owing to a continuous growth in the population of the State. Fourthly, while the traditional methods of agriculture still held good throughout the country, the land, having been in continuous cultivation for more than 3,000 years, had lost much of its productive capacity. Finally, recurring fragmentations of fields owing to divisions in the families of the people, it (productivity) was further going down. (Whether the aforesaid mode of assessment was adhered to along with its merits or otherwise, will be seen later).

At this juncture, the system of land-tenure may be taken into consideration. Ever since the North-western Province (excluding Awadh) passed into the hands of the British bit by bit, attempts had been made at "periodical settlements for short terms"[1], till the famous Holt Mackenzie Minute of 1819, which formed the basis of the Regulation VII of 1822.[2] After the annexation of Awadh, a comprehensive survey-settlement, known as the Cadastral Settlement (*Dakini Bandobast*), involving all the distrcts of the State was carried out in between 1859 and 1876. Known as the First Settlement, it formed the basis for the next two settlements of 1890—91 and 1920—21, each after 30 years (in local language, these are known as *Bandobast Doyam* and *Bandobast Soyam*). Titles to fields (land) were broadly classified into two classes, *e.g.*, (1) proprietory and (2) sub-proprietory[3], which may be looked into their details.

---

1. Misra, B.R., *Land Revenue Policy in the United Provinces* for details.
2. Cf Majumbar, R.D. (ed,), *Britiih Paramountcy and Indian Renaissance*, p. 360.
3. Carnegy- Patrick, *Notes on the Land Tenures*, p. 3. As Settlement Officer, he was incharge of Gorakhpur and Azamgarh (Azimgarh to him) districts.

(The non-proprictory aspect is exclueded here for consideration).

Proprietor Titles : Proprietory titles could be acquired in various ways, *e.g.*, (1) through usurpation, (2) purchase, (3) grant of a charter (sanad), (4) reclamation (of waste land) (5) gift, and (6) hereditament or in manner in which it could pass to the heirs of the proprietor[1].

Sub-proprietory Titles : Sub-proprietory titles could be acquired in various ways and are denoted as (1) *Pukhtadari* (in which the land was held at a fixed rental), (2) *Dihdari* (landed property transferred voluntarily or involuntarily), (3) *Sir* (seer) or (land cultivated by the landholder directly, (4) Nankar land allowance either in cash in return for some services ; when paid in cash, it was known as adai nankar,) (5) Sanklap (properly sonkalap, or land held under a charitaable grant), (6) Birt (land given by landholder for maintenance-often to servants), (7) Bai or Bai-kitat (lond sold by the original proprietor for agricultural purposes specifically) (8) Baghat (groveland very often held under verbal arrangement since earlier times in a family which had divided later and is of various kinds) and (9) Biswi or Biswadar (land under wither mortgage or otherwise but later directly settled with the holder of the land subsequently).

Short of the details, there were, broadly, three types, as pointed out by Dr. Tara Chand.[2] Accordidg to him, there were

1. Carnegy, who was in charge of the settlement work in the districts of Faizabad, and Azamgarh, and has given a detailed account of the proprietory rights, does not seem to have dealt with the rights of certain proprietors who shall be noted later when dealing with certain rights and ccstoms of the villages entered in the *Wajib-ul-Arzes* and *sharah* of families in Awadh.

1. Tara Chand, *History of the Freedom Movement*, Vol. II, p. 54.

three types of tenures, the *taluqdars*, the *zamindars*, and rent-free tenure holders.[1] Most of the sub-proprietory title-holders were under the *taluqdars* and *zamindars* as noted by the settlement officers and detailed by Carnegy.[2] Prior to the annexation of Awadh there was no difference between a *zamindar* and a *taluqdar*, the latter category being a creation of the British, though the word finds mention for the first time in a firman of the mughal ruler, Farrukhsiar.[3] The Mughal system of administration which replaced the earlier set-up, was responsible for introducing various new terms in in its revenue administration like *zamindars, jagirdars* etc., and groups of villages were termed as *parganas* and '*ta'lluqas*'. There does not seem to have been any difference between a *zamindar* and a *taluqdar* in th e earlier stages, as pointed out by Dr. Habib, according to whom "in the latter part of the seventeenth century we come across a new set of terms used practically all over the country, ta' alluqa and *talluqdar*, as substically in certain cases for *zamindari* and *zamindar*."[4]

During the early part of the British rule over the State and particularly after the annexation of Awadh, the term taluqdar gained much currency through it had different meanings or connotations. As pointed out by Carnegy, "In lower province and of the old regulations...... the *talluk* is the smaller, the *zamindari* the larger, property. In Upper India, the reverse is the case ; the ta'alluka is the larger property, to which be smaller *zamindaris* have become attached, or have adhered."[5]

1. *Ibid.*, pp. 54—57.
2. Carnegy, Irfan, *Notes on the Land Tenures*, pp. 3—17.
3. Habib, Irfan, *Agrarian System af Mughal Indta*, p. 172. It may be noted that the term was used in the firman for a tract of land in Bengal (*Ibid*).
4. Habib, Irfan, *Agrarian System of Mughal India*, p. 139 It may be noted that the terms was used in the firman for a tract of land in Bengal (Ibid).
5. Carnegy, P., *Nates on the Land Tenures*, q. 68 ;

The process through which the *taluqdars* came to gain overlordship of the zamindars was quite simple ; the *taluqdars*, during early phase of British regime, contracted to pay revenue for their own group of villages or the taluqas to the British and also stood surety for their smaller bretheren, the zamindars. Whe the latter (*zamindars*), owing to certain stringencies were unable to discharge their obligations in revenue matters, the *taluqdars* quietly appropriated their villages, leaving them some nominal land and sphere of influence in the villages formerly farmed to them.[1] However, in the former North-wastern Province of Agara, there did not develop the *taluqdari* system, as shall be seen later, and it remained a typical revenue feature of the districts of Awadh alone.

It would thus be apparent that the systems of *taluqdari* and *zamindari*, both were prevalent in the State during the early period of the present review. In the North Western Provinces (the Agra part of the State of United Provinces), the Settlement Officers, in their settlement reports, stated that "generally cultivating rights (of tenants) had been "defined and secured" and that the *zamindars* could neither revert to the *Batai* system as long as the cultivators paid their rents in cash" nor can (could) they collect in excess of the rents now fixed".[2] In actual practice. however, both these assertions proved to be wrong.

Thus, through *taluqdars* did exist before 1857, there was hardly any distinction between a *zamindar* and a *taluqdar*. Both were intermediaries and accountable to the Government for the revenue-dues from their respective *zamindars* and

---

1. Habib, Irfan, *Agrarian System of Mughal India*, p. 139 According to the author, this was indirectly encouraged by the authorities "to avoid having to deal with a large number of persons" for governmental revenue dues.
2. Carnegy, P., *Notes on the Land Tenures*, p. 60.

taluqus 'paying about nine-tenths of their entire collections towards State-share, retaining the remaining the remaining one-tenth as their own emolument."[1] But as time rolled on, "in course of time, after accounting to the Government for the assessed amount, they were free to appropriate the surplus amount of rents or (and) profits realised by them"[2]. Due to the unsettled conditions during the declining days of the Mughal rule, all such revenue-farmers, nobles with jagirs, and clansmen (specially *Kshatriyas* claiming possession over villages since the long past days of the Hindu rule but subjugated by the Muslim conquerors) asserted themselves, and as was made home to the British during the days of 1857, the peasantry and the village-men acknowledged their overlordship to the extent of their right to revenues of their cultivated as well as the *parti land* within the villages[3].

Thus, it is clear from the above that there were taluqdars, *zamindars*, proprietory tenants and alsome some titular *rajas* both in the Ceded and conquered Provinces (amounting to Agra, or more precisely, the former North Western Provinces) and Awadh towards the beginning of the nineteenth century As pointed out by Matcalf, the *taluqdars* in the North-Western.

---

1. Pandey, V.D., *Land Revenue Administration of Awadh* : (1856-1921), p. 14.
2. *Ibid.* ; Cf. also Jafri, S.N.A., *History and Status of Landlords and Tenants in the United Provinces*, pp. 81-159.
3. This aspect-the overlordship of the taluqdars and zamindars accepted by their tenantry—was most apparent during 1857 when the rebel taluqdars were given full support by their tenants and has, incidently, partly been responsible for the controversy as to whether the holocaust of their 1857 was 'a war of Independence', Cf. Majumdar, R.C., *British Paramauntcy*, etc., Chapt. 'Revol of the People' and Tara Chand, *History of the Freedom Movement*, Vol. I & II.

Provinces had "no more and perhaps rather less than 20 per cent of the land" whereas 66 per cent of the total land of Awadh was controlled by them in Awadh in 1856[1]. Since there was very few large land-holders in the former (North West Provinces), the task for settlement of land with the village-zamindars and coparcenary communities was undertaken by the British masters with a view to secure a fixed and regular revenue from these areas.

The various experiments tried by the British need not be detailed, as these have already been exhaustively dealt with by various scholars[2]. The short-term (three yearly) settlements were followed by the Holt Mackenzie Minute, in which the policy of 'detail to aggregate' method of assessment was followed; but Bentinck reversed the policy in 1833 when 'aggregate to detail' policy was followed by Bird, his Chief Settlement Officer, and the settlement was to be for a thirty year period[3].

Throughout all these attempts at settlement there was emphasis on raising the revenues of the Government and the policy adopted was one of graduated enhancement in assessments. It (rigorous enhancement) did not stop even when large tracts of the State were laid waste by famines[4]. As

---

1. Metcalf Thomas R., *Land, Landlords, and the British Raj*, p. 54. He submits a detailed account of the policies followed by the British in the following pages (pp. 54-73).
2. Cf. Baden-Powell, *Land System of British India*, Vol. II, p. 204 ff.; Jafri, S.N.A., *History and Status of Landlord and Tenants in the United Provinces*, Chapter II & III. Jagdish Raj, *The Mutiny and British Land Policy in the United Provinces Under British India*, (Introduction).
3. For details. Cf. Metcalf, T.R., *Land, Landlords and the British Raj*, pp. 47-73.
4. Srivastva. H.S., *History of Indian Famines*, pp. 23-27.

pointed out by Srivastava, during the famine of 1801, "the districts of Oudh ceded by the Nawab in 1801, suffered considerably due to the exhorbitant enhancement of the land revenue"[1]. Then again inbetween 1812 and 1815 when the former North-Western Provinces were in the grip of a prolonged famine, the severity of realisation was so great that the '*malguzars*' and the people, unable to meet the revenue demands, "felt better in jails and did not wish to quit them"[2]. Further, the N.W. Provinces and also parts of Awadh were reeling under such distress in years 1832—34, yet there was no let-up and the region "suffered due to overassessment"[3]. Even when the State was suffering from "the most severe famine of the first half of the nineteenth century", the conditions were "aggravated by an excessive revenue demand"[4].

The oppressive revenue policy of the British brought havoc with the landlords and the proprietory tenants. One or two examples would make it clear. In Aligarh, the demand rose from Rs. 19,29,978 in 1804—5 to Rs. 33,14,022 in 1815—16, or more than 70 per cent in those twelve years"[5] in the Ceded and Conquered Provinces for the same period from Rs. 1,88,12,017 to Rs, 2,97,30,997 in 1817—18, more than 50 per cent within 14 years[6]. Since these settlements were made

1. Srivastava, H.S., *History of Indian Famines*, p. 23.
2. *Ibid.*, p. 24.
3. *Ibid.*, p. 25.
4. *Ibid.*
5. *Holt Mackenzie Minute of July 1, 1819* ; *Selections from the Revenue Records of the North Western Provinces*, pp. 156-57. H.S. Srivastava, *History of Indian Famines*, p. 25, fn. 6, observes that the demand from N.W.P. and Delhi rose from Rs. 3,70,38,215 in 1832-33 to Rs. 4,10,08,740 in 1834-35.
6. *Selections from the Revenue Records of the North Western Provinces, 1818-1820* (*Holt Mackenzie Minute of 1919*), pp. 156-57.

with revenue-farmers, the sad lot of the tenantry can only be visualised[1]. Sometimes when these revenue-farmers were ousted for non-payment of the required sum, the British made settlement with the village headman known as the *Mukaddam*, creating fresh revenue-farmers. But in each case there was no hope for relief to the actual tiller of the soil.

It is strange that Metcalf tries to exonerate the British from their harsh and injurious assessments with a view to augment their financial gains at the cost of the peasantry of the State. According to him, "These extra ordinarily severe assessments were a product in part of the ignorance of the new British Collectors, who were confronted with revenue records of doubtful accuracy and a sub-ordinate native staff who revealed nothing to their nominal superiors"[2]. The ignorance of the British Collectors is hardly an excuse to make the people bleed ; nor is the lame argument that their subordinates did not put up the true facts. Further, when settlements were being made, the records could easily have been verified on the spot, as was done later. The plain truth seems to be that the British masters hardly cared for the sufferings of the peasantry and went on pitching the assessments so steeply to raise their revenues. This seems to have been the basic policy of the British in the pre-Mutiny days. For, elsewhere, Metcalf admits that even though "extensive remissions were authorized, particularly following the drought year of 1803—04 the government soon turned to the forced sale of land to recover the arrears"[3].

Despite these glaring defects, settlement work continued in

---

1. Hussain Imtiaz, *Land Revenue Policy in North India*, p. 34.
2. Metcalf, T.R., *Land, Landlords and the British Raj*, p. 55.
3. Metcalf, T.R., *Land, Landlord of the British Raj*. p. 556.

the North Western Provinces till 1949. It may be noted in passing that some of the Lieutenant-Governors, particularly T.C. Robertson and James Thomason, "removed some of the evils" of the earlier practices and the work came to a close in 1949, as stated above[1]. According to Majumdar, "It is justly looked upon as the first complete Land Settlement Gods" and many of the principles enunciated by Thomason were later embodied in the Tenancy Acts of the different provinces of India"[2]. Some of the guidelines laid down by Thomson were, however cancelled in view of their severity in 1854 and the setlement work had come to a close f r the time being.

Meanwhile, Dalhousie (1846—56) had, through his aggressive policy of annexation, brought to an end the role of the *Nawab of Awadh* Much has been written about the merits or otherwise of this highhandedness of the Governor-General and perhaps much more will be penned about this sordid affair[3]. There was nothing to justify this action of Dalhousie the Nawab had all along been obliging to the British and there was no charge of 'contumacy' ; the Doctrine of Lapse did not apply in his case, as he had legal heirs ; According to the advice tendered by Sleeman himself, the administration of Awadh was to be assumed, but its revenue was not to be grasped. Even Lawrence had advocated the same view. But Dalhausie, unmoved by such advice, unmoved by such advice, assumed rather annexed—Awadh 'on grounds of mis rule'.

---

1. Majumdar R.C., *British Paramountcy*, etc. p. 366.
2. Majumdar, R.C., *Bretish Paramountcy*, etc., p. 363.
3. Cf. *Dacoitee in Excelsis or the Spoliation of Oude* : For the British point's justification, Cf. Sleeman, W.H., *Journey through the Kingdom of Onde in the Years 1849-50* (2) Volumes).

The annexation made the British masters of the whole of the State practically in the shape in which it stands today. While the North-Western Provinces were under the charge of a Lieutenant-Governor, Awadh was placed under a Chief Commissioner. As already pointed out, some 66 per cent of the total area of Awadh was under the *taluqdars*, many of whom had risen against the British in the insurrection of 1856-57. As pointed out by Jagdish Raj, they had become very powerful during the effects rule of the Nawabs, subjected the tenantry to every type of oppresston, even alienating them to part with their proprietory rights[1]. Dalhousie soon set about to settle the land problem of Awadh on the pattern of the Panjab and the North West Frontier Provinces (Agra) by drafting men from the N.W.P. and the Panjab[2]. He desired to make summary settlements with parties in the actual possession of land for a period of three years[3]. Further, the Settlement Officers were directed "not to suffer the interposition of *talookadars (taluqdars)*, farmers of revenue, and such like"[4].

This was cause enough for the hitherto tyrant taluqdars to feel uneasy ; but to add to their discomfiture, they were asked to pay off their final instalments along with the balance of what they had not paid to the *Nawab* earlier[5]. This was greatly resented to by the taluqdars and some of them, like

---

1. Jagdish Raj, *The Mutiny and British Land Policy in North India*, pp. 12-14.

2. *Foreign Department, Political Consultations*, 6th June, 1856, No. 189-91.

3. *Parliamentary Papers Relating to Oude*, No. 45, pp. 259-60.

4. *Ibid.*

5. Vide Metcalf, *Land, Landlords, and the British Raj*, p. 169.

the *Taluqdar* of Deara in Sultanpur and Man Singh of Shahganj in Fyzabad refused to comply with the demands[1]. Yet the summary settlement was completed and an impression was generated that the *taluqdars* were unrooted and village communities restored[2]. Meanwhile, the revolt of 1857 broke out before a regular settlement could be carried out.

The events of 1857-58 and the role of the *taluqdars* as leaders of the uprising is too well known to merit any detailed description here. One fact, however, remains uppermost. The rebel taluqdars did receive fullest help from the very masses who they were oppressing till then. Scholars have tried to explain away as oriental mentality to remain loyal to the master, but there were other reasons as well. However, when piece was restored, the British, far from exhibiting animosity to these very *taluqdars*, followed a policy of appeasement and at the same time, inducted many new ones within their fold after choosing from amongst those who had stood with them in the hour of their need.

But the new policy of conciliation and appeasement of the *taluqdars* was at complete variance with that adopted prior to the events of 1857. The result was that the earlier policy of settlement with the village proprietors was reversed. The new Governor-General, Canning, in his proclamation solemnly promised "to view liberally which they (the taluqdars) may (might) acquire to a restitution of their former rights"[3].

Further, the *taluqdars* were also associated in administration which further strengthened their strangle-hold on the

---

1. Pandey V.D., *Land Revenue Administration of Awadh*, pp. 40-44.
2. *Ibid.*
3. *Lord Conning's Proclamation* of 14 March, 1851, p. 41.

peasantry[1]. A new Chapter was opened in the history of the State in which the former North West Provinces (Agra) had slightly different set-up of settlement, the taluqdars reigned supreme in Awadh with administration of the British to back them up in their tyrannical methods to be related in the next Chapter.

1. *Papers Relating to the Administration of Oude*, (1865), p. 35. Six taluqdars, those of Balrampur, Shahganj (Faizabad), Kapurthala, Khajurgaon (Rae Bareli), Hardoi, and Deara (Sultanpur) were made Assistant Commissioners with powers to adjudicate in revenue disputes.

2

Agrarian Conditions

Reference has earlier been made to the institution of the Taluqdari System and the taluqdars in general in the preceding pages while discussing the various systems of land-tenures prevalent in the United Provinces, and it has been noted that the system had been handed down from the declining days of the Mughal rule.[1] However, the connotation appended by the British to the term *'talqudar'* after their experience of 1857—58, and the special rights and privilages heaped upon them by the new masters needs some elaboration in view of their newly gained powers and prerogatives and the treatment of the peasantry under them after having been firmly established as such.

Formerly, a *taluqdar*, for all practical purposes and intent was a revenue-farmer of a 'taluqa' and as pointed out by Habib, there was, for all practical purposes, no difference between a taluqdar and a *zamindar*.[2] But after the events of 1857, when the refractory *taluqdars* had been settled and loyals from out-side been rewarded with fiefs carved out of the taluqas of the rebel *taluqdars*, their position and status was redefined[3]. Thus, "an opulent landholder" and former taluqdars, who were sole proprietors of a village or group of villages, and paid Rs. 5,000/- or more as revenue to the

1. For details see Chapter—I.
2. Habib, Irfan, *Agrarian System of Mughal India*, p. 172.
3. Many loyals like those from the Punjab were awarded taluqas in some districts.

Government for their holding of villages came to be recognised as *taluqdars.*[1] The clause of 'scle proprietorship', laid down by the Chief Commissioner of Awadh, Wingfield, for a single or a group of villages, thus became the determining factor the award of a sanad to a person to be deemed as a *taluqdars*, though this rule was relaxed in certain cases. For instance, if a person had "held the hereditary title of a raja and the rule of primogeniture had prevailed for many generations on his estate"[2], he, too, could be deemed a taluqdar, even if he paid less than Rs .5,000/- as land-revenue to the Government. The said clause also debarred, in many cases, persons assessed for more than Rs. 5,000/- from being granted a sanad to be deemed as a *taluqdars.*[3] There were also cases where *stands* were granted out of 'inadvertence' to joint owners of villages though this had been denied to others. The enactment of Act I of 1869 finally set the seal and, after the lists of such beneficiaries had been received from the

1. *Board of Revenue, Oudh General File*, Letter from Wingfield to Barrow, the Financial Commissioner, 26th June, 1860 and further communication to Commissiner Lucknow, 2nd July, 1860.

2. *Board of Revenue, Oudh General File*, 1964.

3. Metcalf, T.R., *Land, Landlords and the British Raj*, PP. 188—90 ; Metcalf makes special mention of the Nain estate in which the owners of the said estate were refused taluqdari sanad. The writer, on the authority of the Secretary, B.I.A., takes the opportunity to point out that the owner of the Nain Estate is a taluqder ;

   Elsewhere (p. 189, text and fn. 56) Metcalf gives the number of taluqdars as 276 raised to 279 in 1870. But the number has gone on increasing since then, as stated later.

various district officers and scrutinised by the Financial Commissioner, Barrow, a full list of the *taluqdars* was published in the Gazette of India on 31 July, 1869. Some more persons were recognised as *taluqdars* in 1870 and since than the list has been published by the Secretary, British India Association (of taluqdars), of which more to be said later.

The Government seem to have been very anxious to preserve and perpetuate this newly created taluqdar-class of landed aristocracy. Ordinarily, the Hindu law of inheritance should have governed inheritance of property of the family amongst the sons and successors of a taluqdar. But this was. viewed with concern by the British and it was suggested by Wingfield that the title of a *taluqdar* was to go by the rule of primogeniture.[1] Younger sons and dependents were to be given *guzara*, and the absolute control of the estate was later mooted and passed by Canning for the *taluqdar*.[2] Subsequently, this rule was to apply to all *taluqdars* and this measure was finally passed into law in 1869 and is known as the Oudh Estates Act (1869).[3]

The ostensible reason on the part of the Government was that it wanted to create 'a prosperous landed gentry' in the State on the pattern of their homeland aristocrates ;[4] but the real purpose was to win over their loyalty for the future. It

---

1. *Paper Relating to the Administrstion of Oude*, (1856), p. 53.
2. *Ibid.*, Canning to the Chief Commissioner of Oudh, No. 5549, 16 November, 1860.
3. Metcalf, T.R., *Land, Landlords and the British Raj*, pp. 229-30 ; Oudh Estates Act, 1869.
4. Majumdar, R. C. (ed.), *British Paramountcy and Indian Renaissance*, p. 536 ff.

had become quite clear to them during the troubled days of 1857 – 58 that these persons commanded the respect and obedience of the masses owing to blood-ties (*bhaiyachars*) and sentimental attachments of age-long duration between the ruler and the ruled. A repetition of the earlier holocaust was to be avoided at all costs and they were to be sustained within reasonable bounds.[1]

There were certain far-reaching privileges granted to the taluqdars under the new dispensation. Besides being perpetuated in their taluqas,[2] some of the influential ones also enjoyed magisterial power, as already noted earlier. They were to be treated with utmost consideration and courtesy,[3] their court-decisions, howsoever faulty, were to be rectified by the Chief Commissioners with utmost circumspection without causing them embarrassement,[4] and given due respect so as not to bring them down in the eyes of their tenantry. Further, if they incurred debts due to their profligate habits, their estates were put under the Courts of Wards, till the debts were cleared and

---

1. *Foreign Department, Secret Consultations*, 18 November 1859. (Quoted both by Metcalf and Pandey).

   The whole question of primogeniture, *guzara* (maintenance to younger brothers and dependents) etc. shall be dealth with elsewhere in relation to the revolts against taluqdars while discussing the revolt by peasants against the former and the role played by these disgruntled dependents.

2. *Papers Relating to the Administration of Oude* (1859), p. 252.

3. Ibid., Lords Canning's address to taluqdars at Lucknow *Darbar* in November, 1859.

4. Idid., *Circular No. 31, 16 November, 1858.*

the estates handed over again after such clearance.[1]

Such favouritism from the top naturally caused its impression the lower authorities like the *tehsildars*, qanungos, patwaris and other revenue authorities who were expected to extend similar (rather much more) courtesy to the *talqudars* in their official dealings. Likewise, the police followed a similar policy in cases which required their inquiries. The tenantry under the taluqdars was thus at the mercy of this rapacious class and, under the conditions related above, there was full opportunity for them for exploitation, some of which was of the worst and meanest type, as shall be related later. But what was more painful was the fact that, taking clue from their *talqudar* brethren, the *zamindars* also took to similar methods. Like the *taluqdars*, they, too, asserted their rights on tenants' groves,[2] abadi-land trees planted by tenants,[3] in tanks, wells and water channels. Further, there was considerable scope for them to derive sayer income, *tahbazari*, etc., and these rights were fully exploited by them in order to augment their income at the cost of the peasantry.[4]. At the same time, they went on

---

1. The functions and establishmnt of the Court of Wards have been dealt in detail by Metcalf, *Land, Landlords and the British Raj*, pp. 252-54, but, as shall be seen later, the estates under the Courts of Wards were no less opressive to the tenantry, as their main aim was to clear off the debts regardless of the woes of the tenantry.
2. Replies in full to the questionnaire from the Collector, Moradabad, in '*Report of the Committee for the Abolition of the Zamindari System in U.P.*
3. Ibid., The Collector has enumerated the various sources of additional income, p. 98.
4. Replies in Full to the Questionnaire from the Collector, Moradbad, in '*Report of the Committee for the Abolition of the Zamindari System in U.P.* 1947, Vol. II, pp. 96—98. The Collector has enumerated the various sources of additional income, p. 98.

increasing their sir and *khudkasht* land areas at the cost of the latter. Thus the rights and privileges enjoyed by the *zamindars* were also substantial though in no way equal to those of the *taluqdars* (many *zamindars* being under the *talqudars,* as explained earlier). At the same time, by virtue of their being so, they also wished considerable influence with the revenue officers as well as the police, mentioned earlier.

Noticed in the light of the above, it was unfortunate that the Government, while vesting the landed aristocracy with so much power and licence, did not take the interest of the peasantry seriously. After all, it had considerable knowledge of the exacting nature of the *taluqdars, zamindars* and such revenue-farmers who had brought the administration of the *Nawabs* of Awadh to ruin only a few decades earlier. But, as pointed out by Metcalf, the landlords both in Agra and Awadh, further consolidated their positions in land through other means as well, due, largely, to the cold attitude of the Revenue Boards. Some landlords held court-decrees for arrears of rent even against *biswadars* under them ; when the latter were passing through lean days, the landlords calmly prayed for their settlement. The harassed biswadars appealed to the Board of Revenue, but the latter "coldly reported that sale of land for debt was a wide-spread phenomenon and that even newly acquired Biswadri proprietors had no right to expect the Board to rescue them......"[1]. The result was that the landlord himself purchased their land and rights. Obviously the Revenue Board, too, was more inclined to favour the landlords.

1. Metcalf, T.R., *Land, Landlords, and the British Raj* p. 100. The author has pointedly brought to focus this and other means through which smaller zamindars and co-sharers were gradually deprived of their holdings in land and the Government did not come to their rescue (pp. 99—104).

It would thus be apparent that the policy of the Government from the hectic days of the latter half of the nineteenth century till the dawn of Independence had been to favour the landed aristocracy rather than that of looking the interests of the actual tillers of the soil and small landholders. Nor was there any attempt to secure "a definite limitation of the State demand on land"[1] other than what the *taluqdars* and *zamindars* were required to pay to the Government treasuries. In view of the growing pressure on land as already described earlier, the landlords were free to exploit the situation to their advantage. In addition, there was no limit imposed regarding the size of the sir and *khudkasht* holdings of the landlords ; basic and optimum holdings remained unexplained, as was noted by the 'Agrarian Reforms Committee' appointed after Independence to look into the rights of the tenants in the land.[2]

All these factors led the landed aristocracy of the State to unleash an era of peasant exploitation, perhaps the worst, in the milleniums-old history of the country in general and United Provinces in particular. The story of such exploitation and repression of the masses has been related often enough,[3] but in view of some scholars trotting out arguments in the

---

1. Sharma, J.S., *India's Struggle for Freedom*, Vol. I. pp. 1–3.
2. Sharma, J.S., *India's Struggle for Freedom*, Vol. I, pp. 1–3 ;
   The Committee was appointed under the Chairmanship of J.C. Kumarappa by the then Congress President, Dr. Rajendra Prasad, in 1947.
3. Siddiqui, M.H., *Agrarian Unrest in Northern India*, pp. 3–112 ;
   Jagdish Raj, *The Mutiny and the British Land Policy in North India*, p. 27 ff ;
   Baden-Powell, *Land System of British India*, Vol. II.

defence of the *Taluqdari* and *Zamindari* Systems,[1] fresh appraisal of the arguments of the latter and their contentions would, it is felt, not be out of place.

Prior to looking into the merits and demerits of the system thus perpetuated by the British, and the condition of the peasentry—good or bad-it would be advisable to review the socio-traditional, economic and political backgrounds of the peasantry of the state during the closing decades of the last century and the opening ones of the present. The overwhelmingly large masses that were engaged in the occupation of agriculture belonged to the lower varnas or castes which had, since long, been downtrodden, with very little education, and owing allegiance to the upper two classes, the *Brahmanas* and the *kshatriyas*. Their dominance can easily be visualised, as the *kshatriyas* were earlier the rulers though in certain areas they had been displaced by Muslim conquerors. Still the dominantly Hindu population of the state had a caste-ridden society and generally the upper two classes with a small minority of the *vaisya* community had proprietory rights in the land with the taluqdar or the zamindars holding away over the village. The interest of the latter was guarded by the government itself, as its declared policy was to maintain "the old hereditary, chiefs of the clans"[2] and insure their continuance, obviously, at the cast of the pessantry.

1. Jafri S.N.A., *The History and status of Landlords and Tenants in the United Proinces* (India) : Metcalf, T-R., *Land, Landlords and the British* Raj, pp. 237-305 ; The learned author has tried to defend the taluqdars of Awadh and minimised their exploitations therein.

2. Revanue Proceedings, March, 1966, letter to the Chief Commissioner of Oude (Awadh) quoted by Jagdish Raj, *The Mutiny and the British Land Policy in North India*, pp. 37-38.

Traditions, too, have played a very significant role in shaping rural India, as pointed out by scholars.[1] It has very truly been pointed out that, in the India of recent past, prior to its gaining freedom, 'caste-exclusiveness' in relation to agriculture and occupations, has been the main feature of village-India.[2] Even if the families in the villages grew large to the point of division, its members remained wedded to the same occupation and were content to work in the fields of the landlords or perform mannual labour in the same village, and to the same families wnich, too, had grown in size and were on the lookout for such labour, Another age old tradition was that the members of the upper two communities would not till their lands themselves ; taking to ploughing personally was taboo for them and there always was the fear of excommunication from the society if they did so. Further, the peasantry had to depend on the landlords for many things like cattle-grazing, irrigation from ponds and reservoirs, fuel, etc., on the landlords which rendered them all the more helpless. So for as the occupational castes like barbers. tailors, washer-man, etc., are concerned, these had to pepend on the upper castes and also on the landlords largely for those small amanities that they derived from the latter.

The landlords often helped their tenants in certain ways ; if there was a marriage in the family, the *taluqdar* lent out his *shamiana*, tents, and other things needed for that purpose, again, if there was death in the family, he allowed cutting of woods from his trees. But, in return, he was always beneficiary as he could exact begar from his tenants. It has come to the knowledge of the present writer that a token *pan-bida* had to be

1. Cf. welty, *The Asians*, etc., (*op. cit.*), p. 89 ff.
2. *Ibid.*, pp. 90-91. The author has dealt at length on the importance of traditions and traditional values highly prized in the villages prior to their reawakening after Independence.

offered to the landlord before a marriage party went out or if it had to be received in the case of a daughter's marriage. This was traditional sanction and obeisance to the authority of the landlord.[1] Such traditions, it may be surmised, resulted in the mute submission of the ryot to the authority of the *taluqdar* or the *zamindar*.

Economically, the pessantry, burdened with a growing family and no other source of additional income except from the fields, was mostly in debt. The output from his fields mostly depended upon the vagaries of noture. If the rain failed, he was forced to go into the debt of the village *bania*, or the landlord himself and both charged from ¼ to ½ of the amount of the grain lent to him. In case the produce was again lean, the original amount went on increasing at the rate of compound interest. There was no hope of redemption from such debts and in many cases he lost even the small bit of land he owned. Rural indebtedness and its causes have been detailed at considerable length by eminent scholars[2] and need hardly any such mention, but the undue advantages derived from such helplessness of the peasantry boggle the imagination all as shall be seen presently.

The legal position of the tenantry or sub-proprietory rights under a *taluqdar* or a *zamindar* after 1857 needs some elaboration, as it was the root on which the exploitative

---

1. The above account is based on a personal inter-view of Kr. Birendra Singh of Gaura Raj, Rae Bareli. Kr. Singh a highly educated person, offered many other traditions as well that were current in his villages till the abolition of zamindari.

2. Cf. Dutt, R., *Economic History of India in the Victorian Age* (Vol. II of his two works) ;
Anstey, Vera, *Economic Development of India* (Chapter on Agriculture and Co-operatives).

activities of the two rested. After instituting the system, it appears, Canning was conscious of the subproprietory rights of the masses[1]. Yet, as Pandey has pointed out, he "failed to lay down any definite and clear procedure for maintaining such rights." It was pointed out in the First Record of Rights that the rights (subproprietory rights) of those were to be maintained who "were found in possession in 1855, or just before the annexation of the province and no others"[2]. Later, rights in land could only be accepted if the sub-proprietor could prove continuous occupation for 12 or 20 years. (1870)[3]. But, as pointed out earlier, the *taluqdars* and *zamindars* had suddenly become the blue-eyed boys of the British and no more rebels. It was, therefore, very difficult for the sub-proprietor substantiate his claim when the entire governmental machinery—the patwari, quanungo and the divisional officers not excluded—was in favour of the landlords.

Woe betide a person if he ever went to the court in order to establish his claim as such. In the first place, the litigation dragged on for years ; secondly, if the court was that of a *taluqdar* raised to the rank of an Assistant Commissioner, as noted earlier, the decision was bound to go against him, as the latter could easily be influenced by one of his own class ; thirdly, ever supposing that he won, he was unable to get possession against the landlord ; fourthly, if he went to a higher court as an appellant, the issue could drag on for years and in the meantime the poor peasant would have lost everything and be deep in debt. Lastly, there were other

1. *Foreign Department, Political Consultations* 20th May, 1859, No. 254 ; No. 129 of November, 1859.
2. *Ibid.*, (No. 254).
3. *Papers Relating to the Administration of Oude, 1870. Political Despatch from the Secretary of State, 24 April, 1869*, No. 33.

means for the landlord to create enough trouble for him in the village.

It has been suggested that Canning did not intend to leave the tenantry on the mercy of the *taluqdars* and *zamindars*.[1] "In his instructions he provided for securing village occupants against extortion and recognising the rights of the subordinate proprietors......"[2]. It has further been argued that, since he did not lay down any definite and clear-cut instructions or procedure as to how this was to be guaranteed, the lacunae was taken advantage of by the landlords. Further, it has been pointed out by Sharma that in 1862, Canning was in favour of "a definite limitation of the State demand on land."[3]

But a careful scrutiny of both these intended benefits to the under-proprietors and the peasants at large proved detrimental to the cause of the peasantry. Since there were no definite instructions about the process in which the interests of the underproprietors were to be guaranteed and, nor was there any 'deflnite limitation' on State demand the landlords fully exploited this lacuna in the later stages when they had been fully entrenched. The illiterate peasantry did not know about the amount they annually paid to the Government and what actually should have been the demand on them. They were made to pay what was demanded of them by the *karindas* of the landlords, and this not only helped the landlords but often the *karindas* also benefitted for thir own sake.

---

1. Jagdish Raj, *The Mutiny and British Land Policy in North India*, p. 44 ff.
2. *Foreign Department, Political Consultations*, Nos. 284, 20th May, 1859) and 129 (18th November, 1859).
3. Sharma, J.S., *India's Struggle For Freedom*, Vol. I p. 1. According to the author, the same was advocated by Ripon as well in 1882, but Curzon vetoed this in 1902 (*Ibid.*).

A very curious and highhanded procedure seems to have been followed in revenue assessments from the tenants as will be apparent from the following. It appears that, while framing rules for such assessments, caste-considerations were also observed. Section 63 (1) of the Land Revenue Act (Act III) runs as below :

> "When any local area has been brought under settlement, the Settlement Officer or an Assistant Settlement Officer shall inspect every village in the local area, shall ascertain the extent to which caste is taken into account in determining the rent payable by tenants......"[1].

In plain words, this would mean that if a person belonged to a class noted for its industrious methods in agriculture, and could produce more than others mainly due to his labours, was to be assessed at a higher rate than those who were less keen on producing more from their fields. Social implications of this provision of the Act, apart, this led the *taluqdars* and *zamindars* to pick and choose in letting out their land to needy cultivators and grant leases only to those communities like the *Kachhis* and *Karmis* in preference to very needy persons in the villages under them. At the same time they could issue leases to others of land that was not worth cultivation in the hope of making more rent come from the village-land, regardless of the fact that it might have been good as pasturage for other purposes. This provision denied grant of land to the scheduled castes as well, though they were more industrious and every busy in the field of their masters.

Politically, too, the landlords were strengthened towards the beginning of the present century as well (besides having

---

1. Bilgrami, Kazi Azizuddin Ahmad, *An Analytical and Exhaustive Commentary on the Mutation and Correction Sections of the U.P. Land Revenue* Act, III, of 1901 (as amended). (Act, Part III, p. 29).

been given such preferential treatment and powers related earlier). The Act of 1909 needs hardly be termed as a 'Reforms' Act in so far as the larger masses either of the whole country or the State are concerned, as these envisaged representations in the Councils to elected members from the local bodies (mostly dominated by the wealthy and the influential people) and the land-holder class besides others. It is easy to surmise that under such conditions, the landed aristocracy would hardly allow any such legislation which went against their interests, backed as it was by the official members. As for the Act of 1919, though the same story was repeated, its impact and the reaction of the national leaders and that of the masses will be noted elsewhere.

From what has been stated above briefly, it is quite apparent that the British wilfully created a class which was progressively encouraged at the cost of the mass of peasantry. As late as 1921, the avowed policy of the rulers is well reflected in the following words :

> "It is a great thing in these days to have so loyal and important a body, as the taluqdars are, on the side of the Government instead of having them unanimously arrayed against us"[1].

It is not that the Government were unaware of the conditions existing in the State of United Provinces and the harrowing lot of the peasants. But, as pointed out by Jagdish Raj, the aim of the British was to create a bulwark against the rising consciousness of the people, in this landlord--class[2].

---

1. *Revenue Department Proceedings, File No. 588 of 1916.* (the contents are from a letter from the Viceroy, Reading, to Harcourt Butler, Governor of U.P. dated July 5, 1921) (Butler Collection).
2. Jagdish Raj. *Op. Cit.*, p. 33-35.

While it is true that the masses were slow react to the growing tyrannies of this class, a deep undercurrent was already at work as the atrocities had reached a very high pitch. Also, the formation of the Indian National Congress (1885), and in its earlier tages the problems were less highlighted[1]. Meantime, for about a century the *taluqdars* and the *zamindars* reigned supreme till the abolition of the system after the country gained Independence.

Section—II

As noted earlier, the Settlement of 1858 recognised the taluqdar's proprietory rights[2]. The question of the recognition of farmer's proprietor's and of tenants' rights was not altogether dead. In fact, John Lawrence had ordered an investigation into tenant's rights and the Chief Commissioner of Awadh, Wingfield and the Settlement Commissioner, Currie, two great champions of the 'Oudh School' had opined that no inferior proprietarv claims or occupancy rights of the tenants were valid. The successor of Wingfield, Strachey, resolved the matter, by striking the so-called 'Oudh Compromise', by which the *taluqdars* agreed to grant some rights of occupancy to those who had been proprietors earlier. However, the concession was insignificant--only one parcent of the cultivators benefited—the mass of the peasantry was left with no rights of all[3]. The Oudh Sub-settlement Act, 1866, gave legal

1. The Poona Resolution of 1889, embodying 8 points, does not have anything about peasantry (Cf. Comments by Majumdar, R.C., *British Paramountcy*, etc. (Op. Cit.), pp. 762 and 767 specially).
2. According to Metcalf the total number of *sanads* was 276—*Land, Landlords and the British Raj* ; Benett states that 285 deeds of investure (sanads) were made—*Oudh Gazetteer*, Vol. I, Lucknow, 1877.
3. Metcalf, *The Aftermath of Revolt in India*, pp. 188-196.

sanction to subordinate proprietary rights as and when they could be found existing. The recognition of the sub-proprietary rights in no way undermined the dominant position of the Awadh *taluqdars*.

The spectrum of *taluqdari* estates was uneven in Awadh. Out of 23,049 villages 13,161 belonged to the *taluqdars* whose estates and the amount of the annual revenue paid to the Government varied[1] :

	Particulars	*No. of estates*	*No. of villages comprised*	*Average area of each estate*
1.	Taluqdari estate paying over Rs. 50,000 annual revenue.	40	7446½	117,300
2.	Taluqdari estate paying between Rs. 50,000 and Rs. 5,000	104	5165	13,598
3.	Taluqdari estate paying less than Rs. 5,000	48	228½	2,495
4.	Small grantees under Act I of 1869.	159	321½	984

The extent of taluqdari area covered only a little over three-fifths of the revenue area (*malguzari*) of Awadh as a hole. The percentage of the revenue area also varied from

1. *Agricultural Statistics*, 1886-1887.

district to district.[1] The remaining two fifths of the revenue areas were covered and owned by the Zamindars, the second most important land-owing class after the *taluqdars*. The zamindari tenure accounted for over 700 villages out of over 23,000. The zamindari areas were held under different forms of ownership, but there was no basic difference in the them[2].

	Tenure	*Number of villages held under each tenure*
1.	Zamindari	2,956
2.	Pattidari	585
3.	Bhaiachara	168
4.	Mixed or Imperfect	2,738
	Total	7,447

As stated earlier, the third proprietary class of landholders, besides the *taluqdars* and *zamindars*, was that of under-proprietors. They formerly possessed fairly extensive rights over the land but were now eclipsed by the *taluqdars* and *zamindars*. They had to pay revenue either straight or through the superior proprietor. Normally, it was noticed that the Government accounted for fifty percent of the gross rental, the rest fifty percent being divided between the superior landlord and the under-proprietor[3]. Below the *taluqdar* the *zamindar* and the under-proprietors, there lay in Awadh the vast body of tenant—cultivators, who were condemned to lead—"a dim, slow moving and too often a poverty stricken

1. The revenue area under taluqdari in Unnao for example was 20%, in Kheri 71%, Faizabad 72%, Bahraich 78%, Rae Bareli 66% and so on.
2. Baden-Powell, *Land Systems of British India*, Vol. II, p. 227.
3. The under-proprietors were of two kinds—*Pukhtadar* and *Muaafidar.*

and hunger-bitten life......a narrow round of struggle between the rent collector and the village usurer."[1]

The taluqdars absorbed various rights which were formerly enjoyed by the cultivators. The degree of 'absorption', says Baden-Powell, differed. He observed "In some, it in complete, the whole of the villagers, whatever they once were, are now 'tenants', with or without same occupancy rights"[2]. Of the bulk of these tenants only one percent held rights or occupancy which entitled them to pay rents less by two annas in a rupee[3]. Following them and at the bottom of the scale were the so called 'riffraffs'. Their rents could be raised each year and they could be uprooted from their holdings at the pleasure of their landlords. The Oudh Rent Act of 1886. sought to afford them some protection but, as the rule of law was a theoretical postulate, the pro-tenant provisions of the Act could hardly be availed by the supressed peasantry. The 'might' is right or the '*matsya*' law continued to hold its day.

There was yet another class of 'tenant-serf' who worked under '*sewak*' system, Under it a man of any of the four castes—*Lodh, Chamar, Kori* and *Kurmi*—received serfdom for life[4]. He worked as ploughman or reaper, and performed menial jobs.

The hierarchy of the agrarian set-up in Awadh thus comprised ; (a) the *taluqdars* ; (b) the *zamindars* ; (c) the under-proprietors-occupancy tenants ; (d) the tenants-at-will ; (e) tenant-serfs or agricultural labourers.

1. Irwin, H.C., *The Garden of India*, p. 4,
2. Baden—Powell, *Land Systems of British India*. Vol. II, p. 200.
3. Irwin, H.C., *The Garden of India*, p. 33.
4. *Fyzabad Settlement Report* (1898), p. 11.

The consolidation of the stratification within the Awadh society was the result of the British perception of Indian principles of landholding. The taluqdars, as they now were in the safe position of a 'modern landlord', were well set to exploit the peasantry in the 'sunshine of British peace'[1]. The nature of the Awadh rural society was not basically altered atonce but the new policy had long term implications on the rural society and economy.

The last years of the 19th and the beginning years of the 20th centuries witnessed some important changes in the social situation which started influencing agrarian relations. The proprietary mutations, growing impoverishment of small *zamindars*[2], intrusion of the *thekadars*[3], introduction of usurious merchants capital, changing relationship of the landlords with the under-proprietors and the tenantry, etc., were bound to influence the rural scene. The material conditions, such as frowing population[4], unaccompanied by the growth of industries or other avenues of employment, mounting social tensions, soaring prices, fragmentation of cultivated land, etc.

---

1. There were few taluqdars who looked after the welfare of the peasantry also. For details see T.R. Metcalf, *Land, Landlords and the British Raj*, pp. 282-360.

2. "The proprietary body continues to sink in the morass of debt, a fact that was to tell heavily on their tenantry. The loss of proprietary rights by caparcenary owners resulted into gains for the taluqdars whom H.S. Fremantle correctly described as "the principal buyers of the land in the district"—*Rae Bareli Settlement Report*, (1896), p. 37.

3. Contractor or long term lease holder of land.

4. The population showed a steady rise in the period under review.

affected the man—land ratio[1]. The political process of Indian nationalism within colonial constraints helped to highlight socio-economic contradictions.

Rural indebtedness increased rapidly during the last quarter of the 19th century and became one of the acutest problems of the countryside. In the early years of tne 20th century the small tenure holders and sub-proprietors of Awadh began to loss their holdings or sink in debt. Some 21,758 proprietors owned 1,105,000 acres in 1,569 non-taluqdari villages in Hardoi district, "giving an average of fifty acres to each proprietor, of which two-thirds (was) arable[2]". This proprietary body with small holdings went down under a burdensome revenue. This was the 'peasant aristocracy', whom Irwin characterised as "......a class of yeomen consisting of high caste Hindus with a sprinkling of *Musalmans*...... passionately clinging to the remanants of their rights in the soil, at ceaseless war with the rent court and the rent collector, these are the men to whom the task of administration owes much of its difficulty"[3]. Their pride forbade them to work on their fields, and they employed wasteful labour. Their indebtedness increased to such an extent that some-thing needed to be done to save "this enormous body of yeomen"

---

1. The number of ploughs in the district of Sultanpur alone had risen from 106,900 (in 1870) to 141,600 (around 1900)—vide *Sultanpur Settlement Reports* 1873 and 1898, p. *xxiv* and p. 15, respectively. As the cultivation was done by the tenants, and not by land owners, it may be assumed in all probability that the rise in the number of ploughs indicates a growing body of tenants.

2. *Mehta Report* revealed the adverse effect of manland ratio in agrarian relation in Pratapgarh which along with Rae Bareli witnessed agrarian uprisings in 1920-21 in Awadh.

3. Irwin, H.C., *The Garden of India*, Vol. II, p. 5.

lest they would become "a body of needy desperadoes, natural enemies to peace and social order, the elements of agrarian anarchy......"[1]. Their position and numbers varied from district to district. All the same, their holdings were passing into the hands of non-agricultural classes. These were either transferred to *talugdars* or were purchased by bankers, *banias*, sugar-boilers, usurers, distillers, etc. In Rae Bareli, the *taluqdars* were the principal beneficiaries of the growing pauperism of small landholders[2]. Fremantle observed : "It is hardly too much to say that in a purely agricultural tract the happenings of the great mass of the people depends on the consideration or otherwise with which they are treated with (by) the owners of the soil...... the district (its greater portion) is owned by large non-resident landlords, who are chiefly taluqdars. These men are a great help in local administration and are politically important. Local influence is what they chiefly prize, and it is necessary to secure it to them. How to do so without reducing the tiller of the soil to absolute dependence on every whim and coprice of the landowner appear to me to be the great problem of Oudh administration"[3].

The land revenue demand rose steadily in Awadh from 1860 onwards. To quote a few illustrations, the land revenue demand in Rae Bareli in 1880—81 was 974 (in thousand of rupees), and in the years 1900—1901 it rose to 1,502 thousands. Pratapgarh registered an increase of 273 during the above period (from 953 to 1,226). In Bahraich it shot up from 977 to 1153.[4] The incidence of land revenue demand per acre when compared with the average rent that was being charged per acre of tenancy, one finds that rental was three

1. *Hardoi Settlement Report* (1888), p. 50.
2. *Rae Bareli Settlement Report* (1890), p. 37.
3. *Rae Bareli Settlement Report* (1898), p. 37.
4. Whitecmobe, E., *Agraian Conditions in Northen India*, Vol I. p. 200.

times of the revenue demand.[1] On the one hand, the land revenue demand and the rate of rents were increasing due to rise in population[2] while on the other. The burden of increasing money demands in the spape of revenue and rents fell on the tenantry. In 1872, Mac Andrew observed, "the main cause of the poverty of the lowest class of tenants and agricultural labourers is, beyond a question, the density of the population and the disinclination of the people to move to a new spot, for, dense as the population, is, there is land enough in the district itself to give them a large measure of relief, if they would only break it up. But......they multiply their numbers and subdivide their holdings till famine puts a limit to both."[3]

During the period under study, neither more new land was brought under the plough nor the productivity of the cultivated land increased for want of technological improvements. The cultivated area remained almost static. The impoverishment of the bulk of peasantry had become a fact of their humdrum existence.

The first Rent Act in Awadh or the Imperial Act XIX of 1868 bestowed a heritable right of occupancy upon those peasants who were able to prove the possession of proprietary

---

1. The average rent for an acre of cultivated land in Awadh in 1882—83, was Rs. 5—8—0 Baden-Powell, *Land Systems in British India*, p. 194 ; In 1918—19, it was Rs. 6—5—0 in Pratapgarh district—*Mehta (V.N.) Report* in File No. 753/1920, Revenue 'A' Department.

2. In 1899, the average population density per square mile for Awdh was 474—Benett, *Oudh Gazatteer*, p, *xiii*. In 1921, it stood at 504—*Cenius Report*, Part II (1921), p. 451.

3. *Rae Bareli Settlement Report* (1872), p. 76.

rights for thirty years preceding annexation. In a landlord dominated society and with Government solidly behind them, it was no easy task to prove such a possession. If it was proved, these tenants were allowed to pay rents at concessional rates. But they constituted only one percent of the total population of the tenants. The majority of the tenantry was without any rights. Their rents could be enhanced by the land-lord at his sweet will. They could be evicted at a month's notice at the end of each year. Major Erakine's enquiry, into the conditions of the Awadh tenantry, revealed that the landlords replaced 46.4 percent of the tenants by a class of fresh arrivals.[1] The prime motive behind the spate of evictions was the landlords'[2] desire to increses the rent. The landlords in their cold-blooded competion for profits swept aside very larg number of tenants from their holdings. It was reported by Harrington from the Sultanpur district that "...... that rents have risen. are rising and will continue to rise enormously is a fact. Bare subsistence and often hardly that, is the one fixed factor, and the Oudth landlord is with more or less energy and skill, endeavouring to get all beyond that into his hands as rent."[3]

The mounting evictions and increasing rents drove the peasantry into the lap of borrowing agencies—the traditional village *mahajans* and *banias* and the landlord himself.[4] It should be recalled that the exhorbitant rates of interest charged by the rural creditor led to two major evils : interest charged absorbed a large part of the peasant's income ; and the peasant's frequent inability to repay the dept led to the large-scale trans-

---

1. *Oudh Revenne Administration Report* (1872), p. 76, U.P. S.A.
2. Since the following observations hold good in the cases of all types of landlords (*e.g. taluqdars, zamindars*, etc.), the term landlord has been for all these categories.
3. *Oudh Revenue Administration Report* (1885—86), pp. 75—76. Fyzabad Settlement Report (1891) p. 15.
4. *Sultanpur Settlement Report* (1898), p. 18.

fer land to the non-cultivating moneylenders. The last three decades of the 19th century and the beginning of the 20th Century abound in the growth of indebtedness in Awadh. The small landowners were as much in debt, perhaps more, as the multitude of tenants. The vast mass of the tenants-at-will were in varsing degrees in debt to their landlords or the village moneylenders all over Awadh. The Deputy Commissioner of Sultanpur, Young, observed in that "......at least three-fourth of the cultivators are indebted to the *mahajans*', and he added "I should say that their existence is in danger ......".[1] The operations of the usurious merchant capital agravated the economic plight of the tenantry. Seth Raghubar Dayal of Moisuddinpur, a *taluqdar* from Sitapur district knew about "the most galling yoke of the agricultural mass from the hands of the perjuring community of petty money lenders in villages."[2]

The peasants sought relief from the Government by means of the petitions.[3] The Government, it appears, did nothing in the matter except occasional inquires by the Settlement Officers. The landlords, too, were generally blind to the condition of their tenantry. Neither did they make improvents in the land nor allowed their peasanty to do so which would have resulted into increased productivity[4]. One surer way to tide over their

---

1. *Oudh Revenue Administration Report* (1885—86), pp. 75—76; *Fyzabad Settlement Report* (1898), p. 15.
2. *Foreign Department, Revenue Proceedings*, Janauary 1891, Nos. 26—27, NAI. (vide pamphlet the Growth of indebtedness of the Agricultural Community in Oudh, etc.). He started a Bank in 1891 with a Capital of Rs. 25,000 and loaned money to cultivators of the estate at 12 per-cent per annum.
3. *Foreign Department, Revenue Proceedings*, May 1899, No. 56—57, NAI.
4. *Oudh General Files* 394/1882—83, Pt. II, pp 233—234.

independeness was thus barred by the landlords. The condition of the tenants-at-will appeared to be beyond redemption for, "......that they have always the terror of ejectment hanging over them, and cannot provide facilities for irrigation, dig wells, raise banks, cut drains or manure fields. Should a tenant-at-will do so the landlord would forthwith issue notice for ejectment and the unfortunate cultivator is reduced to either pay an enhance rent or vacate the land for another tenant, who will enjoy the fruits of his expenditure."[1]

The nature of the land tenure in Awadh and the greed of the landlord stood in the way of such improvements. The digging of '*pakka*' well bestowed on the tenant a 'quasi occupancy right in his holding'. The landlord found it more profitable to increase rent on each eviction than to share profits accruing through such improvements. The indebedness of the low caste peasantry stemmed not from undue expenditure but from perpetually increasing revenue demands and rents, high prices, pressure of population and the usurious rate of interest on loans. The natural calamities such as floods, famines only added to their miseries. The high caste peasantry owed its indebtendenss to its vanity which prevented from touching the plough themselves.

While the tenants had nothing to fall back in times of distress, the proprietor classes-the *taluqdars* and the co-sharing fraternity-took recourse to enhancement of rents and to other means to ward off their indebtedeness which stemmed from frivolous expenditure and adoption of western style of living.[2] The strugguling cultivator possessed no means to extricate himself from the stronghold of debt and his creditors. His utter

1. *Butler Collection*, from the Secretary Board of Revenue to Chief Secretary, Government of U.P., 1st February, 1921, UPSA.
2. Matcalf, T.R., *Land, Landlords and the British Raj*, (Chapter on the Taluqdari style of life), pp. 341—75.

helplessness found expression in the phrase '*Uppar Parmeshwar, Neeche Sarkar*' (God above, the Government below). The impoverishment of the tenantry and the report on their conditions produced by Major Erskine made it clear to the Government by 1864 that it could ill-afford 'to play fast and loose' with agrarian matters[1].

The Rent Acts passed earlier had proved ineffective in regulating the affairs of the landlord and the tenant. In fact, they contained nothing worthwhile for the tenant, and favoured the landlord at the cost of the former. It drove discontent ment deep underground. The outbreak of agrarian riots were not uncommon. By 1869, as many as eleven riots had taken place in Awadh, the last resulting in several murders, led Secretary Bayley, the Government of India to remark : "The elements of mischief had been seething ever since 1858."[2]. He regretted for not having stationed an extra police force. The 'quarrelsomenss and recusancy' of the tenants was reported from various parts of Awadh.[3] The Government was forced to pass the Oudh Rent Act to regulate the agrarian relations in Awadh. The most important change it sought to make was with regard to the tenure of the tenants-at-will.[4] (*a*) These tenants were now upgraded into statutory tenants in as much as they were secured by the statute in the occupation of their holdings for a seven year term from the date of the last charge in their rent or of the last alteration in the area of their holdings[5]. According to the Act, neither a tenant's rent could be anhanced nor could he be evicted, from his holding till the end of his seven-year-period. However, the landlord was given

1. *Erskine's Report* of 1882—83, Oudh General, File No. 394, UPSA.
2. *Oudh General File* No. 1263/1880—82, p. 189, UPSA.
3. *Oudh Revenue Administration Report*, p. 24 UPSA.
4. (*a*) For details see chapter on Tenance Legislation.
5. *Oudh Revenue Administration Reprrt*, p. 37. UPSA.

the option to either enhance the rent or evict the tenant at the expiry of the seven-year-term. The Act also limited the extent of enhancement, which now could not exceed 6¼ percent or an anna in a rupee of the previous rent. The material advantage to the landlord, so thought the farmers of the Act, would not vary whether the sitting tenant was re-instated or a new one was brought in his place.

The Act stemmed the rising tide of evictions at once. But the happy situation did not last long. The landlords employed their mischief to compensate the loss of income that resulted from the provisions in other ways of the Rent Act, which neither allowed them to evict tenants nor permitted them to enhance rent over the specified maximum. By 1920 may instances of the enhancement of rent as well as of evictions were reported.[1] It was also reported that in the vast majority of cases the landlord and his tenant came to terms "without going into court."[2]

Moreland went into the depth of the matter and, pointing out the weakness of the Act of 1866, he thus wrote that the weakness : "lies in the fact that if the landholder breaks the law, nothing happens to him. In theory he can be sued for penalties for excessive enhancement but no ordinary cultivator should sue his *taluqdar* and the *Kurmi* or *Chamar*, holding land from a resident *Thakur* zamindar... could not possibly stay in the village after taking his *thakur* into Court."[3]

The only alternative to eviction or payment of enhanced rent was a resort to judicial proceedings in the fear of the

---

1. *Oudh Revenue Administration Report* (1887—88), p. 27 U.P.S.A.
2. *Ibid.*, (1888—89), p. 30.
3. Moreland, W.H., *Revenue Administration of the United Provinces*, pp. 64—65.

resources of the contestants. As the tenants were suppressed and poor, the judicial remadies could hardly be expected to be availed. The Rent Act was not to govern the ways of the landlords. The Deputy Commissioner of Barabanki hoped that time, "will set these irregularities right", but with time these irregularities only multiplied.[1]

The landlords found other ways for dealing with these tenants who were not willing to pay increased rents demanded of them. They now resorted to the practice of planting dummy tenants to escape from the legal bindings without violating the law. Another tactics employed by the landlords was the practice of commutation of rent. The Awadh landlords charged rents in cash as the agriculture came to be commercialised. Now the cash rents were commuted into grain rents as the price of grains soared. It was reported from Sitapur district that "every effort is being made by many landlords to change cash into grain rents."[2] As the Act limiteh the landlords' power to enhance rent, he would change a formerly cash rented area into a grain-rented one. At the end of the seven year's statutory period, he would again be able to convert the grain rent into a cash-rent.

The landlords asked the tenants to pay arrears of rent whenever they wished their ejectment or enhancement of rent. The poverty of the tenants had forced them, at some point of their statutory period, to request for a remission of rent which would then be made in the form of a loan. Whenever a landlord desired to eject his tenant, he had simply to ask for his money back. On tenant's failure to pay, he would file a suit for the recovery of arrears of rent invoking section 61 of the

---

1. *Oudh Revenue Adminstration Report.* (1888—89), p. 31.

2. *Ibid.*

Act.[1] The landlords also resorted to what may be called 'straight' evictions. Taking advantage of the section 55 of the Act, the landlord, wishing his tenant to vacate his holding at the expiry of the statutory period, proceeded to evict him. The Government introduced court fee to augment its revenues, and to exercises some restraint on the ejectment of statutory tenants. The court fee equalled half a year's rent of his holding from which the tenant was to be evicted. As the rents would not be allowed to rise about 6¼ percent every seven

1. (*a*) There were tenants of all kinds and some tenants were not always hard pressed. There were tenants who simply wanted to postpone the repayment of their loan indefinitely and when they would see their "ejectment on the point of being finally ordered, pull out the amount with quite a cheerful smile and pay up." But such insolent tenants were few and more the exception than the rule. The Deputy Commissioner of Unnao who likened such tenants to Irish tenants also confessed that his "sympathies were very often on the side of the lanlord"—Siddiqui, M.H., *Agrarian Unrest in North India*, p. 83.

(*b*) Number of evictions in Awadh (1868—78).

Year	*No. of notices*	*Year*	*No. of notices*
1868-69	25,744	1873-74	17,978
1869-70	52,151	1874-75	29,610
1870-71	59,393	1875-76	23,623
1871-72	20,101	1876-77	38,636
1872-73	10,476	1877-78	35,077

Source : *Oudh Revenue Administration Reports* (1868—1878).

years, the Government thought that the landlord would not evict a sitting tenant as he would not like to lose half a year's rent every seven years. The assumption was naive as the rents did rise as part of extra legal devices. The Number of eviction notices, for which court fee was paid, increased enormously between 1887—1921[1]. The court fee enriched the Government treasury by a sum of Rs. 2.2 millions. Ironically enough, it was the incoming tenant, and not the landlord, who would pay the court fee for the eviction of the outgoing tenant.

The practice of *nazrana* (gift payment) was another device to dispossess the tenantry of varying sums. The practice, nazrana, was a legacy form the time of the last King of Awadh, Wajid Ali Shah. Its from, however, was different. Previously, nazrana was what the revenue authorities paid to the minister before they were permitted to enter on their charges. By the 20th century, these 'unauthorised gratuities and perquisites' were being paid by the tenants to the landlords. It was detected in 20th century that another "method by which the landlord continues to evade the law is to take the premium" as a condi-

---

1. Between 1887 and 1891, altogether 9,345 notices were served on which a court fee was charged. The total court for these five years came to Rs. 68,034 or an average of fee about Rs. 7.2 per each notice served. If we assume that the average court fee per notice between 1887—1921 continued to be Rs. 7.2 (although actually it must have been risen since rents rose and the court fee was always half of the annual rent of a holding) then the total sum deposited as court fee between 1887 and 1921 would be : 3,10,000 (the number of notices served between 1887 and 1921 on which court fees were charged) × 7.2=2.2 million. In other words, this sum almost equalled the average revenue of Awadh districts for two years, at the 1900-1901 land revenue demand figures—Siddiqui. M.H. *Agrarian Unrest in North India*, p. 84.

tion for renewing a tenancy or admitting a new tenant.[1] The amounts charged under the head varied from district to district. In Lucknow for the lease of one *bigha* of land, carrying a rent of Rs. 10, the nazarana paid was Rs. 10 to the landlord with *patwari* andziledar getting Re. 1 each.[2] In the district of Pratapgarh the nazrana money varied between Rs. 32 to Rs. 125 per *bigha.*[3] The threat of bedhakli (eviction) was used to extort nazarana money. Such nazrana was usually paid in the months of May, June and July, just before eviction notices for the coming years were prepared and new tenants were let in after the previous year's ejected tenants were formally dispossessed. Many peasants deposed before the enquirying Deputy Commissioner, V.N. Mehta, that they were forced to sell their daughters ageing 7 to 12 years to persons ageing from 40 to 60 years to pay off *nazrana* money.[4] *Kanya Vikraya* is a heinous crime, the punishment of which, according to Hindu customs, was eternal hell for the father. The poor peasantry though it prudent to incur eternal damnation in the next world in order to avoid the living hell. The enormous disparity in the years between the ages of the wives and bushands led Mehta to remark that the marriages of girls were "consecrated before the funeral pyre" of their husbands.[5] (*a*) In this context, Mittal observes, "the wickedness and treachery of taluqdars disturbed the mental equilibrium of a tenant, who had be sent to lunatic asylum while a women committed suicide as she failed to manage *nazrana* money."[6]

The landlords missed no opportunity to inflate rents even the estates managed by the Court of Wards, *i.e.*, by the

1. Mukherjee, R.K., *Land Problems in India*, p. 174.
2. *Iboid.*, p. 176.
3. *Mehta Report*, Exhibit 'S', p. 104.
4. For details see Appendix-B
5. (*a*) *Independent*, 24th September, 1920.
6. *Mehta Report*, p. 11.

Government, were not immune from the tendency of increasing rents.[1] The term '*Murdafaroshi* (literally meaning the practice of selling corpses) bring out the cruelty involved in the fresh letting out of land at higher rents soon ofter the death of a tenant, The Abhyudaya denounced the 'Murdafaroshi Kanun, Mehta reports, "... people describe to me that a new kind of *Mahabrahman* (high priest) has come into being whose one object is to pray for the epidemic, as in popular parlance a grain dealer is supposed to pray for a famine, so that he may have a rich harvest of '*Murdafaroshi* fee and this *Mahabrahman* (the most despised among the Brahmans because he received funeral gifts) is the zamindar. Before the ashes are cold on the pyre that *Mahabrahman* has to be satisfied."[2] this cruel practice was not confined to only *taluqdari* estates but was extant even in the estates by the Court of Wards.[3]

Besides thesethere were the numerous abwabs (cesses, imposts and fines) which weighed heavily on the cultivator community. All petty and trivial pretexts were used to levy exactions on the peasantry. Porter commented "......in fact, the Indian landlord seems to consider that a resident of his village should pay for permission to ado any conceivable action, even for eating, drinking and sleeping"[4]. The realisation of abwabs constituted a prolific source of oppression. The kinds of casses evoke laughter if one forgot about the misery of poor

---

1. *Mehta Report*, Exhibit 'L', pP.98-99.
2. *Ibid.*, pp. 90-99, For Pratpagarh district we have numerous such examples of the inhuman transactions which had resulted from the shortcomings of the agrarian system and the unrestrained exploitation by the landlords.
3. Cf. Malaviya, H.D., *Land Reforms in India*, p. 103; *Allahabad Settlement Report*, (1977), p. 109.
4. *Porter's Report*, p. 97.

cultivators. If a landlord wanted to buy a horse or an elephant or a motor car, the poor teants had to pay cassess like *Ghorwana*, *Hathiana* or *Motorowan*"[1]. A big landlord realised 'gramophoning' cess when his son went round the village with the musical instrument[2]. The landlords held special *darbars* to show off their power and levied '*neota*' money (invitation cess) on the tenants. During festival *darbars* (on Holi or Dussehra) they collected in some cases as much as Rs. 31,000[3]. The other cesses were *nazrana daura* (cess collected during landlord's tour) *Rajauti* (title of King assumed by the landlord), ceremonial cesses on marriages, births, deaths, etc. in the peasants' or in landlords' family[4]. The village society of Awadh was a multiplex occupational society in which, often, a man did more than one kind of work. There was no clear demarcation between "agriculture and other industries[5]. The realisation of cesses taxed a peasant, atleast twice, if he engaged in dual professions to supplement his little earnings. Thus a *Jullaha* (weaver) tenant had to pay a loom fee, the *chamar* (shoe-maker) provided hides, the *Gadariya* (shepered) provided blankets and goats, the kurmies or kumahar (potter) gave khaprails, etc[6]. No one was exempted from these sorts of unnumerable cesses by the landlords in Awadh. Mehta wrote, "......so cruel and hearless were these *taluqdars* that they would not permit the tenants to reconstruct their houses which have been destroyed by natural calamities, unless the peasants paid them 40 to 100 rupees[7]. Similarly, Major Grigg,

---

1. *Mehta Report*, pp. 72-73 ; '*Inquiry Regarding Cesses in Oudh*'—Nos. 271/1922, Revenue 'A' p. 76, U.P.S.A.
2. Malaviya, H.D., *Land Reforms in India*, p. 63.
3. *Mehta Report*, p. 63.
4. *Mehta Report*, p. 73.
5. Crooke, W., *Natives of Northern India*, pp. 129-130.
6. *Mehta Report*, p. 58.
7. *Ibid.*, p. 59.

officiating Deputy Commissioner of Pratapgarh, wrote about the illegal cesses—"the exactions known as Bhait, nazrana, kabuliyatana, Hathiyana, Nachauna, are well known. One name I have heard lately for the first time—Pakwana. A thakurani taluqdar of the district had a fraction on her led, and to facilitate her recovery distributed large sums to *fakirs*. The total expenditure is said to have been 15,000/-. This sum was recovered from the tenants. They refer to it as pakwana. I have never heard of any money exactions being entered in public accounts. They are invariably levied surreptitiously, and in most taluqas the tenants have been directed to deny their existence"[1]. Hari (offering of ploughs) Begar (forced labour) and rased (compulsory supplies), were the parts of tenant's existence. The 'feudal barons' and their kinsmen led luxurious, westernised life and the burden of their high living fell on the poor peasentry. The excesses of the taluqdar, servants, some of them ex-criminals, further exasperated the peasantry. The Press denounced their condcct[2]. Even Butler observed that they "never hesitated in robbing both their masters and the peasantry"[3]. When Baba Ramchandra persuaded reluctant Jawaharlal Nehru to visit the villages of Awadh, the latter was emotionally moved to see the "naked, starving and crushed picture of India"[4]. The various cesses and 'manorial' dues began to be resented by a hard pressed tenantry.

Besides these, the First World War brought fresh misries for the peasants. They had to bear the brunt of the 'larai-

---

1. *Oudh Papers*, Commissioner in Oudh (on special duty) to Secretary, Government of N.W.P. and Oudh, 1st June, 1883, Appendix 'A', Nos. 24-270, Legal Department, October, 1886, p. 33, U.P.S.A.
2. *Leader*, 24th, 29th September, 1921, Abhyudaya, 10th July, 1920.
3. *Butler Collection*, Roll 17.
4. Nehru, Jawaharlal, *An Autobiography*, p. 52.

chandas' (war loans) in the collection of which she taluqdars vied with each other. Meston praised the "admirable" work of the taluqdars in raising money and recruits[1]. The press brought out details and stories exposing callousness of taluqdars during the war[2]. It also pulled up the taluqdars and their protector, the Government for these activities. The Leader characterised Begar as "one of the worst forms of the exploitation of human labour"[3]. The Abhyudaya addressed a letter to Butlar criticising his 'Oudh Policy'[4]. The Independent commented, "The tenant needs are cruelly ignored, the urgency of his work is completely lost sight of, all that the tenant is required to do is to implicitly and unhesitatingly follow the arbitrary will of the taluqdars of his *ziladars* and *sipahis* lest he may bring on him the wrath of the *taluqdars* and be punished with a little shoe beating, fines and *ejectment*"[5]. The taluqdars did not for a moment relent their money campaign, because the Government of the day was with them, and as Mehta observed ; "The possession of unrestricted power has turned the head of the landholder...... He considers that he can maintain his moral health when the rest of the organism is morally diseased and his prosperity is like the beautiful colours of a saprophyte that is flourishing on the decay of others. He has become callous and impervious to the arguments of the other side. He takes recourse to all stratagems to combat the cunning of his helots"[6].

There is a limit to human endurance and it was reached in 1920 when the smouldering fire of peasant discontent broke

1. *Meston Papers* (Meston to Raja Mahmudabad).
2. *U.P. Native Papers*, U.P.S.A.
3. *Leader*, 22nd January, 1921.
4. *Abhyudaya*, 10th July, 1920.
5. *Independent*, 24th September, 1920.
6. *Mehta Report*, pp. 8-11 .

into riots and wide-spread uprisings. As the peasant movement in Awadh had assumed formidable dimensions and got intertwined with the national movement, the Government thought it better to repair glaring abuses of its earlier enactments.

Their overall picture that we get in the preceding narrative of the landlord tenant relationship, and of the condition of the peasantry in general, is by no means an agreeable one. The condition of the peasantry went on deteriorating, year by year, during the period of one study. Sandwiched between the landlord and the money-lender, the poor peasant was utterly helpless, seeking out an unbearable existence. The measures of the Government did not go beyond academic enquiries, and when it passed rent acts, the taluqdars empted them of their pro-tenant sympathies, if any, by their stratagems. In fact, the condition of the peasants became still worse on account of innumerable cesses charged from them.

3

Discontent and Disturbances—I

The saga of the abjectly miserable conditions undeı which the peasants of Awadh spent their days need not be stressed any further. It is not that the British Government were not fully aware of the conditions prevailing in the Awadh areas. But any step taken to improve the peasants' lot was bound to annoy the taluqdars, which the Government could not afford as they were the upholders of the 'Empire' against 'seditious' opposition. Meston, the Lieutenant-Governor of the United Provinces, wrote in 1916, regarding an amendment to the Tenancy laws that, "......the landlord may become a bulwark against the disintegrating forces of swaraj agitation. We should certainly do nothing that will add to or perpetuate any grievance which may tend to throw them into the arms of the advanced and irresponsible politician......At the moment, however, any radical changes of this nature would only provoke intense controversy and set the landlords as a body against us, which is the last thing we wish"[1]. This was the sole reason that the amendament of the Oudh Rent Act, which might have averted the agrarian crisis, was kept

---

1. *Revenue Department Proceedings*, File No. 588/1916 UPSA ; Even after the disturbances when the Oudh Rent Act was being amended Government had the same considerations—"It is a great thing particularly in these days to have so loyal and important a body, as the taluqdars are, on the side of the Government instead of having them unanimously arrayed against us"—*Butler Collection* (Viceroy Reading to Harcourt Butler). 5th July, 1921.

pending. According to this Act of 1886, the peasants were given seven-year-leases on land but they had no hereditary rights or even life tenancies.

The peasants of Awadh were ready to take to any means to achieve redressal of their grievances. They formed a peasant organisation—the Kishan Sabna at Rure in Pratap Garh district under the leadership of poor peasants like Jhinguri Singh and Sahdev Singh, who set up small sabhas which were not able to extract the desired concessions from the taluqdars and their protectors—the British Government. They, however, sought out more educated people than themselves, like Baba Ram Chandra, who agreed to take up the cause of the oppressed peasantry. It should be recalled that the first signs of protest towards the end of 1919, were noticed in the Pratapgarh district, which irritated the landlords—it was "*nai dhobi band*". This meant that all the menial services of cutting hair, washing of clothes, scavenging, etc., services which were essential for the comfortable living of the land-lords and which were provided by the village population, were no longer available to them. Mobilised on the lines of the village caste panchayats these strikes proved most successful[1].

According to Siddiqui, the peasant movement, that grew up in Awadh in course of time, had two distinct origins : "It came about as the result of two simultaneous processes. There was the conscious and deliberate attempt at building up a peasant organisation from the above for drawing the Government's attention to the various forms of agrarian discontent then prevalent, and this was overtly political. The other process through which Kisan Sabhas came into being was the result of grassroot peasant activity. Kisan Sabhas

1. Cf. Gopal, S. (ed.), *Selected Works of Jawaharlal Nehru*, Vol. I, p. 197.

spread in a mushroom growth and under a local leadership from the various villages they first sprang into existence. The grievances around which these Sabhas were organised were the same, nazrana, bedakhli and begar. But what these organisations proposed to do about such and other related matters was determined less by their own independent choice and more by continually changing political horizon[1]".

Siddiqui obviously had in mind the peasant unrest in Northern India, particularly that of the adjoining province of Bihar, where Mahatma Gandhi had taken up their cause in Champaran. In U.P., it was slow to percolate till Nehru and Tandon made on the spot studies of the conditions of oppressed tenants in the Pratapgarh district in 1920. Hence he thinks that the movement was inspired from the above. It was quite natural that the conditions prevailing in that district began to receive more notice. The signs of organised activity were noticed in the Amargarh estate in the Pratapgarh district around the same time. A sabha used to meet at Amargarh, but only to listen to leaders like Jhinguri Singh and Ram Chandra. Ram Chandra came as a saviour with "a message that he would get the law altered if they (the peasants) followed his advice. He worked for them, slaved for them and interceded with people in authority for them and thus, secured their confidence[2]. However, though Ram Chandra proved to be the most illustrious peasant leader, he has at two places in his account acknowledged that the Kisans in Pratapgarh district had already been organised into as many as twenty or twenty-five Sabhas before he came to Pratapgarh. The persons responsible for this were—

1. Siddiqui, M.H., *Agrarian Unrest in North India*, pp. 111-112.
2. *Mehta Report*, p. 53 ; Oral tradition in Pratapgarh confirms the fact that Ram Chandra was immensely popular. Even today he is veritable legend in the villages there.

Jhinguri Singh and Durgapal Singh[1]. Ram Chandra was persuaded by Jhinguri Singh and Sahdev Singh to throw in his weight with them to ameliorate the lot of the passantry through the Kisan Sabhas which was already functioning with headquarters at Rure[2]. A brief account of the early career of Ram Chandra would, it is felt, not be out of place in the present context.

Baba Ram Chandra, whose real name was Shridhar Balwant Jodhpurkar, was a Maharashtrian Brahmin. He was born in the year 1864 in a small village of Gwalior Estate[3]. He left for Fiji as an indentured labourer in 1904 and there he changed his name to Ram Chandra Rao in order to conceal his identity, as the Maharashtrian brahimins were suspect in the eyes of the British. It is difficult to accept the view of Panegrahi that he changed his name "to add to his person some religious and moral colour"[4]. He stayed in Fiji for thirteen years (1905—1917) and took active part in the movement to emancipate the lot of the indentured labourers. He has been referred to in the official literature as "a successful agitator in Fiji[5]". He came in contact with Manilal Gandhi, a close associate of C.F. Andrews, who took keen interest in social and emancipatory movements in Fiji[6]. He led popular demonstrations in Fiji, to focus on the grievances of indentured labourers. He smuggled in to

1. Siddiqui, M.H., *Agrarian Unrest in Narth India*, p. 112.
2. A Small Village in Pratapgarh District.
3. *Ram Chandra's Diary*, p. 4, N.M.M.L.
4. Panegrehi, D.N., *Peasant Leadership*, p. 94 ; He mentions that he had changed his name to Ram Chandra after his return from Fiji.
5. *Mehta Report*, p. 3.
6. *Ibid.*

India an article on the deplorable and inhuman conditions of indentured labourers in Fiji, which was published in *Bharat Mitra*, a newspaper from Calcutta[1]. The Fiji Government was alarmed by this article and was on the lookout for its writer. The article created such a furore that Ram Chandra was advised by his friends to leave Fiji before the authorities were able to lay their hands on him. Ram Chandra returned to India in 1917 because he wished to carry on the battle on behalf of the indentured labourers in India itself[2]. Further, a letter from Bal Gangadhar Tilak adviced him to come to India and carry on the struggle. In India, he started giving discourses on religion which endeared him to the simple and religious minded peasantry of Awadh, who flocked in ever greater numbers to listen to him. The change from social to religious questions was attributed by him to some divine visions he had while asleep[3].

Soon Ram Chandra won the administration of the peasantry which came to look on him as their deliverer. He heard their unending tales of misery and at first contacted the talqudars and sought their help to bring succour to the afflicated peasantry. They, naturally, were found to be unwilling to do away with their tyrannical practices[4] Rebuffed by the taluqdars, he now turned to the district authorities to enlist their cooperation in his mission, but nothing tangible emerged. He than made a direct appeal to the peasantry and urged the kisans to stand on their own feet. He exhorted them to withhold all kinds of cesses, gift payments (nazrana), forced labour (begar), and pay only their normal rents. He gave the example of *Dankani Bandobast* prevalent in Jaunpur district, under which their counterparts, only a

1. *Ram Chandra's Diary*, p. 25.
2. *Ibid.*, pp. 6-7.
3. *Ram Chandra's Writings.*
4. *Police Department* File No. 258/1920, UPSA (G.P. Sinha to Butler, 12th September, 1920).

few kilometres away, were far happier than they[1]. He also advocated an eight-point programme for the upliftment of the peasantry : (1) reservation of jungle tracts for the grazing of cattle, (2) payment of rent in advance of the fix time, (3) sinking of wells and digging of tanks, (4) planning of orchards, (5) half area to be sown with grain crops and half with cotton, (6) establishment of seed or grain depots at every three *kos*, (7) acceleration of female education by the intineraral-updeshikas (teachers), (8) creation of a union among the zamindar, kisans and mazdur (labourers)[2]. The Deputy Commissioner of Pratapgarh commented that Ram Chandra became "a magnet of attraction, who supplied some mental pabulam to a people usually intallectually starved in these out of the way places". The people, he added, "attended his meetings and many fraternised with him[3]".

The peasantry of Awadh was stirred to action in May, 1920, under the leadership of Ram Chandra. Local administration, fearing a breach of law and order, directed Ram Chandra to stop his propaganda calculated to incite class hatred and ill-will. The Deputy Commissioner asked him to forward the complaints of the peasants to him[4]. Ram Chandra instructed Jhinguri Singh and Sahdev Singh to file written complaints with the Deputy Commissioner of Pratapgarh. They marched with one thousand men and women to the office of the Deputy Commissioner to lay their complaints before him. Rure became a centre for receiving the complaints of the peasantry. By this time, the peasantry fear and its had shed its consciousness was growing rapidly. The peasant movement increased its strength because of the cohesion of the *Kurmis* and low caste peasants, who formed the bulk of

1. *Mehta Report*, p. 1.
2. *Ibid.*, p. 2.
3. *Mehta Report*, p. 3.
4. *Ibid.*

the peasantry. They were subjected to extreme ruthless oppression in comparison with the limited oppression experienced by the less numerious high caste peasants.

What made Ram Chandra the leader of the mass of peasantry ? Undoubtedly, the peculiar socio-economic circumstances provided the basis for such an event. The *taluqdars* and *zamindars* were not only unrelenting in their oppression but increased it overtime. The number of evictions increased in Pratapgarh from 1655 during 1918-19 to 2593 during 1919-20[1]. The landowners missed no opportunity to inflate rents on their holdings. The term *Murdafaroshi* brings out the cruelty involved in the fresh letting out of land at higher rents soon after the death of a tenant. Even the charge under the head *nazrana* increased out of all prepositions from the period preceeding 1920[2]. The dispossessed and disgruntled peasantry sought shelter under the Kisan Sabha's umbrella.

The leaders of the movement wished to broaden the movement and, therefore, decided to bring in Mahtma Gandhi and other educated, urban leaders into the movement. Ram Chandra gave the example of Champaran, where the tenants were said to have secured their release from the planter's tyranny due to Mahatma Gandhi's intervention.[3] With this aim in view, Ram Chandra organised a march of five hundred peasants on foot from Patti to Allahabad.[4] It was

---

1. *Mehta Report*, Exhibit 'I', p. 97.
2. *Mehta Report*, p. 19.
3. *Leader*, 23rd September, 1920.
4. The figure of the numbers of marchers varies. Mehta places it 500, Jawaharlal Nehru is also of the same view. Siddiqui gives it as 200. S.P. Sen (ed.), *Dictionary of National Biography* (VIII, p. 132) given 15000. The march took place in early June, 1920.

the first march on foot and must thus occupy a place of honour in the annals of peasant struggle. Jawahar lal Nehru wrote about the march and its leadership : " . . . he (Ram Chandra) had no programme of any kind and when he had brought them (peasants to a pitch of excitement, he tried to shift the responsibility to others. This led him to bring a number of peasants to Allahabad to interest people there in the movement"[1].

Ram Chandra and other leaders hoped to meet Gandhi at Allahabad, as he was scheduled to be there on his way back from Varanasi (Benares), where he had gone to attend a meeting of the A.I.C.C. Throughout the day, the marchers spoke of their difficulties in the city. In the evening, a meeting was held, which was attended by Jawahar lal Nehru, Ram Chandra was anxious to link the peasant movement with the freedom movement, but the bourgeois nationalist leadership, it appears was not enthusiastic and was somewhat reluctant, to take up the cause of the peasantry. Mittal observes : "As Raj Kumar Sukul had tugged at the sleeves of Gandhi and forced him to come to Champaran, so Ram Chandra and other marchers clung on the bourgeois nationalist politicians and would not return from Allahabad without concrete assurance of help"[2]. Ultimately, the returned after an assurance from Jawaharlal Nehru that he would visit them after two days.[3]

The nationalist politicians found an enthusiastic peasantry greeting them at every village they visited in the district of Pratapgarh. Jawaharlal Nehru wrote : "We found the whole country-side afire with enthusiasm and full of strange excitement. They were in miserable rags, men and women, but their faces were full of excitement and seemed to expect strange happenings which could, as if by a miracle put an end to their long misery . . . Looking at them and their misery

---

1. Nehru, Jawaharlal, *An Autobiography*, p. 53.
2. Mittal, S.K., *Social Scientist*, Vol. 4, No. 9, April, 1976 (Raj Kumar Sukul and Peasant Upsurge in Champaran).
3. Nehru, Jawaharlal, *An Autobiography*, p. 51.

and overflowing gratitude, I was filled with shame and sorrow . . . a new picture of India seemed to rise before me, naked starving, crushed and utterly miserable"[1]. Rural India felt elated at the support extended by the city-bred politicians. Their frequent visits created a deep impression on the rural folk. They also ventilated the grievances of the peasantry through the press and from the platform.[2] The Rure based Kisan Sabha stepped up its activities under the impact of these forces. However, while on the one hand, the leaders exhorted the peasants to stand united, on the other, they sought for a compromise between the oppressors and the oppressed.[3] It did not go beyond this nor did it place before the peasantry any concrete programme of action which the latter would secure its release from feudal oppression.

Baba Ram Chandra intensified the struggle and asked the peasantry to stop payment of illegal cases and the cultivation of Sir lands. He also appealed to the peasantry not to accept those lands for cultivation from which their fellow peasants had been evicted.[4] The peasantry by and large, obeyed the exhortation. The very few tenants who were lured by the *zamindars* to occupy such lands were intimidated into following the example of their numerous counterparts. The local Kisan Sabha, under the impetus of Ram Chandra, advised the peasantry to take up 'direct action.'[5] The spirit of defiance and rebellion had permeated the peasantry of Awadh. In the words of Jawaharlal Nehru : "the downtrodden Kisan began to gain a new confidence in himself and walked straight

1. *Ibid.*, p. 52.
2. Independent, 3rd July, 1920 ; *Abhudaya*, 24th July, 1920.
3. *Mehta Report*, p. 3.
4. *Police Department*, File No. 358/1920, U.P.S.A. (Hailey to Keane, 5th September, 1920).
5. *Mehta Report*, p. 3.

with head up. His fear of landlords' agents and the police lessened, and when there was an ejectment from a holding no other Kisan would make an offer for that land."[1] Though outwardly there appeared a full, it was a lull before the storm. The peasants of part of Awadh in those days were "desperate and a mere spark would have lighted a flame."[2]

The menacing situation and the increasing incidents of breach of peace brought the urban 'bourgeois politicians' on the scene. Consequently, several conferences were held to restore peace mostly in the troubled district of Pratapgarh. Despite conferences and efforts, peace did not return to the area. The taluqdars opposed tooth and nail the bestowal of any concession on the peasantry as it would lower their prestige and lead to a loss of face.[3] The situation grew from bad to worse and while Jawaharlal Nehru and P.D. Tandon did not approve the acts of highhandedness by the peasants, they also urged the authorities to withdraw the cases arguing that these might aggravate the situation further. The Allahabad leadership made it clear to the peasantry that if it persisted with such action, it would be deprived of 'bourgeois-nationalist support.'[4] But the disturbances continued unabated. Within the short period of a week about eight cases of high handedness were reported and criminal prosecution followed. Almost in every case Ram Chandra and his lieutenants were involved, not as actual participants but as instigators.[5]

Ram Chandra had wielded an enormous moral authority over the Awadh peasants and had endared himself to them. His organising capacity and his indigenous, semi-religious

1. Nehru, Jawaharlal, *An Autobiography*, p. 57.
2. *Ibid.*, p. 59.
3. *Abhudaya*, 24th July, 1920.
4. *Mehta Report*, p. 5.
5. *Leader*, 5th September, 1920.

methods of propaganda in a backward area without any modern means of transport and communication, enhanced his stature as a rural leader. To the taluqdars and the district authorities he had become a source of positive danger. The Government moved against him and his associates on very flimsy grounds on 28th August, 1920.[1] They were charged under Sections 107 of the Criminal Procedure Code and 379 of the Indian Penal Code. They were refused bail and were lodged in Pratapgarh jail. On the day of the trial a huge gathering of peasants filled the Court Compound. The authorities were at a loss as to what should be done with the arrested leaders. The hearing of the case had to be postponed. Meanwhile, the peasants resolved to secure the release of their leaders. Jawaharlal Nehru and Gauri Shanker Misra briefly addressed the peasants in Patti are a urging them to go *en masse* to the Magistrate and demand the release of the leaders or get themselves placed in jail.[2] The Deputy Commissioner convened a meeting of the local *Zamindari* Association and appealed to the peasants to remain calm. The taluqdars were evasive about the illegal exactions and the petty harassments of the peasants.[3] They pressurised the administration to deal harshly with the leaders, but finally the peasant leaders were freed. The local authorities withdraw all cases. ' For the Kisans this was a big triumph", says Jawaharlal Nenru, "and they began to think that they could always have their way by weight of numbers alone. To the Government this position was intolerable."[4]

---

1. *Police Department*, File No. 359/1920, U.P.S.A. (Hailey to Keane, 12th September, 1920).
2. *Police Department*, File No. 359/1920, U.P.S.A. (Hailey to Keane, 8th September, 1920).
3. *Ibid.*, File No. 358/1920, U.P.S.A. (Fortnightly Report of the Commissioner of Fyzabad for the first half of September, 1920).
4. Nehru, Jawaharlal, *An Autobiography*, p. 60.

The events of August-September brought Ram Chandra such fame that the peasantry of Awadh looked to him as their liberator. Matabadal Kori invited him to Kalkaliapur, a village in Rasulpur estate of Rae Bareli in October. He launched a Kisan Sabha Organisation on 28th October, 1920.[1] He made very frequent vissts to several villages of Rae Bareli, organised the units of the Kisan Sabha and galvanised the masses of the peasantry. He proclaimed 20th December as *Kisan Day* and exhorted the Awadh peasantry to assemble in the largest possible numbers at Ayodhya on that day. The Ayodhya conference and the activities of the leaders infused new life into the meek frame of the Awadh peasantry. Farron commented : "... they returned (from the Ayodhya conference) more than ever filled with a sense of real and fancied wrongs. They fell to discussing these in local panchayats which have since been formed in every village. For the first time in history they had began to realise the power of a united peasantry. If they stood together, *nazrana*, *begari* and other oppressive taxes would automatically cease. The political education ... was progressing. They were learning the value of concerted action."[2]

The new year (1921) began with the revolt of the Awadh peasantry in the Rae Bareli district where large crowds moved from one estate to another destroying the crops of *taluqdars*.[3] The tyrannical yoke of the landed aristocracy had become unbearable. The urban 'bourgeois nationalist leadership' was busy with the Congress programme. The desperate peasantry took to avoilence on a large scale. The movement assumed the dimensions of a class war which

1. *Revenue Department*, File No. 50/ 1921, U.P.S.A.
2. *Ibid.*
3. The crops of the following taluqdars were destroyed--Sardar Nihal Singh (2nd January, 1921), Thakur Ram Pratap Singh (3rd January, 1921) and Rup Singh (5th January, 1921).

climaxed in bloodshed on 7th January, 1921, at Munshiganj. It was reported that four men were killed and two wounded. An additional force of armed police and mounted soldiers had been despatched from Lucknow by train on 6th January, 1921. Several arrests were made.[1] The Munshiganj firing brought to the fore the old, accumulated grievances of the Awadh peasantry. It evoked such an emotive reaction that the brutal incident ended in demanding an enquiry.[2]

Alarmed by this peasant revolt, the Chief Secretary to the Government of the United Provinces, Lambert, reported to the Secretary to the Government of India, Home Department, 13th January, 1921, that "the southern portion of the Rae Bareli district was in a very disturbed state and rapidly approaching anarchy. Serious crimes amounting to dacoity began to occur in alarming numbers."[3]

A correspondent of *The Pioneer* in his report on the Rai Bareli disturbances telegraphed to London press, saying that peasant 'Soviets' had been established all over the area controlled by rebel peasants. On reading these accounts, the Secretary of State for India was greatly alarmed. On 12th January he telegraphed to the Viceroy "Yesterday's and today's newspapers are full of accounts with scare headlines and the terrific posters of agrarian riots in Rae Bareli and Sultanpur districts beginning apparently from January 9th.

---

1. *Home (Political) Department*, File Nos. 195—216/1921 Disturbances in the Rae Bareli and Fyzabad Districts), U.P.S.A.

2. Almost every newspaper demanded it. N.H. Kunzru demanded disciplinary action against men guilty of firing at Munshiganj in the Legislative Council-*Legislative Council Proceedings of U.P.*, Vol. I, pp. 679—704.

3. *Disturbances in the Rae Bareli and Fyzabad Districts*, Telegram No. 41 E, dated 9th January, 1921, U.P.S.A.

It is stated that the trouble is spreading, that civil and police authorities are quite unable to cope with it, that the rioters have a certain amount of justice in their cause, and that the suppression by land-owners of 'Soviets' among tenants is one of the reasons for disturbances. I am once again wholly without news. Please telegraph an account of these incidents."[1]

On 13th January, 1921, the Viceroy stated in his reply that the agitation which had been carried on amongst villagers had been largely, if not solely, the work of non-cooperators though there was no information to show how far the movement had been directly inspired or controlled by Mahatma Gandhi himself. The Viceroy also anticipated the possibility of similar disturbances breaking out in other parts of Awadh as well.

Meanwhile, according to the telegrams of the Indian News Agency and the Chief Secretary to the Government of the United Provinces, agrarian, disturbances involving much damage to property again broke out in the police circles of Barkhari and Jahangirganj in Tanda tehsil of the Faizabad district on 13th and 14th January, 1921.[2]

It may not be inappropriate to recall that the majority of the villages were under taluqdars. The Kisan Sabha movement was very well organised in this area. Its principal supporters and adherents were the small tenants or low-caste labourers employed by the Brahmin taluqdars. On 12th January, 1921, a public meeting was held by Kisan Sabha in

---

1. *Disturbances in the Rai Bareli and Faizabad Districts.* Telegram No. 41-E, dated Lucknow, 12th January, 1921.
2. *Home (Political) Department*, Telegram No. 36, 13th January, 1921 (from Viceroy to the Secretary of State), U.P.S.A.

which the low-caste serfs and tenants were persuaded not to work for the old wages for their zamindar employer. They were also advised to organise a strike. They were also told that it was the wish of Mahatma Gandhi that they should loot. They willingly and readily consented to carry out this behest, amidst sky rending slogans of '*Mahatma Gandhi Ki Jai*'. They were also told that British Raj was coming to an end and Gandhi Raj was about to dawn.

The success of this first operation inspired further action. On 13th January, therefore, large bands of tenants, consisting mainly of *chamars* and *ahirs*, assembled and proceeded to loot and plunder "every person of substance." The taluqdars could not offer any resistance as the peasant bands came in overwhelming numbers. Such bands are believed to have consisted of about five thousand men. For two days 13th and 14th January the looting was through. Many of the houses were completely sacked and the *taluqdars* lost almost all their household possessions.[1]

In the beginning of March, 1921, yet another peasant disturbance broke out in Sultanpur. Not bothering much about the genuine grievances of the peasantry, the authorities embarked upon a policy of repression. Not only were the peasants arrested in large numbers, but they were also also maltreated and beaten and harassed in a manner which could by no canons of justice be upheld. Vehemently opposing this attitude of the authorities. *Independent* of Allahabad wrote on 6th March, 1921 : "It is excessively painfull to inform the general public how the Government has planned the destruction of the noble and sacred movement of the kisans in the district. Police and *zamindars* have been

---

1. *Disturbances in the Rae Bareli and Faizabad Districts*, p. 12.

backed and encouraged by the Government and they work as right and left hands of Government's oppression. The opposition is so great that it is beyond easy description . . . when a person is arrested, he is very mercilessly beaten until he is senseless or unless he promises to make his statements just as the police desire."[1]

Another disturbances ending in loss of some lives occurred in the Rae Bareli district on 20th March, 1921. The facts are as follows : Four peasant leaders, who had been making inflamatory speeches, announced that they would hold a large meeting and make speeches at Karhaiya in the Salon tahsil on 20th March, which was the day of the weekly market. Orders were issued by the authorities prohibiting speeches at the meeting and for arrest of all the four leaders. In the process of arrest the police were attacked by the assembled peasants. To defend themselves the police opened fire. Some were killed and hundreds wounded.[2] Government sources alleged the occurence of another disturbance on 23rd March, 1921 as well. The Prevention of Seditious Meetings Act was extended to disturbed area.

The Governor in Council reviewed the disturbances in the district of Rae Bareli and decided to post additional police in the disturbed locations and make the inhabitants pay the cost of maintaining it. He also decided to prosecute to the leaders. The use of spears and swords was prohibited in the four districts of Rae Bareli, Pratapgarh, Faizabad and Sultanpur

---

1. *Independent*, 6th March, 1921.

2. *Home (Political) Department, Proceedings*, March, 1921, Nos. 334—39, U.P.S.A. (Account based on the telegram sent on 22nd March, 1921, by the Chief Secretary to Government of the United Provinces to Government of India).

for a considerable period.[1] Giving his approval to these repressive steps of the Provincial Government, the Home Secretary to the Government of India, Wyne remarked on 24th March, 1921 : "We must agree. The recommendation is made by the Government of the United Provinces including the ministers and it would be madness to resist them . . . (though the) result of yesterday's debate (in the Assembly) renders the application of extraordinary laws more difficult than at present, we still could not tell the United Provinces we did not agree with their proposal because the members of the Assembly disliked the policy. The prime duty to maintain law and order cannot be superseded by a resolution of the Assembly."[2]

The repressive measures further provoked the peasantry on the night of 17–18th April, 1921 and, the Rae Bareli collectorate was partially destroyed by fire. To frighten the peasants of Rae Bareli district a squadron of the 28th cavalry made a route march of a week's duration through the south of the district. Dispositions had been made which would place additional armed and mounted police at points where their presence was most needed to display the might of British imperialism. Reserves totalling about 600 men had been concentrated at important strategic centres. Thousands

---

1. *Home (Political) Department, Proceedings,* March, 1921, Nos. 334–39, U.P.S.A. (demi-official letter from G.B. Lambert, Chief Secretary to Government of the United Provinces, to the Home Secretary, dated 24th March, 1921).

2. *Riots in Rae Bareli District* : Application of the Prevention of Seditious Meetings Act, 1911, to the Districts of Pratapgarh, Rae Bareli, Sultanpur and Fyzabad in the United Provinces, p. 1.

of armed policemen and mounted police had been drawn off from the more secure districts for this purpose[1].

Effort were made to secure a demonstration of cultivators at the meetings of Allahabad district conference held on 1st and 11th May, 1921. Peasants from Awadh attended in large numbers. According to official sources, one special feature of the conference was the attempt to strengthen the hold of none-cooperators on the Kisan Sabhas, particularly in the Awadh districts which held been proclaimed under the Seditious Meetings Act. The campaign opened with the distribution of a leaflet addressed ta cultivators and signed by Pandit Motilal Nehru. In Pratapgarh district they were distributed among peasants by some youths, who were promptly dealt with under Section 108 of the Criminal Procedure Code[2]. According to local press the youngmen were criminally assulated tortured by the police. This enraged the politically advanced sections of the society. The daily newspaper Independent promptly wrote an editorial on 12th May, 1921, severely criticising the unwanted behaviour of the police. It said, "Lord Reading has been denouncing violence, and quite rightly too. We do not want any favour of Lord Reading as Viceroy but he happens to be a bencher of the Middle Temple and we know he is a gentleman who is interested in fair dealing. We believe that he will recoil from the crude violence of an ill-mannered policeman. May we, therefore, present him with the incident which is reported from Sultanpur ? It is a piece of sheer bullying and torture to which only a wild animal would resort (God forgive us if we do injustic to dumb animals). It is idle to speak of the

1. *Home (Political) Department, Proceedings,* June. 1921, File No. 23, U.P.S.A., (Report on the Political Situation in India during Fortnight Ending 30th April, 1921).
2. *Home (Political) Department, Proceedings,* June, 1921, File No. 63, U.P.S.A.

wickedness of violence in this province as long as the man who commits violence happens to be a government official. We are convinced of the futility of such procedure. The districts in Awadh have been handed over to the torture. Unspeakable things have been done and more will be done. No discrimination can save men from the violence of government, neither age nor youth nor station will be respected. But we thank all the gods that the brave lads who have been put to the torture have refused to band the knee to the torturer or to the tyrant"[1].

Next day Jawaharlal Nehru himself proceeded to distribute the leaflet. But the Government did not dare to take any action against him. The leaflet was immediately prescribed. It was followed by attempts to organise a big mass meeting of peasants at Allahabad.

The agrarian trouble continued unabated for months togethr in Awadh. "There was a quick response", wrote Lambert, Chief Secretary to the Government of the United Provinces on 4th June, 1921, to Gwynne, Deputy Secretary to the Government of India, Home Department, "to the agitators' appeal based on special agrarian grievances".[2].

These peasant conferences and movements along with other activities of non-cooperation movement played an historic role in underming British power and prestige. In his telegram of 13th May, 1921, the Chief Secretary to the Government of United provinces reported to the Home Department in Delhi that the "situation is steadily deteriorating, confidence in power of government growing less ; officers are losing heart ; and the belief that lives of Europeans are in danger is growing"[3]. On 2nd June, 1921, the Viceroy telegraphed

1. *Home (Political) Department, Proceedings,* June, 1921, File No. 63, p. 41, U.P.S.A.
2. *Independent,* 12th May, 1921.
3. *Report on the Political situation in India during the Fortnight Ending 15th May,* 1921, pp. 1-2, N.A.I.

to the Secretary of State about Awadh that there was "little sign of return to settled peace[1]".

Section II

Meanwhile, another peasant movement was also taking roots in some north western districts, and came to be designated as the "Eka Movement". According to Mrs, it was started in Malihabad *tahsil* of Lucknow district in 1921[2]. However, archival material indicates that it was started by the tenants in the Hardoi district[3], towards the end of 1921[4]. The objective was to resist the attempts of the landlords and their men to take more than the recorded rent from the tenants. It was reported that "the Hardoi peasantry have been told that if they stand together and frighten the *zamindars* they will be able to get any concentrations they desire"[5].

It had, however, long been a practice in Hardoi and in the neighbouring districts of Sitapur, Unnao and Kl eri, that the landlords charged their tenants more than the rent that was recorded in the village papers. They did not allow the actual rental to be recorded as they feared that if they did so, the Government would demand a greater sum as revenue

1. *Ibid*, 31st May, 1921, p. 31, N.A.I.
2. Misra, B.R., *Land Revenue Policy in the United Provinces*, p. 213.
3. *Leader*, 3rd March, 1921.
4. Col. Faunthrope, who made a special enquiry into the Eka Movement in Hardoi, "The phrase Kisan Sabha was probably discarded by the Malihabad Congress and Khalafat people because it represented a discreditable and moribund movement". Faunthrope's Report to the Chief Secretary, U.P., dated, Lucknow, 8th April, 1922, and subsequently published in the *U.P. Government Gazette* 13th May, 1922, Part VIII, pp. 271-280.
5. *Faunthrope's Report*, p. 273.

from them[1]. They did not also give receipts for the rents collected and this was another grievance of the tenants[2]. The table below shows the difference between the rents recorded and the rents paid in four cases of the Hardoi district.[3]

S.No.	*Rent as recorded*	*Rent actually collected each year*
1.	Rs. 13,000	Rs. 15,500
2.	Rs. 67,500	Rs. 77,000
3.	Rs. 19,000	Rs. 32,000
4.	Rs. 1,700	Rs. 5,700

It was the general opinion of the officers of the district that "for the whole district a safe estimate would be collection of 50 per cent above recorded rent"[4]. A former Deputy Commissioner of Hardoi who had characterised the system in Hardoi as 'rotten', however, suggested a remedy essentially to the disadvantage of the tenant. He wrote, "I believe, it would be possible in the cases of estates where the *zamindars* are not considered exceedingly oppressive and unpopular, for some friendly settlement to be arrived at. For example, if the rent collected is 50 percent above the recorded rent, parties might agree......to a settlement on the basis of 25 percent, splitting the difference"[5].

The doubts in the minds of the peasants about the legality (as well as feasibility) of having to pay these extra dues sprung to the fore again. As cesses varied 'greatly not only from district to district but......even from village to village in an estate', the question was always alive. In July, 1921,

1. Even the Government admitted, "The main reason why concealment of rent is so prevalent in Hardoi is that the last settlement of that district was a very severe one".
2. *Leader*, 29th March, 1922.
3. *Faunthrope's Report*, p. 276.
4. *Ibid.*
5. *Faunthrope's Report*, p. 276.

a riot over cesses had occured on an estate in Lucknow but this was before the Eka Movement had begun to take shape. This naturally led to resentment on the part of the tenants, specially in those areas where the landlord's share of the produce was two fifths or more. Siddique observes : "Also, the fact that landlords were masters only of all that they surveyed, and not of what their *karindas* surveyed, cut into the landlord's profits. With grain rents as the rule it was difficult for the land-lords to keep an eye on the machinations of their ill-paid *karindas*. The profits thus made by the intermediate subbordinates caused the zamindar to first cry '*batai-lutai*"[1], and then to raise the rents further"[2].

Bahraich was a district of large estates and here too, like in Hardoi, grain rents prevailed. When, towards the middle of January, 1922, the Government through that the non-cooperation was gaining ground, it was only partly correct. Though it could be said that 'unrest had taken an agrarian turn', it could not be asserted as the whole truth. The peasant movement always a tool of the nationalist movement, was always considered by the administraition to have the seditious colour of non-cooperation. As such, it did not always choose to make a distinction between political events and those agrarian. Consequently, the news from Bahraich

---

1. Grain rents in the eastern districts of the United Provinces were of two kinds. In one, Kankut, the standing crop of the tenant was surveyed and a random assessment made of what the actual produce yield was likely to be. And on that basis the shares of landlord and tenant were decided. But as the appraisement of the crop was done by the landlord's servants, the latter were able to manipulate things to their advantage. They would, for instance, agree to assess the crop reasonably only if the tenant assured them of their share. In *batai*, too, where the grain was divided on the threshing floor, the strength of the landlord's men prevailed.

2. Siddiqui, M.H., *Agrarian Unrest in Northern India*, p. 199.

that 'bands of tenants' were moving form village to village demanding the immediate abolition of grain rents was interpreted to mean that non-cooperation was on the rise. Unlike Hardoi, the estates in Bahraich were mostly managed by *thekadars* in the grain-rented areas. This helped the land lord in getting a steady income and the losses that could result from seasonal fluctuations in crop yields were now the business of the *thekadar* . It was against the *thekedars*, therefore, that peasant unrest was directected. Although the Government maintained that hardly any instances in which violence was used occurred[1], but Siddiqui points out that : " . . through an Associated Press report two instances of violence had taken place by 12th January against the *thekedars*. The tenants had gathered together, beaten up the *thekedars* and had carried the grain off"[2]. The same report also stated that politics was slowly taking over the purely tenant's agitation" '. . political agitators have taken advantage of the situation stating that Mr. Gandhi will lower the cash rents"[3]

The Eka Movement had spread from Hardoi as far as Baharaich, although enough information about its form in the districts of Barabanki, Sitapur and Lucknow is not available. But as it had assumed serious proportions, it had to be quelled at all costs[4]. The movement in Hardoi, by the end of January, was strongest in the Atrauli police circle of Sandila *tahsil*. The frequent gatherings of peasants there had frightened the landlords considerably and it was the opinion of two Deputy Cammissioners of Hardoi that matters were brought to a head largely because of the provocative attitude of the *zamindars*. However, once the movement had got off the ground, it became as formidable as the Kisan

1. *Home (Political) Proceedings*, File No. 18/1922 (Demi-official letter No. 124, 18th January, 1922. from the Chief Secretary, U.P. Government to Secretary (Home), Government of India), U.P.S.A.
2. *Ibid*.
3. *Ibid*., 19th January, 1922.
4. *Faunthrope's Report*, p. 273.

Sabha movement not so much in the agrarian rioting that was part of the latter, but in its organisation.

According to Siddiqui, the movement was made strong by the sanctity of an elaborate ritual, a feature not so noticeable in the Kisan Sabha Movement.[1] Before an Eka was formed a hole was made in the ground and filled with water from the well. This hole represented the Ganges and the peasants took an oath over it. A pandit recited some holy scriptures and was paid for his services by the leaders from the collection made by the villagers for the Eka movement. The peasant bound themselves to the following eleven injuctions of the oath :

(1) Not to leave their fields when illegally ejected.
(2) To pay only the recorded rent.
(3) To pay rent regularly at *kharif* and *rabi*.
(4) Not to pay rent without obtaining receipts.
(5) Not to do any forced labour for *zamindars* without payment.
(6) Not to pay the dues of *hari* and *bhusa*.
(7) To use tank water for irrigation without payment.
(8) To graze cattle on jungle and *parti* land without payment.
(9) To give no help to criminals in the village.
(10) To oppose oppression by *zamindars*.
(11) To abide by all decisions of the panchayat without having recourse to the courts.[2]

The Hardoi landlords felt alarmed at the rapidity with which Eka spread in that district. By the end of February, 1922, one police circle alone had reported 21 Eka meetings within a period of three days with attendence varying from

1. Siddiqui, M.H., *Agrarian Unrest in North India*, pp. 201-202.

2. Most of these points were also emphasised by Baba Ram Chandra who, too, had tabled a similar charter aiming at village upliftment.

150 to 2000[1]. As in the case of Bahraich, the Congress workers, who acted as a central organisation for the Eka in its early stages, "were quite annoyed" when the Eka got out of their contol. There was also no coordinating leadership of the movement.

The Eka movement, though primarily a tenants' movement, often had dispossessed landlords participating in it as well. Deputy Inspector, General of Police. Scott O'Connor thought the fact that "a large number of petty *zamindars* are themselves members of the Eka movement indicate clearly that the movement is not purely agrarian"[2]. There was no doubt that the Eka had 'an element of non-cooperation about it', and to this extent O, Connor' judgement was correct. The participations of landlords, however, was motivated by considerations not entirely political. In one instance recorded by Faunthrope, one of the organisers of the Eka had been making, about Rs. 250 a week from subscriptions alone. This aspect of the movement has drawn the following comment from Siddiqui :

"Largely, though notwithstanding deviations of the kind mentioned (above), the *zamindars* of Hardoi and Barabanki participated in two ways. If they were khilafatists, their agitation was only political. If not, then it was primarily the crushing weight of the land revenue demand which made them join the ranks of the tenants"[3].

Obviously Siddiqui makes an oblique reference to the khilafat Movement that was raging throughout India at that time. But the rural masses were groaning under the weight of the exactions of the *taluqdars*, landlords and their agents. As such, the Eka was more an agrarian and less a political movement in nature.

---

1. *Faunthrope's Report*, p. 278.
2. *Faunthrope's Report*, p. 278. (Report by Deputy Inspector General of Police, Scott O'Connor to the Inspector general of Police, U.P. dated 30th March, 1922.
3. Siddiqui, M.H., *Agrarian Unrest in North India*, pp. 206-207.

The Eka movement died out suddenly as it had its origins in spontaniety. The politics of non-cooperation did not influence the Eka to the extent that the earlier movement (Kisan Sabha movement) had been influenced. Even though it was said that the Eka movement was more political in its character and this was said because some non-cooperating khilafatist *zamindars* inadvertantly helped it to get on its foot in the beginning—it was essentially a low caste tenants' movement, which threw up its own leadership in the person of *Madari and Sohrab*[1]. Its level of organisation, too, was much lower than that of the Kisan Sabha movement and this responsible very largely for its short life of approximately four months. It was crushed in lesser time and the *ad-hoc* nature of its organisation prevented its revival.

1. *Leader*, 4th March, 1922.

4

Discontent and Disturbances—II

Kisan Sabha movement was very well organised in Faizabad division, particularly in Faizabad district. Initially, damage to property was reported in the police circles of Bhaskari and Jehangirgunj in Tanda *tehsil* on 13th and 14 January 1921. The major supporters of the movement were the small tenants or low-caste labourers, employed by Brahmin *zamindars* of the district[1]. On 12th January 1921 a Kisan Sabha meeting was held in which the low caste serfs and tenants were persuaded not to work for the old wages for their *taluqdar* and *zamindar* employers. They were exhorted to organise a strike. An attack on the *taluqdars* of Bankara was also demanded. This was immediately carried out and their houses looted[2]. The reluctant peasants were told that it was the earnest desire of Mahatma Gandhi that they should loot. This dispelled their reservations. They willingly and readily consented to carry out this behest admist sky-rending slogans of '*Mahatma Gandhi Ki Jai*'[3]. They were also told that British Raj was coming to an end and Gandhi Raj was about to dawn.[4] The suceess of this first operation seemed to have inspired the belief that there would be no resistance or interference with looting, and on the following day, 13th January, 1921 large gangs consisting mainly of *Chamars, lumirrs and ahirs* collected and proceeded to loot indiscriminately. Every person of substance[5], except at Muhammadpur where the

1. *General Administration Report*, 1920-21.
2. *Hailey Papers*, from Hailey, Commissioner to Lambert, Chief Secretary, 29th January 1921.
3. Nehru, Jawaharlal, *An Autobiography*, p. 61.
4. *Home (Pol.) Department*, No. 17, p. 20.
5. *Ibid.*

villagers turned out and beat off the assailants, no resistance seems to have been offered, the gangs being over-powering in number. During 13th and upto the afternoon of the 14th January 1921, the looting continued. some 30 villages and a *bazar* were looted[1]. The utmost alarm prevailed in the neighbourhood and large numbers flocked into Bhaskhari for police protection[2]. On the 13th January the Sub-inspector of police sent off a message of S.O.S. On the 14th January the Deputy Commissioner and the Superintendent of Police arrived with a few armed police and went in search of the gangs. They arrived at the Ram Nagar Bazar just after it had been looted and found that the gangs had dispersed on the news of the arrival of police reinforcement. A few assests were made at the time of men carrying off plunder.

On the 15th January, more police arrived and a tour was made of the pludered villages. In some only the grain-stores had been looted, whereas in many others the looting was thorough. Many of the houses were completely sacked and the *zamindars* lost almost all their household possessions. Even doors and millstones were carried off. It was observed that "Even the tutors of landlords' children were plundered[3]". In some instances, the women's clothes and ornaments were torn off. Cart-loads of loot were recovered which had been thrown away into wells. In all, the loss was estimated to be of Rs. 2 lakhs.

On the first day the movement was directed against particular *taluqdars* on account of private enmity, but after that the object was loot pure and simple. Choudhary observes that—"The primary object of looting were houses of small *zamindars* ; but *banipas* (money lenders) *sunars* (gold smiths), and *patwaris* (village revenue officers), who were considered

1. *General Administration Report*, 1920-21.
2. From Hailey, Commissioner, to Lambert, Chief Secretary 29th January, 1921.
3. Choudhary, Sukhbir, *Peasants and Workers Movement in India*, p. 141.

the henchmen of *zamindars* were also not spared[1]". The gangs were composed mainly of low castes, it is stated that many of those men had been persuaded not to work for the old wages for their *zamindar* employers and there was some destitution among them as a result of the strike. Several gangs were at work, their strength varying between one thousand and five thousands. The mobs were growing in strength owing to the case with which success was being achieved, and were followed by crowds of women to carry off the plunder. It was only the prompt arrival of the Deputy Commissioner and the Superintendent of Police, with a small force, believed to be the advance-guard of large forces, which prevented the extension of the disturbances over a much wider area[2].

The following days were spent in investigating the numerous complaints filed. There was no difficulty about the identification, as the members of dacoiting gangs were local men, personally known to the complaints, and sometimes residents of same village. Chaudhary writes that "In all, 346 persons were arrested. At first the attitude of the people was friendly to the authorities and a number of villagers assisted in beating jungles in which the dacoits were believed to have taken refuge. With the arrival of some of the leaders of the kisan sabha, intimidation began to be practiced and difficulties were placed in the way of the investigating officers[3]".

On the 19th January, two of these men (agitators) were assaulted and beaten by a small zamindar whose women-folk had their clothes stripped off them, by men of low caste. One of them, Kedar Nath, thereupon addressed a meeting in bazar when he made the following violent speech : "Police who are the servants and get bread from them, on instigation of their white faced Europeans, gets them beaten with *lathis*

1. *Ibid.*, p. 143.
2. *General Administration Report*, 1920-21.
3. Choudhary, Sukhbir, *Peasants and Workers' Movement in India*, p. 150.

and *dandas*. Today they (agitators) will go out and you will see a large gathering at Baskhari. Either we should die or the police will die. Make room and arrangements of food for those who will gather. Mahatma Gandhi will not come, but they will show their strength. I do not think it proper to call Mahatmaji. Either he (Kedar) will die or overthrow the police. These 'Londa Haru' (Sub-inspector and other police) see how they will be treated, and you will see the dropping of bomb in Baskhari. and further, you will see the state of change. Either that *zamindar* (who has beaten him) will remain slave of the English, or Mahatma Deo Narain will remain. He has stopped the *lathis* of the *zamindars*[1]". "The other, Deo Narain, declared his intention of remaining at the thana, until the police apologised[2]". As the language used was threatening to the police, the Deputy Commissioner prohibited the meeting for the following day ; but it was doubtful whether, owing to the shortness of the notice, the prohibitions was widely known. On the morning of the 20th January, crows began to come into Baskhari. The first few ones were dispersed, but they came in greater numbers ; while information was received that larger bodies were advancing from Akbarpur. It became obvious that the small police force was wholly inadequate to disperse them or cope with the situation. The crowd was generally well-behaved and had apparently not much notion of the object for which they had been summoned, but refused to leave except on orders from their leader Kedar Nath.

The situation was relieved by an offer from the latter to dismiss the crowd to their homes on an understanding by the Deputy Commissioner to inquire into the alleged assault ; the result to be announced at a subsequent meeting to be held at Akbarpur on 27th January 1921. The simple peasants

---

1. From Peters, Deputy Commissioner, to Hailey, Commissioner, dated 31st January, 1921, U.P.S.A.

2. From Peter, Deputy Commissioner to Hailey. Commissioner, 31st January 1921, U.P.S.A.

natively agreed to this compromise and the meeting at Baskhari was dissolved[1].

On 27th January 1921, Kisan Sabha was held in a *maidan* in the vicinity of village Gauhana, Police Circle Akbarpur, District—Faizabad, from 11.35 a.m. to 4.20 p.m. The rally comprised of about 40,000 kisans. The meeting was opened with the Sanskrit song 'Bande Matram' recited by a youth. Its essence was that even if a man will be killed in the fight for Swaraj his drops of blood will utter '*Bande Matram*' and if a man is jailed for the same suspicious cause, the fetters will resound with '*Bande Matram*'.

Jawaharlal Nehru was elected the President of the meeting by an overwhelming majority. In his Presidential speech, Jawaharlal Nehru initially said that the kisan of Awadh had now awakened and taken a vow not to sit at ease till they do not remove their chronic gravience of ejectment, *Nazrana*, and multiple illegal cesses etc. They knew that Mahatma Gandhi and other leaders had started a potent war, either to correct or uproot the Government which was oblivious of the religion, lives and respect of Indians. It was the solemn duty of every Indian to take part in the suspicious war to attain their cherished ideal of Swaraj. Then Jawaharlal Nehru expressed his sorrow on the events of dacoity and loot which had recurred in Faizabad district[1]. The only expiable feature was that the *kisan* had been deceived by some people that Mahatma Gandhi had ordered the loot. Nehru exhorted the kisans, if they were serious and earnest about Swaraj, to take a pledge not to resort to violence or looting. Criticizing the 'babas' or messianic leaders like Ram Chandra and his imitators who were preaching extremism, Jawaharlal warned the peasants not to believed that every person in coloured was a real 'Sadhu' and a messenger of Mahatma Gandhi, for Gandhi would never advise irreligious or unlawful activities[2].

---

1. Nehru, Jawaharlal, An Autobiography p. 61
2. Gopal. S., *Jawaharlal Nehru : A Biography*, p. 53.

Those who had taken part in dacoities should purge themselves of their sin by expressing their sympathy with those robbed and their hatred of the robbers. Every kisan should take a vow not to loot, injure or abuse anybody[1] but to remain firm and fearless in the cause and agitation which they had started[2].

In the meeting a resolution was passed. It said that this kisan Conference expresses its abhorrence at the action of the looters in this district and expresses its hearty symathy with those who had been looted. Masud Alam of Faizabad in moving the above resolution said, that Mahatma Gandhi or none of the muslim leaders were in favour of looting. If any person induced them to commit dacoities in the name of Mahatma Gandhi, he was not their friend. His chief object was to spoil their cause. The object of this gathering was to get rid of the atrocities committed upon them by the *taluqdars* by means of ejectment and *nazrana* etc. and their cause would surely fail if they would commence looting. Looting was condemned by their respective religions. Besides they should also sympathise with those who have been looted, be they *taluqdars* or others. In conclusion the speaker advised the kisans, never to commit looting. Their grievances were going to be redressed soon and they had so far succeeded in their endeavours. They would soon be relieved from the boundage of *taluqdars*.

Kedar Nath seconded the resolution. He said the kisans should express horror at the looting. The kisans were so simple that when they were asked by Nehru to raise their hands, about two dozen of hand went up in the very presence of numerous police officials, that meant certain trouble for them.[3] The whole property in India belonged to Gandhi hence he would never say to any person to have his own

1. *The Independent*, 26th January, 1921.
2. The speech of Nehru at Akbarpur as reported by Lakhte Hasan, Inspector, C.I.D., 27th January 1921.
3. Nehru, Jawaharlal, *An Autobiography*, p. 61.

property looted. They should never be afraid of going to jail In the (ause of country and truth, but they should never go to a jail nnder the affeuce of abusing marpit and looting[1]. Sarju Pande supported the resolution and warned the kisans not to believe in usurpers. The resolution was put to vote by the President and was passed unanimously[2].

Lallanji of Faizabad in moving the 2nd resolution regarding the expression of sympathy for those who had been killed in Rae Bareli said they should express their sorrow for those who had been killed in Rae Bareli in connection with the repeal of the Law of ejectment. They should express abhorrence for those who fired these innocent people. They should always be ready to suffer gunshot in the cause of *Dharma* as without sacrifice their '*yajna*' (mission) would not be fulfilled. They should remain firm in their *dharma* otherwise their future will be marred. They should also sympathise with the families of those who had sacrified their lives in the cause of *dharma*[3].

Pandit Vishwanath Sharma then made a speech in which he seconded the resolution. The speech was unconnected with the substance of resolution so he was asked to finish his speech soon[4]. Musammat Ram Devi. wife of Kedar Nath of Faizabad supported the resolution in a speech in which she said that there was no harm if the Rae Bareli kisans suffered the troubles. The present agitation had taken the shape of 'Mahabharat War'[5].

Pandit Tribhuvan Dutt of Faizabad in supporting the above resolution said that in former times there was no law of ejectment. There was 'Ram Raj' in Awadh. The British were taking their loaves and butter on account of the kisans. The wheat was produced by kisans, but the miserable

---

1. Jagannath, Inspector, C.I.D., 27th January, 1928.
2. Lakhte Husain, Inspector, C.I.D. 27th January 1921.
3. Jagannath, Inspector, C.I.D., 27th January 1921.
4. *Ibid.*
5. Lakhte Husain, Inspector, C.I.D., 27th January 1921.

kisans of Awadh could not even taste it. The kisans of Rae Bareli were dying without food, hence it was their duty to help them with money[1]. The resolution was also passed unanimously.

Pandit Deo Narain Pande then moved the third Resolution about forming a committee to enquire into the affairs of the decoities committed by kisans. He said that he had been to Baskhari where any property recovered in the house of kisans were claimed by the *zamindars* as their property looted in the dacoities. The police were committing various oppressions there. The speaker had got a list of about two or 2.50 thousands of money taken by the police in bribery. He also spoke about it to the Deputy Commissioner he too paid no heed. So a committee of the following persons be formed to reach at the spot and atleast to check the oppressions of the police in further enquiry. (1) B. Lallan ji of Faizabad, (2) S. Masud Alam of Faizabad, (3) Deo Narain the speaker, (4) Sarju Pande, (5) P. Tara Chand, (6) Ram Kuber Pandey, (7) Rampal Singh and (8) Tribhuvan Dutt.

Nageshwar Lal (perhaps of Sultanpur District) seconded the resolution and said that since the occurrences in Baskhari, the Kotwal, the inspector and the sub-Inspectors of Sultanpur committed oppressions in the Hanuman Ganj. The *khufia* police committed burg-laries and the *daroga* demanded Rs. 150/- and Rs. 200/- as bribes from the *mahajans.* The *darogah* afterwards returned some bribes when he came to know that some disciples of Gandhi had also reached the spot. The kisans should be careful of the cheats, sent by their opponents, the taluqdars etc. to deceive them for commission of deeds which would mar their reputation. Taking part in crime was against the principles of non-cooperation. The resolution was also carried unanimously.

---

1. Jagannath, Inspector, C.I.D., 27th January, 1921.

It was also mentioned that the bureaucracy was very much perplexed with the present agitation and the Viceroy requested the moderates and the *taluqdars*] to suppress the agitation. The disciples of Mahatma Gandhi—Deo Narain Pande, Kedar Nath and Tribhuvan Dutt have perplexed the Deputy Commissioner and the Commissioner and numerous telegrams had been sent to the Governor. They had been stopped under Section 144 C.P.C. to speak in Bhaskhari and Jehangirganj circles[1].

"This Sabha is convened that Swaraj is the only remedy for the redress of the grievances of the Indians and requests the kisans, cultivators and the traders to advance the cause of non cooperation fearlessely and peacefully as desired by the Congress". Kamaluddin Jafrai in moving the fourth resolution said that the atrocities of the Government had gone to such an extremity that no reform could be expected from it ; hence Swaraj should be established. Even by the repeal of the law of ejectment, their grievances would not be over as every 30 years the land rent would be increased, as the object of the Government was to extort money from India and send it to England. The announcement was simply to weaken the agitation, The only way to get Swaraj was to observe non-cooperation on the lines of Mahatma Gandhi.

Hafiz Alam in seconding the above resolution said that by Swaraj, the land cultivated by them would belong to them and the *taluqdars* won't be able to reprees them. In the attainment of Swaraj they should suffer all hardships and should not mind going to jail. The men killed in *Jalianwala Bagh* and Rae Bareli had brought the Swaraj nearer to them[2].

Pandit Debi Dutt of Allahabad in supporting the resolution said the audience should (1) Bycott courts and settle their

1. Lakhte Husain, Inspector, C.I.D., 27th January 1921.
2. The speech of Hafiz Alam was rather violent—Jagannath Inspector, C.I.D., 27th January, 1921.

affairs by panchayats (2) Bycott foreign goods, (3) organise volunteers and Seva Samitis and (4) be united.

The President then made his speech on the resolution and said the root cause of all troubles was the foreign Government in India. He then explained the items of non-cooperation and took votes on each separate items viz ; (1) bycott of courts, (2) bycott of Government services, (3) bycott of titles (4) bycott of foreign goods and encouragement of country cloth etc. People should not co-operate with the Government as it had become sinful. All the people carried the resolution unanimously.

Pandit Gauri Shanker of Allahabad then moved the Fifth Resolution. He advised on eight things to the *kisans* and these eight things may be considered the ingredients of the resolution as the seconder of resolution, Baba Ram Chandra took votes of the *kisans* on those eight points. In the resolution, Pandit Gauri Shanker made an eloquent and pathetic speech on the grievances of *kisans* in Awadh where in the time of Lord Rama they had every convenience. The eight points on which he asked the *kisans* to act were as follows :

(1) To stop giving *nazarana* henceforth.

(2) To stop doing *begar* and working on very low rates.

(3) To stop giving *bhusa, patai*, cowdung, etc.

(4) No other kisan, except the ejected one, should again take the ejected fields.

(5) To establish Panchayat system in villages and boycott courts.

(6) To encourage *Swadeshi* and spinning wheel and boycott foreign goods.

(7) To commit no robbery etc. on the instigation of spurious sadhus.

(8) To follow no spurious Baba Ram Chandra.

Pandit Gauri Shanker said that in acting upon the principles they should not fear of the Pratapgarh litigation against *kisans* or use of fire arms in Rae Bareli. They may be sent to jail or their hands may be cut, but they should not pay *nazrana* with their hands. If anyone instigates on Gandhi's name or even if God comes and preaches them to commit robbery etc., they should not act on such advice. The *kisans* should not think that they were born for getting illtreatment of others. They had equal rights of human beings. If any other *kisan*, except the ejected one, accepts the ejected fields, he should be socially boycotted. He should not be stopped from pulling water out of the well, but no one should drink water from his hands and no barber or washerman would shave him or wash his clothes.

In settling cases in panchayats, accused should not be beaten or illtreated. Rent should not be stopped as long as the lands cultivated by *kisans* belonged to *taluqdars*. In the end, he said that Deo Narain Pande had pardoned Alopi and they too should not be angry on Alopi, but if he meets them they should be given his message that Deo Narain had pardoned him. He will thus mix with them and become their friend for ever. Baba Ram Chandra in seconding the fifth resolution said that in several meetings, he told them to pay their rent and not to create any disturbance. He also told them not to pay *nazrana* etc. He did not understand why they created disturbances, which showed that they were not *kisans*. They had brought a band name upon him and Mahatma Gandhi. A Sadhu who called himself Ram Chandra had asked them not to pay rent. The Government would surely think that it was the speaker who was doing all these. They should never be misled by such men and they must pay their rent (the *Kisans* promised to pay rent). They should never attend the *sabha* with *lathis*. The speaker further said that it was the native who fired upon them. These *doglas* (illegitimate sons) were hinderances in their way of getting Swaraj and if their minds were turned, they would get Swaraj in a day. The speaker advised them to boycott courts and establish panchayts and comply with the orders of the Panches. By so doing the Government machinery would become futile. He further advocated the cause of Swadeshi and the boycott of foreign goods. The speaker took the pledges of the *kisans* in a convincing manner on the points explained by him. In conclusion, he appealed for funds for the relief of the *kisans* killed and wounded in Rae Bareli affair and said that those who could not pay at pressent, should send the amount by money order to Jawaharlal Nehru at Allahabad. The resolution was carried unanimously. The kisans then gave subscription.

The president, in his concluding address, thanked the audience and requested them to give practical shape to the resolutions passed by them. He said that it was a religious warfare and they should not do anything wrong, but they should advance their cause fearlessly.[1]

Peters, Deputy Commissioner had informed Deo Narain that he would deliver his finding at 12.00 hours at Akbarpur on 27 January, 1921 and it was thought that Deo Narian would turn up as threatened with a very large number. As a matter of fact, he came without a crowd. He was not excited but said that he had taken no food or drink since he was beaten and that he would no longer be responsible for the life of Alopi, the man who had beaten him. The presence of Jawaharlal Nehru and Gauri Shanker was highly significant that no violence would be attempted. These leaders were anxious to restrain the more violent of the adherents such as Deo Narain and Kedar Nath and purposely came to restrain them. Further they were attempting to throw the blame of the recent looting on *badmashes* and it was doubtful whether they would countenance further efforts at stiaring up the low castes. They were determined to curb the activities of Deo Narain who, though told Deputy Commissioner, Peters, that he would not be responsible for Alopi's life, stated that he had pardoned him.

1. Lakhte Husain and Jagannath, Inspector, C.I.D., 28th January, 1921.

They were quite indignant at the proceedings of the pretended Ram Chandra and this in itself was a sign that they regarded themselves as having some sort of responsibility.[1]

In his autobiography, Jawaharlal writes that after Akbarpur meeting when he spoke to the cultivators privately later and heard them artless story of how they had been mislead, he felt very sorry for them and regretted having exposed these foolish and simple folk to long terms of imprisonment. The people who suffered were not just two or three dozens. The chance was too great to be lost and full advantage was taken of the occasion to crush the agrarian movement in that district. Over a thousand arrests were made and the district jail was overcrowded and the trial went on for the next part of the year. Many died in prison during the trial and many other received long sentences.[2]

Whether Jawaharlal was aware of it or not, his attitudes at this time implied information collaboration with the Government in the maintenance of law and order ; and the United Provinces Government were shrewed enough to realize this. As they recorded "serious as these (*kisan*) distrubances have been, they would undoubtedly have been for more serious, had not the leaders considered that the time had not yet come for pushing things to extreme."[3] *The Independent* was of the same opinion. "For one part, we believe that ; but for the timely appearance of Pandit Jawaharlal Nehru on the scene, the situation would have become more complicated'. Sir Lowrence Porter, the Finance Member, who was rather unperceptive, was too easily persuaded by the *taluqdars* to prohibit the

1. *Hailey Papers*, From Hailey, Commissioner, Faizabad to G.S. Lambert, Chief Secretary, 29th January 1921.
2. Nehru, Jawaharlal, *An Autobiography*, p. 61.
3. *Hailey Papers*, From Hailey, Commissoner to G.B. Lambert, 29th January, 1921.

meetings addressed by Jawaharlal and his friends ; but Butler over ruled him.[1]

On the morning of 29th January, 1921, the arrest of a man giving his name as Ram Chandra, was effected at Goshainganj by the Superintendent of Police of Faizabad District. He was immediately rushed to the Goshainganj Railway station. On the way Ram Chandra and the peasants who were arrested with him advertised their journey to the Railway station in the usual manner, that was by yelling out various 'Jais' in every village they traversed. The people arrested were sent to Faizabad by the 11.45 a.m. train.[2] This prompt operation was commendable and paid rich dividents ; as late as 1·00 p.m. a number of people gathered together on the railway line and sat on the railway track, shouting and cheering. In half-an-hour, at 1.30 p.m., the peasants' number reached a formidable 2,000. This number swelled as the day progressed. At about half past one, the Station Master, Goshainganj, notified Warren, the Superintendent of Police, that a goods train was due in his station and was held up by people sitting on the railway track. The Superintendent of Railway Police persuaded the people to clear off the line. Various members of the crowd told him that they wanted to go to Faizabad to see Ram Chandra, but could not afford to purchase their tickets. The peasants were told that they could not travel without tickets and if they attempted to do so, they would be stopped. Other peasants ingenuously complained about their *zamindars* to which Warren non-commitantly replied that they should report to the Deputy Commissioner concerned.[3] The crowd then moved off the line, and promised

1. *General Department File* No. 50—3/1921, U.P.S.A.
2. Report of Warren, Superintendent of Police, Faizabad District to Deputy Commissioner, Faizabad, U.P.S.A.
3. Report of Warren, Superintendent of Police to Peters, Deputy Commissioner, Faizabad, 29th January 1921, U.P.S.A.

Warren before going, that they would make no further attempt to impede the railway traffic. They then moved to the other side of the platform, the Akbarpur end, and to Warren's dismay they again sat on the line, this time directly in front of the goods train that was about to leave the station. The 11 UP to Faizabad had been signalled and the line had to be cleared. The attitude of the mob then became obstinate and truculent. In reply to this recalcitrance, Warren sent troops of mounted police. The latter were directed to go along the line, one behind the other. The mob waited till these troops were almost on top of them. With the exception of four or five, the crowed cleared off the line. The four or five were ridden-over but none were seriously hurt. They then cleared off the line. The whole mobs then went outside the plateform wire-fencing and started throwing bricks and stones at Warren and the police *sawars*. The *sawars* were unable to manoeure further owing to the wire railway fencing. According to Warren, the principal brick throwers were small boys and *bad-mashes* (the leaders of the mob).[1] The *Sawaras* which consti-tuted the majority of Warren's force were thus rendered in-active. At the same time they were exposed to the bricks and stones hurled by the mob. They were withdrawn and 25 armed police were spread out for volley firing. The firing was withheld in the hope that the fusilade of bricks would stop. It did, but only after a great number of bricks had been hurled. The mob then cleared off to the other end of the platform and again took position on the line. At this time, Dupty Commis-sioner, Deputy Inspector General of Police and armed police they had brought, disembarked.[2]

The threads of the tale were then picked up by Peters, Deputy Commissioner. Alongwith Deputy Inspector General,

---

1. Report of Warren, Superintedent of Police to Peters, Deputy Commissioner, Faizabad, 29th January 1921, U.P.S.A.

2. *Ibid.*

Scott—O' Conner, he was proceeding to Faizabad by the 2.30 p.m. train from Akbarpur. Before starting from Akbarpur, he received two telegrams from Baker, Additional Superintendent of Police at Goshainganj, reporting the assembly of crowds and holding up of a train and five minutes later that no serious trouble was anticipated and that the force present was sufficient.[1] Just for safety, 50 extra armed police were entrained. Their train was stopped outside the distant signal at Goshainganj, Warren, Superintendent of Railway Police came running to meet them. He confessed that he was at the end of his tether and on the brink of firing.[2] A goods train was held up at the station, a crowd was collecting on the platform, and considerable crowd were collected both in the station area and outside the railings. When the Deputy Commissioner and Deputy Inspector General approached the cluster on the platform, the crowd dispersed. Soon the crowd collected in front of the passenger train and were collecting bricks on the railway line. As they were not dispersing, the Deputy Commissioner and the Deputy Inspector General want to them and warned that firing would be ordered.[3]

As at that moment both Deputy Commissioner and Deputy Inspector General were in the midst of the crowd, bricks began to be thrown at them. The demeanour of the crowd was extremely threatening but the actual ring leaders appeared to have been few. The greatest forbearance was shown by the police and the casualties amongst the crowd was surprisingly light.[4] It was reported that one man, wearing the uniform of

1. Baker, Addl. Superintendent of Police, at Goshainganj to Deputy Commissioner, Faizabad.
2. Warren, Superintendent of Police to Peters, Deputy Commissioner, 29th January 1921, U.P.S.A.
3. Report of Peters, Deputy Commissoner, Faizabad, U.P.S.A.
4. Report of Peters, Deputy Commissioner, Faizabad, U.P.S.A.

the Brahmins, with war medals was taking a leading part in the crowd, which contained other *sepoys* or *ex-sepoys.* A Bengali dressed in Sadhus clothes known to be one Mitter, a dismissed Station Master, was seen with the crowd from time to time. Baker reported that he heard him saying after the firing '*Abhi mauva nahin hai*'.[1] The crowd gradually dispersed and they returned to the station. The inspector with a guard of 1 sub-inspector, 2 head constables and 20 constables, had been left at the station at Goshainganj as a precautionary measure. It was difficult to give an estimate of the numbers of the crowed as it was perpetually shifting but was probably 5,000.[2]

In a official Report to the Chief Secretary Lambert, Hailey reported that on the night of 30th January 1921, he was compelled to call on Colonel Grogan, commanding the station, for military assistance.[3] On the night of 30th January 1921 he was informed that a certain number of Ram Chandra's supporters had arrived in the city and that a massive number were following. Colonel Lopsley informed the Commissioner that jail guard was insufficient to prodtect the jail. Perhaps they could hold the front gate, but it would be impossible to prevent the crowd from scaling the walls which was facilitated by the fact that the jail was under repairs. It was ascertained from the Deputy Superintendent of Police that there was no armed police other than the treasury guard in the lines. So if an attack was made, the Commissioner would have been forced to call upon the military for aid and it seemed more logical the bring them at once in such force as would prevent

1. Report of Baker, Addl. Superintendent of Police at Goshainganj.
2. From Peters, Deputy Commissioner to Hailey, Commissioner, 29th January, 1921, U.P.S.A.
3. *Hailey Papers,* from Hailey, Commissioner to Lambert, Chief Secretary, 30th January, 1921, U.P.S.A.

any attack taking place. Colonel Grogan, accordingly sent a company of the 11th Rajpur, which remained till the morning of 31st January, 1921, when they were relieved by police, which the Deputy Commissioner, Peters, had brought in from Akbarpur. Nothing happened during the night, though at about 10.30 p.m. there was one of the leaders outside the jail compound and he probably considered any attempt inopportune. Hailey wrote that under these extenuating circumstances, he had not complied with the orders to refer to Government before calling upon the military for aid.[1] These villagers had already shown great determination in their attempt to rescue Ram Chandra, the crowd consisted largely of landless labourers or men ejected from their holdings, who had been given by Ram Chandra, land in Gandhi's name,[1] reinforced by the bad characters of the neighbourhood who had been living on the country by extortion. It seemed unlikely that they would have walked from distances of 30 to 35 kilometres, if they did not mean business. It is hardly essential to point out that the effect of the capture of the jail would have been ignominous.[3] Hailey, Commissioner, informed the Chief Secretary, that pretender Ram Chandra was a beggar in Faizabad and had then started the crusade of his own.[4] The pretended Ram Chandra was out for loot pure and simple. The pretender went round the country with a following, and levied black mail in the name of Gandhi. He and his followers were living in the country.[5] Before his arrest, the

1. *Hailey Papers*, from Hailey, Commissioner, to Lambert, Chief Secretary, 30th January 1921, U.P.S.A.
2. *Hailey Papers*, from Hailey, Commissioner, to Lambert. Chief Secretary, 30th January 1921, U.P.S.A.
3. *Ibid.*, 31st January, 1921.
4. *Ibid.*, 29th January, 1921.
5. *Ibid.*

pretender had been inciting the peassantry in areas close to Goshainganj not to pay their rent. This preaching was not in consonance with the charter of Awadh Kisan Sabha. Hailey cogently informed that : "The pretended Ram Chandra was followed by crowds simply because he had got hold of a saffron robe and posed as a holy man. These people (Sadhus) exercise a more potent influence than the old class of vakil leaders, who were half mistrusted. They (Sadhus) claim to be followers of Gandhi and speak in his name, but their preaching certainly not on the lines of Gandhi's, as they advocate non-payment of rent and doctrines such as the land for the cultivator. There be no doubt, of course, that they make the strongest appeal to the low castes and landless labourers who are always little removed from starvation and are lured that a millenium in the shape of Swaraj in coming through the intervention of Mahatma Gandhi". Hailey further conveyed that to some extent Ram Chandra was able to put his programme into action.[1] He distributed holdings to peasants who had been evicted and ordered the expulsion of others who, he declared, were not true to the cause. But if a small *zamindar* was willing to pay a subscription fee to the movement he was permitted to retain his land.[2]

It is manifelt that the two Ram Chandras were very much sundered both in doctorine and in practice. In fact, both the Ram Chandras shared nothing but the name. The real Baba Ram Chandra was arrested on 10th February, 1921 at Benares (Varanasi). The Ram Chandra who was taken into police custody on 29th Jauuary, 1921 was a pretender. The following points will dispel any doubts :

(1) Account of the arrest of the pretender Ram Chandra in the *Leader* of 2nd February, 1921.

1. *Hailey Papers*, From Hailey, Commissioner to Lambert, Chief Secretary, 1st February 1921, U.P.S.A.

2. *Ibid.*

(2) Arrest of Ram Chandra himself reported in the *Leader* of 14th February, 1921.

(3) Account of the Kisan Sabhas meeting at Akbarpur which the real Ram Chandra asked the tenants not to follow any spurious Baba of the same name.[1]

(4) Above all, Ram Chandra's own record of his arrest at Varanasi in his memoirs[2].

With the passage of time, the movement underwent a charge from *Nazrana* and ejectment, to Swaraj and Swadeshi. Despite this, Ram Chandra embraced change in the Congress programme with spontancity. This is evident from the agitation he pursued. During the riots Ram Chandra was in Barabanki, on the plea that his very presence would only serve to fan the flames of revolt.

Baba Ram Chandra was ultimately arrested at Varanasi on 10th February, 1921. He had gone there to attend the opening ceremony of the Kashi Vidyapith where Gandhi, Jawaharlal Nehru, Abul Kalam Azad and other nationalist leaders had assembled. Ram Chandra's arrest in the presence of Congress luminaries and 80,000 persons, had generated a great deal of controversy.

The daily *Independent* commented that the arrest of Ram Chandra in a crowd of 80,000 persons was a deliberate act of provocation on the part of the Government[3]. The same newspaper also commented, "The spectacle of the *Kotwal* followed by an armed European Inspector, a few sub-inspectors and a large number of constables armed with loaded

1. Meeting at Akbarpur on 27th January 1921.
2. *Ram Chandras Diary*, p. 41.
3. *The Independent*, 12th February 1921.

rifles may have been calculated once to arouse and to meet strong indignation, and even violence"[1].

Kapil Deva Malviya, Secretary of United Provinces Kisan Sabha, saw in the manner of arrest of Ram Chandra, multiple motives. Elaborating, he writes: "How was it that Benaras (Varanasi) where he (Ram Chandra) went on just a day's visit should have been deemed a more convenient place for his arrest. Mahatma Gandhi was at Benaras at the time of the arrest. Could it be that the Government arrested him at Benaras so that they could discredit Gandhi, if any disturbance followed the arrest? Or it may be that Government were really afraid of arresting so popular a worker anywhere except under the protection and with the indirect help of Gandhi"[2]. It was a fact that Jawaharlal Nehru urged the excited crowd to obey Gandhi and allow Ram Chandra to be arrested quietly[3]. Ram Chandra too, twenty years later, was of the opinion that had not Gandhi, Nehru and others helped the police, he would have evaded them at Varanasi, just as he had been able to, in the other districts[4].

An authentic source informs us that it was only in an embittered state, having fallen out of favour with the Congress leaders, that Ram Chandra established the view that the Congress actually connived with the police to have him arrested. However, the larger evidence points to the fact that Ram Chandra then was as much of a non-cooperator as a Kisan worker and at that time did not consider the two interests to have been incompatible. This is apparent from

---

1. *The Independent*, 13th February 1921.
2. Letters to the Editor of *The Independent*, 13th February, 1921.
3. Sri Prakash's Article in 1921 Movement Reminicences, p. 199.
4. *Ram Chandra's Diary*, p. 41.

the slogans he used in which the emphasis was clearly that were not for the British government, the landlords would not be in a position to oppress the peasants[1].

In the warrant for Ram Chandra's arrest, it was particularly ordered by the Deputy Commissioner, Barabanki, that all possible means should be employed in affecting the arrest to avoid a demonstration[2].

However, this instruction failed to be implemented as Ram Chandra was arrested before an audience of 80,000. The police could hardly have been more indiscreat. With the dessimation of the news of Ram Chandra's arrest in the whole of the United Provinces, there was widespread resentment. In District Bara Banki, where he was primarily agitating, there was instant and ubiquitous *hartal* (strike) ; Earlier there was a grandiose plan to rally support for securing the release of their Baba by physical force. As the helm of this valiant mission were Mustafa shopkeeper and Kashi Prasad. The plan could not be excuted for lack of valour in the multitude. On the contrary the political leaders were happier with Ram Chandra behind bars, not because he had a programme of action that was different from their own, but because his mere presence at meetings might have led to a recrudescence of *Kisan* violence[3]. Also it was in accord of the non-co-operation Movement that arrest of leaders was insignificant so long as they ceaselessly strove for the ultimate goal-Swaraj. Hence Gandhi called it a sacred incident[4]. So the 'opening ceremony was turned into a *Yaqna*......... because he who worked for the welfare of

1. Inteligence Bureau Records in the custody of the C.I.D. Offices, Lucknow.
2. *Ibid.*
3. Intelligence Bureau Records in the custody of C.I.D. Office, Lucknow.
4. *Home (Political) Department*, File No. 87, U.P.S.A.

Kisans had been arrested"[1]. The United Provinces Kisan Sabha published a leaflet endorsed by Motilal Nehru as President and Gauri Shanker as Vice President underscoring the need to remain unperturbed by Ram Chandra's arrest[2].

The leaflet pointed out that to remain under foreign rule was slavery. Freedom was achieved only by going to prison. This was Gandhi's firm conviction. That is why Baba Ram Chandra has become free to-day and his holy sacrifice has been offered for the national cause. The bet way to get him released is to non-co-operate peacefully. The more peaceful your non-co-operation will be, the sooner will you obtain Swaraj and through that Swaraj will his release be sanctimonious and according to his desire. Meanwhile, do not violate peace in thought, word, and did. Do not attempt to see him in the jail. This only violates peace, delays Swaraj ; and, therefore, his release[3].

Motilal Nehru drafted a leaftet for distribution to the Kisans, urging them to join the Congress, take up spinning, settle disputes in their own panchayats and not the law courts, subscribe to the Swaraj fund and promote caste and communal harmony. Nothing was said about rents or evictions, and a positive directive was given to avoid gatherings in districts where public meetings had been prohibited. But above all, it was most necessary that all *Kisans* should follow the path of righteousness, should speak the truth, should not indulge in any looting and should refrain from every violence in word and deed, and should commit no excesses of any kind[4]. These instructions, far from being revolutionary, were to the benefit of authorities. Yet the Government arrested

1. *Ibid.*
2. Intelligence Bureau Records of 1921, U.P.S.A.
3. Intelligence Bareau Records of 1921, U.P.S.A.
4. *Kisan ka Sandesa*, English translation in the *The Independent*, 3rd May, 1921.

six young men who were distributing the pamphlet and sentenced them to jail for six months on the ground that the pamphlet attempted to excite disaffection and to bring the Government into hatred and contempt. The harsh action was clearly meant to proclaim that the Government had recovered their nerve, and intended no longer to tolerate intervention by Congress men in *Kisan* affairs. The pamphlet itself was later prescribed, but significantly no aetion was taken against its author, Motilal Nehru, or against Jawaharlal, who distributed the pamphlet in the court-room itself and wrote formally to the Magistrate that he would continue to give the widest possible publicity to the pamphlet which gave expression to his views[1]. The failure to be arrested, at a time when his followers were receiving savage sentences for carrying out his orders, acutely embarrassed Jawaharlal[2].

Section II :

The authority of the *taluqdars* had crumbled at a stroke where the Kisan Sabha movement had spread, and very few of them did any thing else but shut themselves up in their houses or leave for the nearest town. The *Kisans* had, to a large extent, lost all fear of the police, and the efforts of the Congress had succeeded to the extent that the Kisans were now prepared to defy not just the landlords but even the Government. It was believed by the officials that the leaders of the non-co-operation party had built up an enormous organisation which they could start working whenever they pleased, and that they were steadily using their influence to instil hatred of Europeans and Indian officials. No longer could the authorities comfort themselves with the belief that the *Kisans* had no grudge against them, but sought redress from them[3].

1. *The Independent*, 30th April, 1921.
2. Gopal, S., *Jawaharlal Nehru, A Biography,* Vol. I, p. 56.
3. Note of Commissioner, Faizabad Division, 1st February, 1921 ; General Department, File No. 50-3/1921, U.P.S.A.

In Sultanpur district, there were a number of high-caste tenants who were generally inimical to their landlords. Many of them took advantage of the agitation to refuse to pay their rents and in this district, at any rate, the movement was far more political than in Pratapgarh[1]. The Commissioner, Faizabad wrote to Chief Secretary that Indian cavalry could clear any mob without doing them much damage and added, "I consider the effect of bringing down Indian Cavalry into the district would be admirable"[2]. A mobile column consisting of one squadron Indian Cavalry, 2 companies British Infantry and a section of guns marched in Sultanpur District from 23rd February to 28th February, 1921. They entered the district at Dostpur on the North-Eastern border, on 23rd February, 1921. They marched as follows :

24th February 1921—Dostpur to Kadipur
25th February 1921—Halt at Kadipur
26th February 1921—Kadipur to Deora
27th February 1921—Deora to Baraunsa
28th February 1921—Baraunsa to Sultanpur

The troops entrained at Sultanpur on the 28th February for their respective stations. The troops were played into the district by the infantry band through Dostpur, one of the longest villages of the district. A strong band was considered a very important adjunct to such a march. The march from Dostpur to Kadipur was uneventful and at Kadipur a large number of people saw the camp while the sub-divisional officer sat opposite trying cases under Section 107 I.P.C.

At Tajiuddinpur, six miles from Dostpur, 'Swaraj' was proclaimed and a parallel Government was set up for the

---

1. General Administration Report, 1920-21.

2. From Hailey, Commissioner, Faizabad to Lambert, Chief Secretary, 29th January 1921, U.P.S.A.

proceeding few days[1]. The ring leaders were arrested and convicted at Kadipur on the 25th February, 1921. On the same day while troops were at Kadipur, an enquiry was re-installed into some looting of payal at a court of ward village near by and a case instituted. Owing to lack of evidence and failure of ziledar to report, it had been thought impossible by the sub-divisional officer and local police to get on with the case, before.

On the 26th, February 1921, the infantry and guns marched along metalled road, direct from Dostpur to Deora. while the cavalry under Major Hawley and the Deputy Commissioner, swam through Gomati twice, to do a patrol of 30 kilometres through Chanda and Lambhua which was considered as the worst effected part of the district. This patrol was of the greatest service, the small crowds of villagers on the roadside were called upon to stand up and salam, as the head of column reached them, and in only one case there was any hesitation. The insolent young man was arrested under Section 55. The enquiry showed that he was not a wondering agitator but only a prominent member of the local sabha. Accordingly, he was released with a warning. At Lambhua *gur* and milk was provided for the troops, as some offering of respect. As it was not an authorised issue of rations, the payment was made by Deputy Commissioner. A *bania* (shop-keeper) at Lumbhua during the halt for refreshment filed a complaint of intimidation against four of the local leaders, and after statements were duly taken on oath, three of them were arrested on the spot and sent for trial to the subdivisional officer. This incident during the actual presence of the troops undoubtedly helped to drive home to the crowd that Government was determined to put down this form of law

1. Report of Deputy Commissioner, Sultanpur disrrict, 1st April, 1921, U.P.S.A.

breaking. On the 27th the troops marched to Baraunsa, a village which had for some months harboured a number of ordinary *badmashes* (bad characters) for whom warrants of arrest had been issued. This was considered a very truculent village and had given much trouble to the police in the past. It provided a large amount of *rasad* (food-grains) without trouble.

On the 28th February the troops marched to Sultanpur and on arrival, each unit marched round the town, through the Chowk, and to a shady space in the Civil lines where they rested. The Government High School was on the line of march and the whole school much enjoyed turning out and standing at attention at the salute while the infantry passed with band playing. The band also made a due impression through the Chowk[1].

To restore peace in the district, the Deputy Commissioner took various other measures which are enumerated below :

(1) Leaders Kedar, Deo Narain and Raghunandan Sadhu were arrested on the 4th and 6th February. The effect of these arrests was increased tenfold by the fact that these persons disappeared completely and no demonstration was allowed in respect of them. (2) The stiffining of Government policy towards violent agitation and the consequent restriction of mass meeting in the district. (3) The punishment of six other leading disaffected persons for specific crimes which had been committed by them during the month. (4) As operation by the armed police when an attempt was made to hold a forbidden meeting. Fifty armed police were quickly put into two motor buses and conveyed to the spot. The Deputy

1. Report on passage of troops through Sultanpur District by Deputy Commissioner, 4th March, 1921, U.P.S.A:

Commissioner and Superintendent of Police, accompanied them on horess. The meeting was an utter fiasco. One person was arrested on the spot under Section 55 C.P.C. as he was an agitator and a twice convicted thief. (5) The collection of *rasad* for the troops in due legal form under the Regulation of 1806 and 1825 from the village where looting and the worst agitation had taken place and the distinct demonstration to the people that *rasad* is a right of the Government inforceable by law, and not to be taken with argument and apology. (6) Extensive proceedings under preventive sections and section 506 I.P.C. against minor agitators and heads of sabhas which had used intimidation. (7) The announcement that the Oudh Rent Act had been definitely taken under consideration for amendment, and the holding of a series of quite open and informal enquiries into grievances at which *vakils* and cultivators took part. (8) Propaganda : (*a*) A series of durbars were held all over the district for presentation of stars, (*b*) Extensive distribution of leaflets both by officials and non-official agency.

The Deputy Commissioner wrote that the general result of the march through this district, was an unqualified success and that its effect on the local feelings was excellent. The vast majority of the people were pleased that decisive action had been taken and law and order was restored.

He further wrote that the performance of the effect remains to be seen and it was to be driven home by some what stern measures for a few months against all criminal intimidation, sedition and agitation of the nature that had led to such violence in surrounding districts[1]. Not bothering much about the genuine grievances of the peasantry, the British authorities

1. Report of Deputy Commissioner, 4th March, 1921 on passage of troops through Sultanpur District on 23rd-28th February, 1921.

embarked upon a policy of repression. Not only were the peasants arrested in large numbers, but they were also mal-treated and beaten and harassed in a manner which could not by the law of justice, be upheld.[1]

The Independent wrote on 6th March, 1921, "It is excessively painful to inform the general public how the Government has planned the destruction of the noble and sacred movement of the Kisans in this district. Police and zamindars have been backed and encouraged by the Government and they (zamindars) work as right and left hands of Government's oppression. The oppression is so great that it is beyond easy description......when a person is arrested, he is very mercilessly beaten until he is senseless or unless he promises to make his statements just as the police desire (In accordance with the 'Plans' of Government it is obvious Innuendo)"[2].

In a note prepared by Jawaharlal Nehru for Mahatma Gandhi in June 1921, he wrote "A very determined and persistant effort has been made by Government to kill the Kisan movement. Early in February Ram Chandra, Kedar Nath and Deo Narayan were arrested. There was no disturbance of any kind and Government was emboldened to total concerted action to crush tho kisans. Columns of cavalry, artillery and infantry were marched through the districts and people were forced to supply *rasad* etc. to the troops. School boys were made to salute the European troops. Hundred of Panches and Sarpanches were in jail or have been made to give security. The usual offence charged against them was "you are leaders of the sabha and you compel people to attend it."

---

1. Choudhry, Sukhbir, *Peasants and Worker's movement in India*, p. 191.
2. *Home (Political) Department*, File No. 63, p. 27, U.P.S.A.

Sometimes "Even barbers and washermen have not been spared." False cases were started on these allegations and conviction almost invariably followed. Most of these cases were instituted by private parties at the instigation of the local police or *zamindar*.

The Seditious Meetings' Act has been forced (according to the Act, all public meetings were banned and any person taking part in organising such meetings was liable to arrest without warrant). Before the Act was applied, all meetings were prevented under Section 144. This order was obeyed and no meetings were held. In spite of this, the Seditious Meetings Act, was enforced. The workers in these district were harassed in a variety of ways. A number of C.I.D. men and uniformed policemen followed them and preceded them. Villagers were threatened lest they join the Congress or help leaders in any other way. They have been told orally that the use of *Charkha* was against the law, to shout 'Mahatma Gandhi ki Jai' was a heinous offence, to sign the Congress form was illegal etc. Men who had signed were threatened with legal proceedings and bribes were extracted to hush matters up. Six young student workers were sent to jail for distributing leaflets. Two workers have been sentenced to six months rigorous imprisonment on a false charges of breaking the provisions of the Seditious Meetings Act. One of these was beaten and kicked by a policeman. It is difficult to give a proper idea of the hundred and one methods by which Government tried to crush the insans. Tho taluqdars, zamindars and the few local persons who call themselves moderates have allied themselves with the Government and have succeeded in making the life of the average kisan a burden almost too great to be borne[1].

---

1. Note prepared by Jawaharlal Nehru for Mahatma Gandhi in June 1921 on 'Repression in U.P.'

There was a vehement demand that the Oudh Rent Act of 1886 be rescinded or modified. It had worked fairly well in Northern Awadh, where the population was thin and there was no pressure on the soil, but it had completely broken down in the densely populated area of Southern Awadh where there was great competition for land. This led to *Nazrana*, ejectment, *begar* and various other grave abuses. The loop-holes had to be plugged.

The position of the land and the people has two aspects : the relation of the Government with the landlords and the relations of the landlords and the tenants. Both these aspects have come into prominence in the last few years. There had been on the part of the landlords of both provinces, a presistent demand for the revision of the settlement policy ; and on the part of the Awadh tenantry a demand, equally presistent and asserted more violently for greater security of the tenants. The tenantry of the Agra Province had also, in some districts, expressed dissatisfaction with their position. The Oudh Rent Amendment Act of 1921 attempted to put the relations of the landlords and the tenants in the Province on a more satisfactory footing.

The endeavours of the Government in amending the Act was directed mainly at obtaining for the tenant a degree of protection which would give him a reasonable security of tenure, subject to the payment of a fair rent, and which would remove the two main evils of the existing system, namely arbitrary ejectment by notice and the exaction of nazrana. Occupancy rights could not be obtained for him in view of the undertaking vien by the Government after the Revolt and embodied in what is known as the 'Oudh Compromise' that no right of occupancy would be created. The ordinary tenant in Awadh never had any kind of occupancy or hereditary rights. The question of amending the Act was undertaken, and an amending bill was drafted in the summer of

1921, and was introduced into the council by Porter, the Finance Member, on the 4 August, 1921, and became Law before the end of the year. The act was admittedly a compromise as it was found impossible to reconcile the demands of these members of the Committee who advocated greter concessions to the tenants with those of taluqdars. The latter, however, made large concessions and the Act of 1921 relieved the tenants from their chief grievances, and secured to them life tenure at a fair rent with 5 more years' tenure for their heirs.

The Act was attacked in the Council and outside, chiefly on the ground that it conferred on the tenants no hereditary rights. In the circumstances of the case, this was not found possible. Referring to the controversies which the act had raised, Harcourt Butler, in his farewell speech to the legislative Council pointed that the Act "has introduced a new and important principle in regulating the relations between the tenant and the landlord, the principle of giving general tenant—right without the consent or acquiescence of the landlords in regard to individual tenancies"[1]. He went on to say that that was a principle which had never been introduced in the Province of Agra. So recently as 1917, Lord Meston had admitted in regard to the general question of the reactions of the landlords and the tenants that the position was unsatisfactory. The proprietary right undeniably carried the right and power to give or withhold occupency rights, while rack-rents and instability meant agricultural impoverishment but said Lord Meston, that no ideal solutions could be immediately attempted. Some especial consideration was due to the landlord, and it was not possible for the time to eliminate certain of the more obvious causes of friction. Butler concluded by saying that "the Oudh Rent Act of 1921,

1. Awasthi, D., *History of Modern India*, p. 47.

goes much further in the protection of the tenantry of either provinces than has ever been attempted before. Considering the past history of the question in Oudh, the pledges given to the taluqdars and the strong majority of the landlords in the (Legislative) Council, I think, although none can foresee the working the Tenancy Act in practice, that there is good reason to be satisfied with the result, and I shall not be surprised if, when the Agra Rent Act comes again under revision, the compromise that was reached over the Oudh Rent Act affords the prospect of a settlement of the question in Agra in regard to tenants-at-will".

In the press also the Oudh Tenancy Legislation came in for severe criticism. Leading papers, both in English and the vernaculars supported the cause of the tenants and warned the taluqdars and the zamindars of the dangers of adopting an illiberal attitude towards them. The vernacular press generally considered the Bill a retrograde measure, and likely to strengthen the hold of taluqdars and zamindars over the tenants. The extremist papers generally held the view the problem could not be solved without the attainment of Swaraj in India and, therefore, urged the people to concentrate their energy in that direction.

The violence and volume of seditious print and speech increased so greatly during 1921 that the number of prosecutions under the criminal procedure Code and the Indian Penal Code for such offences increased from 7 to 93 ; while the number of publications which it was necessary to proscribe under the Press Act rose from 6 to more than 100. Thus despite the fact that the policy of Government has continued to be one of utmost forbearance and that only the most dangerous and persistent agitators have been brought to book. It is no exaggeration to say that a large proportion of the hundreds of speeches which are made at non-co-operation meetings every month would justify prosecution. Similarly the number of publications proscribed represents only a fraction of the objectionable matter which has pured out of the presses.

Generally speaking, the tone of the press became more bitter and more anti-British than it was in 1920 Of the English papers *The Independent* of Allahabad had been easily the first in point of bitterness and had assiduously supported the non-co-operation movement. It ceased publication late in December as a result of the confiscation of its security deposit. *The Leader,* while continuing to be relentless critic of non-co-operation and insisting on the necessity of supporting the reformed council, had condemned the application of the criminal Law Amendment Act and doubted the expediency of Government action in dealing with the revolutionary movement towards the end of the year as likely to strengthen the hands of the extremists. Hindi papers had been very bitter in their attacks of the Government specially *Pratap* of Karpur and *Swarajya* of Unnao. A new paper *The Kisan* of Allahabad appeared during the year. It aimed at being the organ of tenants and was occassionally bitter against the landed classes.

Nor despite all the hopes held out, did the revision of the Oudh Rent Act improve substantially the condition of the tenantry ; on the other hand, it strengthened the authority of the landlords, giving them the rights to evict undesirable or non-resident tenants, to increase the area of land under their own cultivation and to acquire lands for a wide range of developmental purposes. Cesses also continued to be exacted, while some landlords refused to give receipts for rents paid, as they were collecting more than that was recorded in the village accounts[1]. In November 1921, the All India Congress

---

1. Gopal, S., *Jawaharlal Nehru : A Biography*, Vol I.

Committee permitted full civil disobedience including non-payment of taxes but not rents.

The *bazar* of Chauri-Chaura in Gorakhpur District had been for some time the scene of vigorous picketing, foreign cloth was totally excluded from sale and the liquor shops had no customers. This was resented and resisted by the local landlord, the owner of the *bazar*. On 1st February, 1922, the local sub-inspector of police, notorious for his bad temper, was alleged to have visited the *bazar* with a police force and to have beaten some of the peasants and volunteers engaged in picketing. This provocative behaviour of the sub-inspector led to the assembly of the kisans of the surrounding villages on 4th February 1922. They marched in a big crowd to the police station. There the peasants wanted to know why the Sub-inspector had chastised their leaders. They expressed their determination to picket the *bazar* that day and dared the police to prevent them in their intrepid resolve. So far as the Sub-inspector of police was concerned, the peasants had thrown down the gauntlet. However, some neutrals acted as peace-makers and managed to pacify the angry procession, which then moved on. Some persons who were in the rear were roughly handled and abused by the police constables. They retaliated with brick-bats. A scuffle took place. The constables opened fire and killed a few. The rest raised an alarm. Being thus stabbed in the back, the peasants returned, this time, in a grip of fury. They started brick-batting the police station. Majumdar observes : "The armed police fired on the mob. How long the firing lasted is not known, but dead bodies of only two rioters were later found near thana. It is not unlikely, however, that some wounded persons were removed by the mob. After some time the firing ceased, presumably because the police had exhausted their ammunitions. As soon as the crowd realised this, they rushed towards the than a building shouting 'through Gandhiji's kindness even the bullets have turned into water'"[1]. The policemen who attempted to run out of the police station were caught, beaten, soaked in kerosene and hacked to pieces. The mutilated bodies were thrown into the raging fire. The railway communication between Chauri Chaura and Gorakhpur were cut-off. The century old ruthless oppression had forced the Chauri-Chaura peasants to express their indignation in violence against the 'administrative apparatus of colonial oppressors[2]'. The 'mailed-fist' measures adopted at Chauri-Chaura, provoked Gandhi's displeasure. Instantly, a mandate was issued for the suspension of Non-co-operation Movement.

Thus, the peasant movement in Awadh had a number of characteristic features. It was a considerably mature and organised action of the Indian peasantry during this period. Appraising the dynamic character of the movement, *The Times* wrote on 6th March, 1922 : "Formerly the tenants crushed by requisitions of all kinds were in no condition to effectively express their protest, but in connection with the recent political awakening of the masses they began to put a fight for their rights".

The class nature of the movement was very clearly defined. Unlike the Peasant movements in other provinces, religion was kept completely out of picture. The recourse by Baba Ram Chandra to arouse the kisans through recitations of *Ramayana* at various places was merely a ruse to collect the masses at a particular time and place.

---

1. Majumdar, R.C. (ed.). *Struggle for Freedom*, p. 241.

2. Chaudhari, Sukhbir, *Peasants and Workers Movement in India*, p. 201.

Heavy exploitation by the landlords and the fact that the majority of the peasants in Awadh were fluidus, also played a certain role. In the course of the movement caste differences faded into the background. The acknowledged leaders of the peasants in Awadh generally came from the lower castes.

By a quirk of fate and circumstances, this movement against the 'feudal barons' who were in league with British authorities, assumed an anti-imperialist character and on many occassion got mixed up with the anti-British demonstrations going on in the urban areas at that time. The peasants actively supported the political agitations of the city people, and the latter responded by giving similar support to the peasant movements. Sometimes they even led these movements. It is self-evident from the report submitted on 14th January, 1921, by the Deputy Commissioner of Rae Bareli to the Chief Secretary to the Government of the United Provinces. He stated : "The non-co-operators, finding their efforts to stir up trouble among students and the general public unsuccessful, had to look round for some more promising field for their operations. They failed to influence the general public and students to any extent, because they had no real grievances. They had succeeded in stirring up the cultivators of Oudh to a state of considerable excitement, because the cultivators have in many cases considerable grievances against the landlords ...... what the kisans are interested in is their own condition and in particular *nazrana* and ejectments."[1]

A resolution setting forth their version of the peasant disturbances was issued by the Government of the United Provinces. It alleged that the 'local agitators' had exploited the feeling against 'coolie labour'. It also added that there had been some increase in extremist activities since the return

1. *Disturbances in the Rae Bareli and Fyzabad Districts*, p. 27, U.P.S.A.

of the Congress delegates from Nagpur Session. It alleged that school masters, chaukidars and students showed signs of restiveness. With the first two classes the trouble was principally economic. But the students were 'being made cats' paw agitators as in other cases..

Thus, the peasant upsurge in Awadh, as in other parts of India, merged with the nationwide anti-imperialist struggle producing a very tense situation throughout the country. The British authorities were compelled to pay considerable attention to these revolts. In a report of the military command responsible for suppressing them, it was admitted that the movement was very serious and "...... endangered the basis of the traditional land tenure system and administration."[1] To put an end to the movement the authorities started making concessions to the Awadh tenants. Pretending that they considered the complaints of the peasants against the landlords justified to some extent, the government arranged a special investigation into the collection of rents in Awadh. It enacted the 'Rent Act for Oudh, 1921'. Owing to the half-heartedness of the Act, however, neither of these aims was achieved. The discontent of the peasants grew and the deterioration in agriculture continued.

---

1. Jafri, S.N.A., *History and State of Landlords and Tenants in the United Provinces*, p. 181.

5

No Rent Campaign

The United Provinces was a small part in the collosal machinery of the vast British Empire. It is coherent that when the economy of Britain incurred a malady, the economy of the United Provinces would also be affected. The province envisaged an unprecedented slump in the prices of agricultural produce sinking prices created cluster of agricultural imbalances. Consequently, the foundations of the rural economy received a formidable jolt. The cultivator was crippled and was not in a financial position to pay the escalating rents demanded by the taluqdars and zamindars. The Provincial Government can be held culpable for aggravating the distress. Without a critical scrutiny of the causes, it resorted to repression for tackling the agricultural problems. Innumerable atrocities were committed on tenants and harrowing accounts emanated from the provincial districts. In their endeavour to mitigate the Kisan distress, the Congress workers had to undergo serious ordeals. They were lamentably harassed, gagged, imprisoned and mercilessly chastised in other ways. The Congress patriots could not countenance such acts and resorted upon a No-Tax campaign, in the province.

The prices of agricultural products began to show a tendency to fall in January 1930 and continued doing so month by month throughout the year. The value fell by 50 percent between January and December, 1930.

If we compare the figures for December, 1929 with December 1930, we find that the prices per Kw. (maund) had fallen from 5·33 to 2·35 and that instead of 7 kg of grain that was available per rupee in December 1929, one could get 17 kg, in 1930. The steep downward march continued unabated so that in May 1931, the price per maund had fallen to 2·3 and the rupee value stood at 18 kg. In many places the price that the cultivator could get for his produce at harvest time was appreciably less. This unparalleled slump as was inevitable completely shattered him.

An inquiry made in over 300 U.P. villages in the eastern region revealed that the price of the produce in 1931 did not even cover the rents payable and this made no allowance for the cost of cultivation. In the case of wheat the tenant produced on an average 10 Kw worth Rs. 30/- to produce which he spent about Rs. 62/-: These unprecedented development shook the very foundations of rural economy; the situation was unmistakably grave and clamoured for immediate redress. The cultivators had been nearly crippled by the successive failures of crops and was suffering from the cumulative effects of a series of bad seasons even before the crash and due to the collapse of the prices which overtook them. Even before the depression there was sure signs indicating that the pitch of rents was not suitable.

A survey of the economic conditions of the cultivating classes was made made in 1931. The data collected can admit of only one invariable deduction namely that the cultivator has been maimed and his produce is not at all sufficient at the present rates even to meet the cost of production.

It must have occurred to the meanest intelligence that in the face of the tremendous decline in the prices, it would be preposterous to expect from the cultivators the rents they used to pay in the previous years, the money value of this produce having diminished by more than 60 percent in the course of a few months. It must have been obvious that any delay in dealing with the situation was fraught with serious danger. It was the duty of the United Provinces Government to take initiative in the matter and to adopt adequate and liberal measures atonce. The value of the Kharif harvest had been reduced to about one-half. The Government ought to have stopped in atonce when the Kharif crop was garnered with satisfactory solutions in the matter of rent and revenue demands. But the Provincial Government showed complete apathy.[1]

The No-Tax campaign was part of the Civil disobedience programme of the Congress. Speaking at Taugan, district Rae Bareli on 5th February, 1930, Jawaharlal apprised the people of the fact that Gandhi had put forth a resolution that the Congress did not wish to have any relationship with the British people as they want nothing but exploitation of poor men. The more English men came here more the poor Indians exploited. Part of this programme comprised the non-payment of taxes as they had been doing at that time. The British Government was run by the peasants money, realized as tax and revenue from the peasants. Other Indians helped it with their co operation. Nehru said that on coming to Taugan he had learnt that the revenue was enhanced and ejectment was increasing. The peasants wanted that they should be stopped. Hence Gandhi had appealed to the Indians for the non-payment of taxes. This involved all sections of society, professional classes, land owners and tenants, etc.[2]

After the Gandhi-Irwin Pact of 5th March, 1931 the No-Tax campaign was discontinued. During this time Gandhi was having his conversations with the Viceroy regarding the

---

1. *Report by Uttar Pradesh Congress Committee.*
2. *Home Department* (Political), File No. 90/1930. N.A.I.

terms of the provisional settlement, it was pointed out to him that even on the withdrawal of the political no-tax campaign the economic distress in united Provinces would persist and it would not be possible for the tenantry to pay the full demand.[1]

A full scale establishment by the United Provinces Congress Committee was improvised to meet the agrarian crisis in the province. The Congress organization in tehsils acted as agents of the peasants in negotiations with the landlords. G.B. Pant was made liaison officer and established at Lucknow. In the beginning the tenants were advised to pay what was possible, which in general appeared to be 50 per cent by occupancy tenants and 40 per cent by statutory tenants, provided the landlords gave receipt of the whole amount.

On 21st March, 1931, G.B. Pant sent a copy of the resolution of the Executive Council of the Provincial Congress regarding agrarian situation to Sloan, Revenue Secretary to U.P. Government. He stresses the urgency for the announcement of the policy regarding remissions and wrote that so long as this question was not settled the state of suspense and uncertainty which must be embarrassing to all concerned was bound to continue. The resolution noted with grave concern that coercive and oppressive measures were being taken to recover rent and revenue and that the assistance of the police and the tehsil staff was being given to *taluqdars* and zamindars for forcible collection of rent in some districts and a very large number of ejectments were made. Remission suggested was 60 percent and it was also recommended that all collections of rent and revenue should be suspended till the decision of the Government. The Council also recommended

---

1. *A.I.C.C. File* No. 4/1931, Part I, pp. 61—65, N.M.M.L.

that land from which tenants had already been ejected should be restored to them and pending suits should be withdrawn.

The Revenue Secretary to United Provinces Government had long discussion with G.B. Pant and told him that they were prepared to issue orders to their officers that they were not to interfere between the taluqdars and zamindars and the tenant. It was also stated that if the Congress took the line of advising tenants not to pay rents or only a very small portion of their rents, it was going to be very difficult for the Government to stand aside. As a public man, Pant, claimed the right to advise tenants who, in his opinion were not able to pay their rents, to pay only a portion of this. He was not prepared to admit that would infringe the spirit of the truce[1].

The U P. Government pursued their inhuman and pragmatic approach : "If the tenants are made to realize that by with holding the payment of rents, they will also lose their holdings, they will be less likely to follow the advice and dictates of those who advocate the non-rent campaign, and who are in most cases not personally affected, as they are not cultivators themselves. With all the authority of coudign power the Governor noted : "If tenants refuse to pay, they must be ejected. I do not see how we can leave the landlords in the lurch......".

Nevertheless the Revenue Secretary issued a circular to all the Deputy Commissioners enquiring statments of ejectments in their districts. Since it had been asserted that the taluqdars and zamindars procured the assistance of police and tehsil staff for collection of rents its veracity was sought.

The Deputy Commissioner, Agra, reported that there was no reason to suppose that improper use was made by the

---

1. Note of the Revenue Secretary, T. Sloan to Finance Member, U.P.S.A.

landlords of Sections 52, 61, 62 and 127 of the Oudh Rent Act. Of course the total number of institutions under these Sections had risen to 1299 and number of decrees to 711 as compared with 493 and 395 in 1928-29 and 781 and 577 in 1929-30. The landlords had been advised to take action in Court only against coutumacious tenants who could pay but did not, and there were reasons to believe that most landlords had followed this advice, otherwise in view of the economic crisis and non-payment rent compaign the number of cases would have been much longer.

Another reason for the number of cases being smaller than expected was that most landlords were not in a position to incur the expenditure filing suit against the tenantry who had combined to withhold rent and considered it hardly worthwhile to file suits against only a few. As an example of the refractioriness of the tenants and the futility of the ordinary process of the law, the Deputy Commissioner mentioned that even before the truce-since when the situation had considerably deteriorated strong action was taken under Section 12-A, Oudh Rent Act with the sanction of the Government nineteen villages on the ground of general refusal of the tenants to pay rents, which had, therefore, to be collected by the revenue staff with the help of a strong police force. The Deputy Commissioner also said that ejectment decrees passed in each of the three years in Rae Bareli being 711 in 1930-31 as compared with 395 in 1928-29 and 577 in 1929-30[1].

J.H. Darwin, Collector of Agra wrote that there were 2008 ejectment decrees in 1930-31 in comparison with 1119 in

1. *Revenue Department* File No. 465, extract D.O. No. 74/4, dated April 1931 from Deputy Commissioner, Rae Bareli, U.P.S.A.

1928-29 and 1941 in 1929-30. A comparison of the figures of 1930-31 with those of 1929-30 showed that Section 81 had been less used in Karauli, Fatehbad, Ferozabad and Agra tehsils and more in Bah, Khairagarh and Itmadpur tehsils but the differences were not very striking and they did not indicate that excessive use was being made of the section if regard is made to the continuance of bad agricultural conditions. The low figures in 1928-29 were due to the fact that the *tehsildars* were directly under local orders to discourage applications in Court for realization of rent.[1].

Naqsuddin Khan, Collcctor, Mainpuri, said that there were 902 ejectments in 1930-31 as compared with 229 in 1928-29 and 364 in 1929-30. These figures showed that the number of ejectment cases under Section 79 had almost doubled as compared with average of past two years. Cases under Section 81 showed a similar increase. The percentage of ejectments actually ordered to number of cases decided under either Section has also considerably increased, considering however the circumstances of the year, the increase in institutions and ejectments were not excessive. The number of relinquishment of holdings by tenants has increased four times. Instructions have been issused to *tehsildars* to slow down the procedure in cases of ejectments.[2]

The Deputy Commissioner, Fatehgarh stated that there were 862 ejectments in 1930-31 as compared with 775 in 1928-29 and 736 in 1929-30. The statement showed that excessive use was made of Section 81 of the Tenancy Act.

---

1. *Revenue Department File* No. 465, Box No. 509, Letter of J.H. Darwin, Collector, Agra, to Revenue Secretary No. 160-S, dated 23rd April, 1931, U.P.S.A.

2. *Revenue Department*, D.O. of Maqsuddin Khan, Collector, Mainpuri to Marsh, dated 23rd April, 1931.

The police had not been used to assist zamindars in the collection of rents[1].

The collector, Kanpur intimated that there were 2062 ejectment cases in 1930-31, 831 in 1928-29 and 883 in 1929-30. There was a considerable increase under Section 81. They resulted from the fact that under Collector's orders *zamindars* were encouraged to fight suits against well to do tenants who could afford to pay rent but refused to do so from political motives. The Deputy Commissioner did not think that the Section was abused to any considerable extent. In some villages which had been badly affected—by Congress agitation and refusing to pay any rent, revenue and the police officers took joint action during winter, *i.e.*, a few arrests were made and tenants were induced to pay some of the rent at the same time such action was very necessary at that time Now *tehsildar* and police officers had nothing to do with the collection of rent. It will not be possible in this district to maintain a policy of leniency towards that tenants for long[2].

The Collector Fatehpur stated that he had issused orders to the tehsildars that tenants who had paid reasonable portion of the arrears were not to be ejected from their holdings. The police force was never used in that district to assist *zamindars* in the collection of rent. In tehsil Khajuha the *tehsildar* was given armed guard for protection. This tehsil was much affected by the No-rent campaign started by the Congress. The *tehsildar* went to the villages and presuaded tenants to

1. *Revenue Department,* Extract of Confidential D.O. No. 249, dated 18th April, 1931, from Collector, Fatehgarh to Maharaj Singh, Commissioner, Allahabad.

2. *Revenue Department,* Extract of D.O. No. 159-B/31, dated 21st April, 1931, from Collector, Kanpur, to Maharaj Singh, Commissioner, Allababad, U.P.S.A.

pay rents to the *zamindars* to the extent of 10-12 annas (60 to 75 NP) in the Rupee on the threat of immediate ejectment proceedings and unfortunately, the tehsildar met with an organised opposition from the residents of Nonara on 26th February, 1931 in which he lost his life. Since then no police had been given to any of the revenue officials for protection. The *tehsildars* since then did not take any active part in assisting zamindars in the realization of rents. In the district, genererally speaking, no orders of ejectment were passed against these tenants who had paid their rents to the extent of 10-20 annas (60-75 N.P.) in the rupee[1].

The Deputy Commissioner, Etawah wrote that the tehsil Bidhuna was especially effected by the Civil Disobedience Movement and there were 1036 ejectment decrees out of 2259 in the whole district. There had been no appreciable increase in Etawah and Aurayah tehsil while the condition in Bharthana tehsil had remained normal.

The Collector, Allahabad, wrote as follows : "It is quite clear that a great many tenants will lose their holdings because of the Civil Disobedience Movement. I enclose a statement showing how things stand in Government estates in this district. For your information similar figures are given for the principal Court of Wards estates. Harper is, of course wrong in saying that ejectments cannot be given effect to until 1st April. This provision applies only to applications under Section 81 of the Agra Tenancy Act. Execution of decrees under Section 79 of that Act can be taken out any time. It is impossible to say how many of the tenants who have been ejected have refused to pay for political reasons, but, as only 18 percent of the Kharif kist has been collected

---

1. *Revenue Department*, Extract of D.O. No. 61/C, dated 12th April, 1931, from Mussanna Collector, Fatehpur to G.M. Harper, Revenue Secretary, U.P.S.A.

from the Court of Wards tenants and as there have been several in Government estates in which tenants who have paid have had their crops destroyed by the agents of the Congress. I think it may safely be said that the great majority of these who have not paid have been influenced either by political motives or by fear of the consequences of paying. I donot see that the Congress can take any objection to tenants being ejected. They invite them not to pay rent and to suffer the consequences and have promsied them their land back, if they are ejected. For this purpose they are said to have opened a register at their headquarters in the city where tenants who have been ejected are inivited to come and record their names and the details of their holdings. In a great many cases tenants have not appeared in Court to answer suits applications for ejectment. In such cases ejectment must automatically follow. Where they have appeared and offered to pay anything *tehsildars* have all along had orders to treat them with greatest leniency."

"As regards ejectments a statements is enclosed showing the number of cases in which ejectment had been ordered and in which it has already taken place—the latter of course, are all under Section 79. There has been a large increase in the number of ejectments. The greater increase in the number of ejectments ordered is due to the political propaganda and the Congress promise to restore fields to recalcitrant tenants. It will be seen that the prominent Congress leader who estimated that 800 ejectments had already taken place in Karchchana tehsil, was not far out there have been over 700.

Zamindars and Police. It is not quite clear what is meant by "the use of the police to assist *zamindars* in the collection of rent." Police in this district, have, of course acted as agents on behalf of the *zamindars* but as you know Government have sanctioned extra police in Soraon because of the trouble that had arisen owing to the tenants refusal to pay rents. The object of sending extra police to Soroan was to 'assist the *zamindars* in the collection of rents. "In fact, the whole problem of the administration of the Allahabad district at the present time is to "assist the *zamindars* in the collection of rents." The no-rent campaign is both anti-Government and anti-*zamindar*. Unless the no-rent campaign is actually called off it is unfair for Government to tell the *zamindars* that they have made peace with the Congress and the *zamindars* can now fight their battle alone. If the present state of affairs continue, the general estimate of the rabi revenue collections is 4 annas in the rupee. I mention this because at present there is only one real problem in the district and that is to break the no-rent campaign. Harper's letter seems to ignore this, or atleast its tone suggests that the problem in this district is to protect tenants from the rapacity of their landlords".[1]

Mahatma Gandhi was frightened by the officials with the bogy of a class war being let loose by Nehru. He liked the idea of Congress tehsil committees acting on behalf of the tenants, but disapproved of the advice to withhold payment of rent even in part. The appointment of Congress tehsildars and attacks by tenants on taluqdars and zamindars.[2] He even, to the Government's delight, practically withdrew claim of the Congress to be an intermediary between the Government and

---

1. *Revenue Department*, Extract of D.O. No. 1896/S.T. dated April 8/10, 1931, from Mudie, Collector, Allahabad to Maharaj Singh. Commissioner, U.P.S.A.

2. *Revenue Department*, Emerson's report of his interview with Gandhi on 6th April 1931. Home Department Political File No. 33/11 of 1931, U.P.S.A.

the people.[1] Gandhi was also pressed to throw his weight against his wild men[2].

Gandhi met Hailey, the Governor in Nainital and issued a manifesto to the *Kisans* : "During the last struggle, in some districts the non-payment of taxes was being organised as part of the Civil Disobedience for the attainment of purna swaraj. But by reason of the settlement between the Congress and the Government civil disobedience was discontinued and, therefore, also the non-payment of taxes but then there was dead economic distress amongst you. Concentrated work was done in Agra, Mathura, Rae Bareli, Gorakhpur, Kanpur, Lucknow, Partapgarh and Etawah and it had been found that there should be a remission for the year 1338 *Fasli* of 8 *annas* (50 N.P.) in the rupee in the case of statutory and non-occupancy tenants and 4 *annas* (25 N.P.) in the case of occupancy tenants. He also appealed that all ejectments made during the struggle and afterwards, should be restored to create proper atmosphere.

Gandhi appealed to *taluqdars* and *zamindars* also that inquiry made in over 300 United Provinces villages in the eastern sector showed that the price of the produce at the present rate did not even cover the rents payable and this made no allowance for the cost of cultivation. He quoted Hooper, once a Settlement Officer as said to have given the following landlord definition of the U.P. tenants : "One is who is ready to live on one meal a day and in native phrase to sell his wife and children to pay the highest possible rent for his holding, who submits to any ceasses it may please the landlord to demand and who is always willing to work for him without

1. *Home Department*, political file No. 33/11 of 1931, Emerson's report of his interview with Gandhi on 6th April, 1931.
2. *Hailey Papers*, Crerar, Home Member to Hailey 6th May, 1931.

payment, to give evidence for him in court and speaking generally, to do any conceivable lie is told."

Gandhi said that this description was not flattaring to the zamindars but since Hooper's time the zamindars idea had gone a revolution. Many of them were sympathetic to the tenants but the process had to be much faster than it had been. They should become trustees and trusted friends of their tenants. They should limit the privy purse and forego questionable perquisites they took from the tenants, in the shape of forced gifts on marriage and other occasions or nazrana on transfer of holdings from one kisan to another. They may themselves become Congressmen and know that the Congress was a bridge between the people and the Government.[1]

It was hoped that Gandhi's efforts would be welcome by all parties and things would become to settle down but they had just the contrary and almost provocative effect on the Government. His concerete formula was attacked on the grounds that it did not take account of local variations. The critics lost sight of this important point that the money value of the out turn in the cases of all classes of tenants in all quarters of the province was brought down by about 60 per cent. This was invariable source of distress which was of equal potency in the case of all classes of cultivators whether in Bundelkhand, Gorakhpur, Partapgarh, or Meerut [2]

So when Jawaharlal came back to the U.P. (after his illness) in the middle of June, he found the situation and atmosphere much worse than in March. The *taluqdars* were terrorizing the peasants with the help of the police. Congress volunteers were

1. Gandhi's article in *Young India*, dated May 1929, addressed to U.P. *Zamindars*.
2. *Report of U.P. Congress Committee on Agrarian Condition*, p. 17.

being beaten up in many places, and even activity such as peaceful picketing permitted by the settlement. was in places banned by over-enthusiastic district authorities. Jawaharlal no intention of submitting meekly to this despite letters from Gandhi,[1] seen in the mail by authorities, deploring the element of violence in the Congress ranks and urging him not to break any law himself but to seek an interview with the Governor or with Emerson. "On your side", Gandhi wrote to a U.P. Congress man,[2] "it is all well, so long as you hold the *kisans* in check." Jawaharlal in reply to Gandhi and also to Government said that the Government was breaking the truce and using the *taluqdars* and zamindars to crush the kisans, and the Congress would have to take drastic action in reply. *Taluqdars* who preferred to bask in official sunshine rather than to be on friendly terms with their tenants had no place in India, and those who were guilty of oppression would have to answer for it before the nation.[3]

The authorities adopted a policy of indifference to the Congress representation and if they did not connive at, or encourage the landlords excesses, they certainly did nothing tangible to put a stop to them. This attitude of apathy prepared the way for an organised campaign of repression. The office of the Provincial Congress Committee was flooded with diaquieting commuications from various parts of the province. They held a special session of 14th June and appointed a number of committees to enquire into and report on the agrarian situation in the districts as noted below.[4]

---

1. 20th and 24th June, 1931.
2. Gopal, S. (ed.), *Collected Works*, Vol. 46, To Mohanlal Saxena, 15th June, 1931.
3. Speeches at Delhi, 22nd June, '*The Bombay Chronicle*, 29th June, 1931 and at Lucknow 26th June, 1931.
4. *Report of U.P.C.C. Committee, on Agrarian Distress in U.P.* pp. 48—49.

(1) Barabanki Inquiry. Committee.
Dr. K.N. Katju, Mr. Rafi Ahmad Kidwai, Mohan lal Saxena.

(2) Rae Bareli Inquiry Committee.
Dr. K.N. Katju, Rafi Ahmad Kidwai, Mohan Lal Saxena.

(3) Pratapgarh Inquiry Committee.
Gopi Nath Srivastava, Chandra Bhanu Gupta.

(4) Mathura Inquiry Committee.
Srikesh Dutta Paliwal, Nemi Saran Jain.

(5) Gorakhpur Inquiry Committee.
Achrya Narendra Deo, Sampurnanand.

(6) Gonda Inquiry Committee.
V.N. Tewari, Rafi Ahmad Kidwai, Mohanlal Saxena.

(7) Bahraich Inquiry Committee.
V.N, Tewari, Rafi Ahmad Kidwai, Mohanlal Saxena.

(8) Unnao Inquiry Cammittee.
Pt. Balkrishna, Hari Har Nath Shastri.

(9) Sultanpur Inqiry Committee.
Gopi Nath Srivastava, Chandra Bhanu Gupta.

(10) Basti Inquiry Committee.
Acharya Narendra Dev, Sampurnanand.

The gentlemen noted above conducted careful personal inquiries in the areas allotted to them. The reports suumitted by them were considered by the Council of the Provincial Congress Committe on 18th July.

The impression which was sedulously fostered by those who want to stem the tide of the Congress, that it was opposed to the taluqdars and zamindars, was wrong and mischievous. The Committee passed the following resolution :

"After taking into careful consideration the reports of committees, the council is definitely of opinion that the terms of the truce are being persistently violated by the local authorities and strong efforts are being made to undermine the Congress organisation. Atrocities of the various kinds are being committed on the tenants. Office-bearers and members of Congress Committees and Congress volunteers are being arrested in large numbers. Notices under Section 144 are being issued to suppress Congress activities, that bodily assaults, arson and looting of property, are being freely resorted to ; and that there are authentic cases of rape. and of women being subjected to inhuman tortures. The council feels that this state of affairs has now become intolerable. It, therefore, requests the working committee of the Congress either to bring about an immediate cessation of this condition of affairs or authorise this council or the U.P.C.C. to take such steps, as it may deem necessary under the circumstance."[1]

The U.P. Congress Committee by a resolution of 28th July, 1931 appointed a Committee comprising of Govind Ballabh Pant, Rafi Ahmad Kidwai and Venktesh Narain Tewari with Mohan Lal Gautam as Secretary. The Committee submitted its report on 2nd September, 1931. They wrote that there was chronic poverty in peasants and because of agricultural calamities and slump in prices the foundations of rural economy had shaken. The cultivator was crippled and unable to pay rents and the Government was apathetic. Its attempt to face realities was belated and the remissions granted very inadequate and disappointing. The Government was responsible for aggravating distress and relied on repression for the settlement of agrarian problem. Innumerable atrocities had been committed on the tenants and harrowing accounts had reached the

1. Extract of Resolution passed by the Council of U.P. Provincial Congress Committee on 18th July, 1931.

committee from several districts. Congressmen had been harassed, gagged and imprisoned. The Committee asserted :

"The country is to-day faced with a difficult problem, mere remissions in rent and revenue will not solve it. We will have to devise and introduce a system, which will ensure to the tenant his subsistence. Unless this is done the problem remains unsolved. Remission or similar device might ease the situation for a year or two, or even for a decade but the problem will remain there. The more the solution is delayed the more is the danger of the situation getting out of control. If those on whose power it is today do not give the necessary relief to the distressed cultivators, hunger and starvation will force them to seek relief for themselves. And then who can tell what may happen ? Millions of *Kisans*, and almost 35 millions they are, will not meekly submit to starvation. They are bound to seek relief, they are bound to get it, we can today solve it peacefully. How it will solve itself tomorrow, no one can dare foretell."

"The bulk of the population some how manage to eke out a meagre subsistence out of land as agriculture is practically the sole industry. The density of population is very high. The pressure on land is ever increasing. There is no room for extension of cultivation except in very unhealthy tracts. Large number have only uneconomic holdings ; the size of the average holding is uncontinuously going down, and owing to destruction of indigenous arts and crafts and the dumping of cheap articles from abroad, agriculturists are continuously losing their subsidiary vocations, and there is an incessant flux of people from industries to agriculture. The indebtedness of the agricultural classes is another serious handicap. Most of the people somehow manage to exist and very few people are possessed of any resources on which they should draw in times of stress. As a rule the agricultural classes are dreadfully poor, deeply in debt, and illiterate. Their standard of life is inconceivably wretched"[1].

The Government and the landed proprietors insisted on extracting 'blood out of stones' and they had recource to all conceivable devices for this purpose. The real cause which gave rise to the tenant's penury was ignored and the myth was circulated that political forces of a dangerous character were leading to an outburst which could be checked only by an iron hand.

The Government was abusing the law, and oppression in the garb of law was hard to resist. The Section 107 Cr. P.C. was being misused. A person was issued with a notice confronting him with the alternative of either going to jail for a year or severing connection with congress. Several persons were involved in a case under this section. When the case came up for hearing, the accused were discharged as by that time they had paid all their rents[2]. Other preventive sections had also not been forgotten. A prominent Congress worker was bound down under Section 109. The bonds were, however, cancelled on his giving on understanding for future good behaviour.

In Mathura[3] most of the Congress workers of one village came in for their share under Section 107. Action was also taken under the non-political sections in a number of cases through they were purely political reasons. Eighteen persons were affected in village Bijhari on the allegation that they had obstructed the Quark Amin in the execution of a process of Court. The Magistrate bound them down under

1. Chalhpathi Rau, *Govind Ballabh Pant : His Life and Times*, pp. 102, 103.
2. *U.P.C.C. Committee Report*, p. 38.
3. *U.P.C.C. Committee Report*, p. 53.

Section 144 Cr. P.C. On appeal the Sessions Judge found that the case was entirely false and had been colluded by the police, the revenue staff, and the *zamindars* against the appel-lents. The magistrates not unoften allowed their minds to be influenced by extra judicial considerations.

In Rae Bareli, the well known order of the Deputy Commis-sioner was served on about a score of Congress workers under Section 144 Cr. P.C.[1].

In Sultanpur, every office-bearer and practically all the members of the district Congress Comittee were gagged.

In Barabanki, a large number of villages were similarly dealt with under Section 144. By one single order several villages were covered. Blank forms with the magistrates signatures were given to the police to be filled in as occasion demanded. It was admitted by the Government also that such blank forms were issued. It was a shameless abuse of law[2].

In Ghazipur a notice under Section 144 was served on all Congress workers on 11th July, for one month, and then further extended by another month.

Official resources hit upon other devices also. A general policy of granting attachment before judgement was adopted all over Awadh and in several districts of Agra province. There were grounds for believing that instructions were issued from the Council House (main office of Chief Secretary) directing the district officers to adopt this course. Police

1. The Deputy Commissioner, S.S.L. Dar issued these orders under Section 144 Cr. P.C.
2. The provision of Section 144 are of an exceptional nature and even all magistrates were not authorised to put it into effect.

and revenue staff were placed at the disposal of the *talugdars* and *zamindars*. Just as Section 107 served as a shield for criminal courts, so the legal processes were utilised for making a display of force in the villages to overawe the tenantry.

The Deputy Commissioner, Rae Bareli, wrote "......if the revenue staff needs police protection in execution of legal processes, it will be given and you can utilise this opportunity and the presence of the revenue staff and the police in the villages to push on your collection[1]. The Deputy Commissioner, Rae Bareli, imported 200 armed police and sent them in a procession in the city and later used them in villages[2].

Mauza Garhi Shahja in Agra was visited by the Quarak Amin, the police sub-inspector and about a dozen police constables and *tehsil* peons accompanied by zamindars and thirty of their men on 27th June. Some cattle were attached and ultimately it led to a dispute with the result that one villager Kishore was belaboured with *lathis*, and Gajadhar Bahori and Tula Ram got bullet shots. A number of villagers were arrested.

At Panwari in Rae Bareli district Gayadin and Sitaram were killed and serious injuries were caused to Mahabir.

Section 12 A of the Oudh Rent Act which enables the Government to realize rents directly from the tenants was also applied to certain places for example the whole of the Rae Bareli district.

---

1. *Revenue Department*, Letter of Deputy Commissioner, Rae Bareli, Dar, dated 19th June, U.P.S.A.

2. Dar, Deputy Commissioner, Rae Bareli, on his return from Nainital where he had an opportunity of meeting his superior officers, U.P.S.A.

At Baraipur, there was a regular siege of the village which lasted for three days. Houses were entered into forcibly property removed from them, women beaten and illtreated[1].

Raghvendra Pratap Singh, the son of Raja of Maukapur, a prominent Congressman was threatened with a case under Section 363 Indian Penal Code, also reminding him that he was holder of a licence. The Deputy Commissioner was reported to have told him that he would harass him in various ways if he would continue Congress work[2].

Mathura district had a good net work of Congress Committees in the villages. Congress work continued expanding even after settlement. On 20th May, three buses full of armed police raided Bijhari[3] apparently to arrest eighteen congressmen under Section 107. The police party broke flag posts, destroyed national flags, assaulated women, and took hold of the ornaments and cash they could find.

A Congress meeting was forcibly dispersed by the police at Naujhil on 26th June. Gherelal was seriously injured and others were also hurt. Curious defence by the Government was that the villagers prevented the meeting being held and a scuffle ensued[4] on 20th June, 1931, the sub-inspector pulled

---

1. This incident was included in the Charge Sheet submitted by Mahatma Gandhi to the Government of India.
2. Deputy Commissioner told Raghvendra Pratap Singh in the course of an interview on 6th June. (As per statement of the latter).
3. Bijhari is one of the village centres of Congress in Mathura.
4. Sessions Judge, Mathura supports the allegations made by the Congress that a peaceful meeting at Naujhil was forcibly dispersed on 26th June, 1931.

down the Congress flag, arrested five villagers and took Congress registers from Bhudaria[1].

On 20th June, some Congress workers were beaten by the Quanoongo in Dedra. A report was sent. On 27th June, 1931, the Deputy Commissioner and Superintendent of Police, Barabanki, visited Dadra. The Deputy Commissioner called the tenants together, had their Gandhi caps removed and warned them against the use of Gandhi cap and Khaddar. He asked them to severe their connection with the Congress and got them sign a declaration to the effect.

A number of volunteers belonging to Panwara village were beaten. Thakur Bhagwan Singh who paid Rs. 800/- revenue annually and was president of Maharajganj *tehsil* Congress Committee presided at a Congress meeting on 20th and 29th June and entertained a party of volunteers. The same night the Deputy Commissioner, Superindent of Police and the tehsildar with about forty policemen, entered his house and demanded the arrears of revenue. On his asking for two hours' time, he met the retort "where do get the time and money for the volunteers to feed" and was taken into custody[2].

In Agra when villagers applied for remission, their applications were referred to the *Aman Sabha*. Remission slips were withheld from the villagers who had taken part in civil disobedience and no rent campaign and they could get them only after they gave understanding about future good behaviour[3].

---

1. This incident was mentioned in the Congress Charge Sheet.
2. J.C. Donaldson was the Deputy Commissioner and Punwara village was situated in Maharajganj Tehsil of district Rae Bareli.
3. Babu Ram Yadav the Publicity Officer and Secretary of *Aman Sabha* and editor of mouthpiece the '*Agra Samachar*' published this in the Samachar.

In Bulandshahr, some people sought the help of the police in connection with the executi›n of some process, and the civil court ordered it. When it was brought to the notice of the court that decree-holder was an active Congressman, he cancelled his previous order and directed that the guard should be called back if it had left.

The Government has claimed more than once that it was guided only by one governing principle in its attitude towards the agrarian question and that was to hold the scales even between the tenants and the *zamindars.* Bhagwanta and a few others filed an application under Section 107 against zamindars of Karau in district Rae Bareli that they had been beaten. The sub-inspector also supported some allegations. But instead of taking any action against the *zamindar*, the sub-divisional officer started proceedings under Section 107 against the same applicants.

In the concluding paragraph, the committee wrote that they had referred to the hardships which the tenantry had borne patiently. They had seen tenants complaints recoiling over their heads, being consistently thrown into waste-paper basket. They were not aware of any steps or action taken against the worst member of the *taluqdar* or *zamindar* class and they wondered how long the Government would be able "to hold the scale even", in this manner and how long people will let this Government mishandle such vital questions[1].

In a statement to the press Jawaharlal Nehru said that there was no improvement, and the agrarian situation continued to be bad. The time for collection was long past, but coercive processes continued. In the district of Mathura, during August, over 2,000 processrs had been issued and the

---

1. *Report of U.P.C.C. Committee*, 2nd Scptember, 1931, p. 79.

cattle of the tenantry attached in large numbers. Prominent workers were being removed one after another under Section 103 Cr. P.C. The main trouble, however, was the ejectment of the tenants in large numbers. There could be no solution on the problem till this matter was attended and relief was given[1].

In an article 'How they manage things in Mathura District'[2], Jawaharlal Nehru wrote that the district of Mathura had grained a measure of notoriety in recent months and it had found prominent mention in the charge-sheet against Government framed by Gandhi. The truce had been observed there by numerous arrests of Congress workers and by police raids on villages and assaults on villagers and Congress workers. The complaints in regard to Bijhari, Nojhil and Rayah[3] mentioned in the charge-sheet, were denied by the local government. The judgement in appeal in recent cases showed clearly that the governments reply was wrong and the charges in the main, correct. Congressmen convicted by the first court had been acquitted on appeal. In the Bijhari case, the Sessions Judge had held that the sub-inspector of police, the *amin* and a *zamindar* colluded to bring false charges against the accused. In the Nojhil judgement the judge says ; "I cannot finish my judgement without observing that it is to be regretted that while the complainant and other Congressmen were holding a meeting some policemen, two of

1. *Bombay Chronicle*, Ahmedabad, 11th and 12th September, 1931.

2. An article published in *Young India*, dated 19th September, 1931.

3. A Congress volunteer was beaten with shoes by the police at Rayah and ordered to leave the village on 10th July, 1931.

whom were Gandhi and Yusuf Ali, had surely assaulted one Ghurelal, most probably under the very nose of the S.O. (Station Officer) of the police, Nojhil......".

But the most revealing document is judgement of another Judge in the Kosi Kalan case. This case was made out to have arisen out of communal quarrel between Hindus and Muslims. The judge was a Christian. He has written a judgement running into two hundred ten typed pages and has discredited the attempts to drag in the Congress into it. "I may state at the outset" he says, "that a prosecution case so wretched as this it would be impossible to imagine". Perfectly innocent persons, who had themselves suffered from looting and had been seriously injured, he further says, were implicated "in a serious offense so that bail might not be granted to them and they might thus be prevented from bringing complaints". About a police officer, he says "it is disgusting in the extreme to find a pclice officer in his position telling deliberate lies". Referring to the Congress meeting, the j dge says, "the authorities could have prohibited the meeting . . . there was no need to prevent it by hooliganism". The police "first arrest everybody whom they wanted to arrest and after that the witness was brought to say that they had all taken part in the riot".

In spite of the great economic distress, coercion processes, ejectments and attachments continued. Jawaharlal wrote that things were pretty bad beating and assaults continued. while acknowledging Mehta, Commissioner, Allahabad[1]. letter of 22nd[2], Jawaharlal mentioned about the instance of

1. *A.I.C.C. File* No. G-40 (K.W.)(*iii*)/1931, p. 105, N.M.M.L.
2. Mehta suggested that the District authorities should be approached first for redressal of any kisan grievance.

Badarpur village in Karchchana tehsil[1]. Three persons, like Purshottamdas Tandon, Venkatesh Narayan Tiwari and Kamla Nehru visited the village and personally investigated the matter. A report was sent to the District Magistrate, an offer was made to send one of our member with him to the village. He preferred to go alone and forthwith issue a press statement denying our version. This kind of cavalier treatment may be the government's method of doing work. "P.D. Tandon will soon be sending you another case of village Sakrawal in Karchchana *tehsil* where men and women were beaten for the recovery of a paltry sum like Re. 1 or Rs. 5" Jawaharlal on 24th September, 1931 wrote to Chief Secretary[2] that in Bareily new developments had taken place which were quite alien to the city and district before[3]. Congress meetings were interferred with and stones were thrown and threats used. Income instance dancing girls were brought to the meetings and were made to perform in order to interfere in order to interfere with the meeting.

On 4th October 1931, Jawaharlal wrote to Gandhi[4] in London that he had time to find out a little more about the agrarian situation. The tenantry had lost hope to a large extent of any real relief being given to them. Their passion for land was amazing and especially the fear of being

---

1. On 1st September 1931, the police, while helping a zamindar to realize rent harassed the tenants of Badarpur in Karchchana. As a result the villagers left their houses.

2. *A.I.C.C. File* No. G-40(K.W.)(*iii*)1231 pp. 97-99,. N.M.M.L.

3. The Chief Secretary in his reply dated 26 th October, 1931, denied any harassment.

4. Gandhi Smarak Sangrahalaya, Serial No..17973.

dispossessed with the crops ripening had made many of them do almost anything to stick on. A large number of the dispossessed tenants in Allahabad, probably 25% or more, have raised money somehow, by sale of property etc., and paid up the dues fully and thus get back the land. This was bad enough as they would soon find out what was worse was the effect this was going to have on future remissions. There was a clause in the report of the official rent committee that these proposals would not apply to cases where the *zamindar* and the tenant had mutually agreed to a fresh arrangement. Altogether position was not most unsatisfactory. Stray reports of beatings of kisans continued to come.

On 15th October, 1931 Jawaharlal Nehru in a letter addressed to Chief Secretary[1] with facts and figures challenged the statement of R.F. Mudie[2] Collector, Allahabad, that the remissions he was giving were fair and in accordance with the principles laid down by local government. It had been told that every consideration would be shown to the tenant and every facility would be afforded to him. The experience during these past months and even now had been unfortunate. The revenue staff seemed to look upon the tenant as the enemy of the society to be harassed in every way and made to pay up by any means. For him the period following the Delhi settlement had been one of the intense suffering. Gandhi had discussed the matter with Emerson[3] and the U.P. Government had been continually informed about this. The general depression and the economic situation were

1. *A.I.C.C. File* No. G-25/1931, pp. 123-129, N.M.M.L.
2. Chief Secretary, U.P. Government 1939-43, Home Member, Viceroy's Executive Council 1944-46. Governor of Sind 1946-47, after 1947 served in Pakistan.
3. On 15th and 16th July, 1931-

against the tenant. To this was added the treatment he got from his landlord and from the revenue staff. The period of the Delhi Settlement had been one of ceaseless war against the tenant. The new scales of remissions were inadequate. The prospect ahead of the tenantry was again, therefore, one of coercive processes, ejectments, harassment, attachments, sale of cattle or property if they still possess any. The Allahabad District Congress Committee had after anxious and prolonged consideration decided to approach the U.P. Provincial Congress Committee and Congress President, Sardar Vallabh Bhai Patel, for permission, should need arise to advise withholding payment of rent till relief was given in regard to various matters connected with it. This referred to one district but this might have for reaching consequences. The question of payment or with-holding of payment of rent was vital and an urgent one for the tenantry and it could not afford to be shelved till the conclusion of the Round Table Conference, which Gandhi was attending in London.

A cable was sent to Gandhi on 16th October, 1931 regarding[1]: "Agrarian situation becoming critical. Coercive attachments, forcible collection of rent continued right through without interval. Many ejected tenants proceeded against for criminal trespass. Many for fear permanently losing land sold cattle, belongings, borrowed money. Paid f.ll demand plus extras. Fresh demand was made for current season. Inadequate remissions. Threat that if full payment not made within one month remission might be cancelled. Also no objection considered on behalf tenants till full payment made. Condition of Kisans deplorable. Throughly exhausted after past six months continuous harassment forcible measures. Apparently process likely to be repeated this year also. Allahabad district Congress Committee resolved under circumstances ask permission start satyagraha if necessity arises by advising with-holding payment rent.

1. *A.I.C.C. File* No. C-140/1931 (Part III), pp. 167-168 N.M.M.L.

Application for permission made to Vallabhbhai and provincial committee representative District Kisan Conference being held next week to decide question. Decision likely have far-reaching consequences but question payment or withholding payment must be decided soon vital urgent problem for kisans admitting no delay[1]".

The summit of the crisis was now reached. The kisans losing all hope of redress from the Congress and the Government, was desparately raising money to avoid eviction and the loss of their crops. They sold their cattle, dumped their grain on their grain on the markets thus further reducing the price, and borrowed from money-lenders and paid not only the current rent in full but often some arrears and heavy cost. Those who had been evicted paid very much more to recover their land than if they had paid in full rent without any remission at the start, and in the process they lost their occupancy rights and became life tenants[2]. Moreover their direct transactions were regarded by the authorities as mutual arrangements between the tenants and landlords which dispensed with the need for remissions. All out efforts were made by the U.P. Government to impede Jawaharlal Nehru. In the villages of district Gonda, there were serious allegations of harassment, ditches were dug across the road and in Bahraich district to prevent attendence at Jawaharlal's meetings, the kisans were directed to stay in their villages on those particular dates to receive the remission slips[3]. In

1. Gandhi on 18th October, 1931, cabled back "You should unhesitatingly take necessary steps meet every situation. Expect nothing more".

2. Gopal, S. (ed.), *Selected Works,* Vol. 45, Jawaharlal to Gandhi, 16th October, 1931.

3. *The Leader,* dated 14th October, 1931.

many districts the peasants were informed that their remissions would be cancelled if rent for the current Kharif crop was withheld for over a month. It was only when rent had been fully paid, moreover, that any objections of the tenant regarding the rent would be considered, But it was obvious that money once paid would never be returned, and clearly the purpose was to terrorize the peasant into peasant into paying all he could. In Allahabad district, the population had increased over the years, while the cultivated area had declined, so that the pressure on holdings, already uneconomic, was acute. The Kharif crop was also well below average because of untimely rains. But heedless of these considerations, as well as of the public opinion to which the district was exposed, the Collector, R.F. Mudie, granted remissions for 1931 of only Rs. 9.5 lakhs. Out of a total cash rental of Rs. 57 lakhs for both the Kharif and rabi crops, as against Rs. 11 lakhs in 1930 for the rabi crop only[1], on the ground that there were a large number of occupancy tenants whose rents had not been raised in recent years. The collector also contended that the rental demand in 1915-16 had been the same as in 1901, the base year selected by the U.P. Government, and on this wrong premise, assumed without checking or publishing the figures, further reduced the remissions[2]. So the remissions were only 17 percent although the prices of cereals had fallen by 55 percent, and grain formerly worth a rupee was now worth only half rupee.

---

1. Though for 1930 the U.P. Government had sanctioned remissions of Rs. 12.3 lakhs, the Collector granted only Rs. 11 lakhs.

2. Press interview of Collector, Allahabad, 14th October. *The Leader*, 16th October, 1931, Jawaharlal to Jagdish Prasad 15th October, 1931 (two letters), *A.I.C.C. File* No. 54, Part III/1931.

Jawaharlal was at last forced to contemplete a no-rent compaign. He wrote to the Chief Secretary, : "Thus the outlook for the tenant is about as black as it could well be and there seems no way out. If the government policy is enforced he is doomed to even greater sufferings than he has passed through. We have been anxiously considering this and the Allahabad district Congress Committee have felt that they can be no parties to the continuous oppression of the kisan leaning to his economic death".

So it became imperative to council withholding of payment of rent by the tenantry, till a congenial solution was negotiated. Nehru informed the Chief Secretary that they were convening a representative Kisan Conference to consider this momentous question and simultaneously communicating with the provincial and the All-India Congress. In a concerted move both the Allahabad District Congress Committee and the Kisan Conference recommended the cessation of payment of rents[1].

With the collections of rent impending from 15th November, 1931, the U.P. Congress Committee with the authorization of Congress President, Patel, directed the Kisans of Allahabad district to withhold payment of rent and revenue while negotiatons were in progress.[2]

This was a rational step, for it was pointless to pay rent and revenue while the whole question of the quantum was under discussions. But the U.P. Government utilized this resolution to call off the parleys with the Conservative party dominating the polls in Britain and the Second Round Table Conference a failure, the Government of India had manifestly decided to turn their backs on Irwin's settlement, and

1. *The Leader*, 19th and 25th October, 1931.

2. *The Leader*, 18th November, 1931,

the harsh Bengal Ordinance and drastic policy were parts of a general return to a policy of brutal repression. *The Pioneer,* which had access to official sources even referred to the possibility of deportations[1] of the Congress leaders ; Some retribution was demanded on 6th December, 1931, the district Congress Committees in Rae Bareli, Etawah, Kanpur and Unnao in addition to Allahabad, were authorized to commence their no-rent campaigns.[2] Payment in these districts came to an almost a complete standstill.[3] Other districts of the province were also lining up, and it was manifest that once the movement commenced it would encompass the whole province. Unlike in the previous year, this no-rent compaign had no obvious political overtones and was motivated and justified by economic causes."[4] Hailey, the Governor was apprehensive that the situation might slip out of control and if Gandhi, upon his return decided to support the agitation no rent or revenue at all could be collected.[5]

At this precarious juncture, Governor Hailey who had so far demurred at repressive measures, advised by the Government of India, acceeded to the latter's impolicy. The Congress and its affiliated parties were outlawed, the instigation ordinance repromulgated and the leaders ordered to be arrested. Notices were served on Jawaharlal Nehru and other leaders prohibiting them from speaking or writing in

---

1. *The Pioneer*, 27th November, 1931.
2. *The Bombay Chronicle*, 7th December, 1931.
3. *Fortnightly Report* of U.P. Government for the first half of December, 1931.
4. Gopal, S., *Biography of Nehru*, Volume I, p. 168.
5. *Hailey Papers*, Hailey to Verney Lovett, 14th December, 1931, and to Irwin, 2nd January, 1932.

support of the no-rent campaign. Jawaharlal served with a mandate not to leave Allahabad without official permission and the United Provinces Provincial Conference scheduled to be held on 26th December, 1931, was banned. Still the Congress struggled to avoid battle, and postponed the Conference.[1] Jawaharlal was arrested on 26th December, 1931, for violating the order restricting him to Allahabad. Significantly, it was a national event and when the prominent Congress leaders of India endeavoured to revive the Civil Disobedience Movement, they were also imprisoned. Every possible effort of traumatic repression was resorted to, to crush the Congress and subdue the national movement.

1. *The Leader*, 25th December, 1931.

6

Congress Ministry and Tenure Reforms

One of the major reforms initiated by the Congress Ministry during the Governorship of Haig related to the upliftment of the downtrodden peasantry of the Provinces which had, for long, been groaning under the tyrannical exactions of the landed aristocracy thereof.[1] The actual tillers of the soil had been reduced to a state of utter distraction and chilling penury under the existing tenancy laws which governed the two parts of the Province of Agra and Awadh.[2] While the tenantry in Agra was, comparatively, on firmer footings, a tenant in Awadh, where the pernicious *Taluqdari* system was in vogue, was not sure whether the same piece of land that was under his cultivation would remain with him (for his cultivation) during the next cropping

---

1. *Agrarian Distress in the United Provinces* : Report of the Committee appointed by the Council of the U.P. Provincial Congress Committee to enquire into the Agrarian situation in the Provinces, 1931 ; also, *Report on the Agrarian Situation in the United Provinces, 1931* Offi- also, *Report on the Condition of Tenantry in Oudh (Awadh)*, Vols. I and II, 1933 ; also, Misra, B.R., *Land Revenue Policy in the United Provinces Under British Rule* ; also, Pande, V.D., *Land Revenue Administration of Awadh : 1856—1921*, Chapter—IV.
2. For Agra, *Agra, Tenancy Act*, 1926 ; for Awadh, *The Oudh Rent Amendment Act, Act VII of 1921* ; also *U.P. Tenancy Act, Act III of 1921.*

season.[1] Amid such conditions it was not surprising that the Provinces witnessed several kisan movements like the Eka Movement and the organisation of Kisan Sabhas in almost all the districts of Awadh,[2] till the Congress took up the cause of the suffering peasantry in real earnest[3] which ultimately voted it to power in 1937.

The malaise did not altogether lie with the landlords themselves as the petty revenue officials like the *patwaris, qanungos* and *tehsildars* aided and abetted them in their nefarious and illegal exactions for their own petty gains[4]. Also, it would

---

1. Srivastava, Gopinath, *When Congress Ruled*, p. 22 ff. ; also p. 38 ff.
2. *Report*, 1921—22, pp. *xvii—xviii*. According to it, the *Eka movement* was started in Malihabad by one, Madari Pasi and spread to Sitapur and Hardoi districts. But see Pande, *Land Revenue Administration* etc. (op. cit.), for another view.

   The Kisan Sabha Movement started from Pratapgarh and spread to other districts of Awadh. Cf. Baba Ram Chandra's *Diaries*, (microfilms in the State Archives : pages indistinct).
3. Cf. Nehru, Jawaharlal, *Towards Freedom*, pp. 65—67. According to him, after the Calcutta Session of the Congress in 1920, Mahatma Gandhi "brought about a complete change in (the Congress) constitution" and "made it democratic and a mass organisation ...... Peasants rolled in and ...... it began to assume the look of a vast agrarian organisation......" For Nehru's first contact with the peasantry, see Norman, Dorothy, Nehru—*The First Sixty Years.* (Volume—I), p. 52 ff.
4. Pandey, V.D., *Land Revenue Administration in Awadh : 1856—1921*, for the role of *patwaris* and *Quanungos*, (Chapter—VI), p. 346 ff.

not be out of place to mention the apathetic attitude of Hailey, the Governor of the Province (1928—1934), predecessor of Haig, towards the peasantry in so far as revenue realisations are concerned. Despite the fact that the Provinces had visitations of several natural calamities like hailstorms, locusts and even paucity of rains in some regions, he established an enviable record in revenue realisations amounting to 99.9 per-cent in the fiscal year 1933—34, or just before he relinquished office.[1]

It is not that the existing state of affairs was not known to the Governor. For, soon after the formation of the Interim Ministry, he thus wrote to the Viceroy ; "The main item (of the programme of the Interim Ministry) will be tenancy reform. They (the Ministers) are intending to set up a Committee very shortly to recommend immediate action. The main item . . . will be the grant of occupancy rights to all tenants-in-chief . . . this will probably be supplemented by a number of measures directed to removing the many grievances in small matters (sic) and the petty tyrannies from which the tenants suffer . . ."[2] Evidently, Haig, the Governor of the province, does not seem to attach great importance to the 'tyrannies' and 'grievances' of the peasants which were in the form of *hari* (unpaid tilling of the landlord's fields), *begari* (wageless labour) realisations of *bhusa* (chaff), *ghee*, *Ghorawan* (contribution for purchase of horses), *hathiawan* (contribution for purchase of elephant), etc., which were highlighted by the Mehta Report and which the hapless peasants were subjected to.[3] Haig was also fully aware of

1. *Report* (Administrative), 1933—34, No. 6551, pp. 7—16.
2. *Haig Papers, Private and Confidential* letter to the Viceroy, dated 23rd April, 1937, para 4.
3. Cf. *Mehta Report* (Summary), pp. 2—5, now in the State Archives. The full *Report* is in the *State Archives*, File No. 753/1920, *Revenue (A) Department.*

the "arbitrary powers of landlords in matters . . . such as grant of land for building houses or the right to plant trees . . . (and) the opportunities for the landlords' servants to bully the tenants, etc. . . ."[1] Yet he makes light of these and calls them 'small matters' and 'petty tyrannies' at a time when prices of agricultural produce were falling[2] and the peasantry, in utter desolation and the binding demand of the revenue and canal dues, had been thrown into the laps of the moneylending Shylocks from whose clutches there was no hope for their redemption.[3]

---

1. *Haig Papers*, letter dated 23rd April, 1937, para 4.

2. *Report*, 1933—34, p. 7 ff. ; also Srivastava, Gopinath, *When Congress Ruled*, pp. 24—25. According to him, "After 1929, agricultural prices fell precipitately and made it impossible for the tenant to meet his rental obligation." (*Ibid.*) For the real condition of the peasantry in Agra and Awadh, see two booklets by Pande, Mata Badal, entitled *Kisanon Ki Phansi* and *Awadh Ke Kisanon Ki Durdasha*, cited by Siddiqi, M.H., in *Agrarian Unrest in North India*, pp. 201—7 ; also Siddiqi, *A Note on Some Sources for the Study of Peasant Movement*, in the *Proceedings of the Indian History, Congress*, 1972 (*Ibid.*).

3. Cf. *Report*, 1936—37, p. *xvii*. According to it, "The first step taken by the (Congress) Government ......was to consider reform of the tenancy and land revenue law while the other was to examine the proposals for relieving rural indebtedness and for framing new debt legislation." (Ibid.). The moneylenders charged from *sawai* (quarter of the sum lent) to *derhi* (half of the sum) as interest and, failing repayment after a year, calculated the debt on compound-interest-basis. (I owe this information to Kr. Birendra Singh of Rae Bareli).

Beside the problem of insecurity to tenants throughout the Province, there were two other factors that plagued the life and living of the peasants in general. These were the pitch of rent and indebtedness. These had also attracted the notice of the Governor and his Interin Ministry, though the latter was fully composed of landlords, as already noticed. With regard to the first—the pitch of rent, Haig, instead of advising his Ministers to announce some immediate relief in view of the prevailing conditions, felt satisfied that "the matter is (was) already being tackled by the comprehensive re-settlement and revision (of rents) programme . . . "[1]. He was even against the small concession to the peasants through lowering of the exhorbitant canal rents, and, though the Ministry desired to make some concessions in the rates, he prevailed upon them not to do so[2]. As for the second—rural indebtedness—the Ministry had hardly any time or opportunity to take any positive steps in that direction due, perhaps, to its short stay in office[3]. To Haig, "any reductions in the land revenue or lowering of canal rates . . . would involve the province in bankruptcy unless new resources of taxation falling inevitably on the landlords were introduced"[4]. And, since any new taxes on the landlords were out question in view of the composition of the Interim Ministry which would have opposed

---

1. *Haig Papers*, Letter to the Viceroy, dated 23rd April, 1937, para 4.

2. *Ibid.*, ; Also another letter dated 7th June, 1937 para 7, referring to it. Finally, Haig noted in yet another letter dated July 21, 1937, that "after considerable discussion they (the Ministers) decided, to my (his) relief, not to reduce canal rates." (para 2).

3. Cf. Foot note Vo. 1.

4. *Haig Papers*, letter to the Viceroy, dated 23rd April, 1937, para 4.

any such suggestion tooth and nail, thete were out of question. Meantime, the peasantry of the province which accounted for more than 80 percent of its population was to suffer patiently hoping for the Congress to assume the reigns of government of the provinces.

Something may be stated about the landlord community as well. According to Haig, the Governor of the Province the result of the 1937 Elections had left them "in varying degrees, bewildered, frightened and angry" and blamed their defeat to the "British connections"[1]. Haig also noted that, amongst them, there were some who were of the view that "their bes of saving anything out of the wreck is (was) to hasten to tender their submission to the Congress"[2]. But, in the assessment of Haig, if they did so, "the Congress, after using them and reducing them to practical impotence, would then finish them off"[3]. He hoped that they "will try to pull themselves together and organize resistance[4]. When Pant declined on 29th March, 1937, to form a Ministry, their hopes were raised with the formation of the Interim Ministry headed by the *Nawab* of Chhatari—their kinsman. There were rumours also in the air that the Ministry might try "to secure a majority in August"[5] when the Houses were tentatively scheduled to meet.

But, when there was a turn in the course of events and the Congress assumed office after the resignation of the Chhatari Ministry, as noted earlier, their desperation, born of panic,

---

1. *Haig Papers*, letter (Confidential) to the Viceroy, dated 17th February, 1937, para 1.
2. *Ibid.*
3. *Ibid.*
4. *Ibid.*
5. *Haig Papers*, letter (Private & Personal), dated 7th April, 1937, para 6.

knew no bounds. For, immediately after the assumption of office the Congress Ministry passed a series of regulations which added to their worst fears. On 2nd August, 1937, Pant announced "the Government's intention to form two committees of the legislature to consider the forms of tenancy and land revenue law (in the Provinces) and to examine the proposals for the relief of rural indebtedness"[1].

It should be noted here that even the Interim Ministry had toyed with the idea of introducing certain reforms in these directions. The interim Ministry, as noted by the Governor without going in for "pretentious promises" wanted to devote themselves "to a programme which could be reduced to practical measure (s). The main item will (would) be tenancy reform" for which they (the Interim Ministers) were "intending to set up a committee very shortly to recommend immediate action"[2]. As such, the landlords shouldr not have been alarmed unduly and prepared themselves fo the inevitable. Instead, they organised '*The United Province Zamindars' Conference*' which was held at Lucknow on 29th, 30th and 31st October of which more later.

The Congress Ministry was quite alive to the pressing problem of the tenantry which was unable to pay off its rental dues due to several factors. Prices of agricultural products, as already noted earlier, had been falling since 1929[3]

1. *Proceedings of the Legislative Assembly*, dated 2nd August, 1937 (hereafter referred to as Proceedings); also Srivastava, Gopinath, *When Congress Ruled*, p. 22. (for the quote); Cf. also *Report*, (1936-37), p. *xvii* (44).

2. *Haig Papers*, letter to the Viceroy, dated 23rd April, 1937, para 4.

3. Cf. Srivastava, Gopinath, *When Congress Ruled*, pp. 24-25. Also *Report*, 1933-34, Report No. 6551, pp. 7-16.

and the peasantry was hard put ; the landlords had filed thousands of cases for ejectment of tenants and hundreds had been ejected while the rest were involved in litigation with their landlords[1]. At the same time, poverty of a peasant being proverbial, he was often deep in debt and, in many cases, peasants had to sell off even their daughters to meet the demands of the money-lenders[2], or else, their small tracts of land under their cultivation often passed into other hands[3]. The situation called for immediate action.

The Congress Ministry, therefore, took two important steps : (1) The "Board of Revenue was asked by the Government to issue instructions for the stay of Proceedings for recovery of arrears of rent previous to *Rabi* 1344 *Fasli*[4] by ejectment or otherwise"[5] and (2) it issued instructions also for "the stay of Proceedings for the liquidation of debts under the Encumbered Estates Act[6]". Two stay of Proceedings Acts, one affecting Civil Courts and the other affecting Revenue Courts, were also passed so as "to validate the stay orders for old rental and civil debts"[7]. At the same time, the expert

---

1. Cf. *Report*, 1936-37, p. 6, for the number of cases decided and under litigation. The figures cited therein are staggering, pointing to the helplessness of tenants to pay off their revenue dues.

2. Cf. Pande, Mata Badal, *Kisanon ki Phansi*, and *Awadh Ke Kisanon Ki Durdasha.* (Noted earlier and cited by Siddiqi).

3. *Baba Ram Chandra's Diary*, (pages indistinct), microfilm in the *State Archives*, reel No. 2.

4. *Report*, 1936-3[7], p. *xvii* (44) ; Srivastava, Gopinath, *When Congress Ruled*, p. 24.

5. *Ibid.*

6. *Ibid.*

7. *Ibid.*

Committee referred to earlier was to fully examine "rural indebtedness and the existing Debt Acts."[1]

Though the above two steps were taken in the best interests of the tenants these had, ironically enough, adverse effects both on the landlords and the tenantry. Such of the Zamindars who were habitually disinclined to pay off their revenue dues (unless coercive measures were adopted) or delay payment till the last day, "took advantage of the position" while others did not attempt to collect the dues. There were also some of the same class who, after having made the collections, withheld payment to the Government.[2] On the other hand, the tenants thought "that there was no need to pay rent or that if they paid, they would loss the benefit of subsequent legislation."[3]

It is perhaps this situation which led *Majumdar*[4] to make some pungent and adverse criticism of the functioning of the Congress Ministry in the Provinces. According to him, "hopes were raised very high when the Congress accepted Ministry, and the disappointment equally keen as there was no immediate relief by way of substantial reduction in rents and legislation for tenancy reform and debt relief . . . there was frustration among the *kisans* . . . and in some places, notably in Bihar and U.P. where the land revenue system was most oppressive, there almost open revolts."[5]

It may, however, be pointed out that the Congress Ministry did not possess a magic wand which could, in one waving

1. *Report*, 1936.37, p. *xvii* (44), Srivastava, Gopinath, *When Congress Ruled*, p. 24.
2. *Ibid.*, p. *xviii* (45).
3. *Ibid.*

Majumdar R.C. (ed). *Struggle For Freedom*, p. 600.

5. Majumdar, R.C., *Struggle For Freedom*, p, 600.

remove all the ills that had accumulated during the course of a rule of some two centuries by the British who, after their experience of the Revolt of 1857, had all along favoured and nurtured landlordism.[1] Nor could it come in confrontation once again with the Governor by enacting any law which it could not successfully carry in the House. As for the confusion arising out of the above two proclamations, it was soon dispelled by the Premier and the Minister for Revenue and the "land revenue demand for 1344 Fasli was collected almost in full."[2] As such, to us, the Scathing criticism of Majumdar seems hardly warranted. The confusion regarding the two proclamations was confounded by the petty *zamindars* themselves who refrained from paying off their revenue dues and illiterate tenantry followed in their footsteps for sometime till the situation was explained to them by the Premier and the Minister for Revenue, as stated above.

Outmanoeuvred, the landed aristocracy began organising a series of Conferences, beginning with the one at Lucknow, to which reference has been made earlier. The United Province s *Zamindars*' Conference held (at Lucknow) towards the close of October, 1937, passed a series of resolutions heralding that "they, on no account, would allow their legitimate vital interests of suffer", that they "strongly disapproved" the Stay Orders which were "deliberately unjust to *zamindars*" and "condemned the activities of those avowed object was destruction

---

1. Cf. Pandey, V.D., *Land Revenue Administration of Awadh : 1856-1921*, Chapters II, III and VI.

2. *Report*, 1936-37, p. *xviii* (45). Cf. also Srivastava, Gopi Nath, *When Congress Ruled*, according to whom "The land revenue and rent collections were full by the end of 1937." *Ibid.*

The *fasli* year starts from July 1, every year ; all field and debt transactions in the villages begin from that date even to-day in rent and revenue realisations.

of the propertied class."[1] The next day, 30th October, 1937, they urged the Government "to respect the terms of contracts" in permanently settled districts of U.P."[2] ; reduce the pitch of land revenue by 15 percent[3] ; "adopt suitable measures for the protection of rights of the *zamindars*"[4] and finally, resolved to throw "themselves as a class wholeheartedly into the struggle for political and economic freedom of India..."[5]

Later, when a new Tenancy Bill was introduced in the Legislature on 20th April, 1938, and whose merits or otherwise will be detailed later, the landlords of Agra held a Conference at Agra on 3rd July, 1938, reiterating their grouse that "grave injustice ... was being inflicted on the *zamindars* of the province."[6] Yet another Conference of the zamindars of Agra was held at Allahabad on 10th July, 1938, which also condemned the socialistic' approach of the Congress and blamed an alien rule for the exploitation and miseries of the tenants.[7]

However, the din and dust raised by such protests on the part of the landlords soon subsided and Haig seems to have been impressed by the way in which the Ministry had started functioning. He makes certain interesting observations about its personnel. He regarded Pant and Katju as "much the ablest" but "the two Muslim Ministers do (did) not seem to be

---

1. *Haig Papers*, Resolutions Nos. 1, 2, and 3 passed on 29th October, 1937.
2. *Haig Papers, Resolution Nos.* 1 & 2, passed on 29th October, 1937.
3. *Ibid., Resolution* No. 7.
4. *Ibid., Resolution* No. 9 (*e*).
5. *Ibid., Resolution* No. 10.
6. Cf. *Indian Annual Register*, 1938, Vol. II, p. 399 ff.
7. *Ibid.*, pp. 402-3.

very bright (meaning Kidwai and Hafiz Muhammad. Ibrahim)."[1] About the former (Kidwai), he wrote that though he was in charge of Revenue, "...it is clear that it is not he who thinks out and decides on the big issues of revenue policy."[2] In summation, he considered "the outlook of the Ministry... reasonable, and their policy sane", for it had, "shown so far no signs of taking up unpractical ideas..."[3] and the "prestige of the Ministry stands high...", obviously because of the two ameliorative steps taken in the direction of easing the pressure of landlords on the long suffering peasantry of the peasantry of the Provinces, as detailed earlier.

While the landlord community maintained its sullen attitude "becoming more and more emphatic in their protests against the action taken by the Ministry in suspending further proceedings in suits for arrears for rent"[4], the Ministry calmly introduced the Tenancy Bill in the Legislative Assembly on 20th April, 1938, which was piloted by Kidwai with "the very able support of Ajit Prasad Jain"[5] and which was yet another nail in the coffin of the obsolete, pernicious *zamindari* and *taluqdari* systems.

1. *Haig Papers*, letter (Strictly Confidential), to the Vicerory, dated 23rd August, 1937, para 1.
2. *Haig Papers*, letter (Strictly Confidential), to the Viceroy, dated 23rd August, 1937.
3. *Ibid.*
4. *Haig Papers*, letter (Fortnightly Report), deted 6th September, 1937, para 11.
5. Srivastava, Gopinath, *When Congress Ruled*, p. 40.

8

Epilogue

Attempt has been made in the foregoing pages to present the case of Agrarian unrest in United Provinces with special reference to Awadh region during the period 1901-1939. The province, which has been the cradle of Indian culture and civilisation and played a no mean role in the history of the country in the past, had, all through the ages, agriculture as the stanchion for its economic support. Its industrial potential, whatever it was, was obliterated by the British who believed in the policy of exporting poverty to India in the interest of their own industries. Unfortunately, even the agricultural base of the State was corroded by imperfections in its system of land-tennure much to the distress of the actual tillers of the soil. After the Revolt of 1857, the British enacted tenancy laws in 1859 for the first time with an everemphasis on the retention of intermediaries and these continued to operate with amendments from time to time till the dawn of the present century. The feudal system, thus retained by the British, had mean time, crystalised into two main categories, viz., *zamindars* and *taluqdars* in the two contiguous parts of Agra and Awadh with pronounced ownership in land and the tenantry was left to their mercy and exploitation.

The peasant in Awadh, as elsewhere in any other part of the country, was traditionally bound to a family system in which the father, mother, married and unmarried children lived together along with his parents, if alive. All shared a common mud-hut and a common Budget labouring constantly and intensively to wrest a living from out of their meagre holdings without, however, any suitable opportunities to augment their income through any handicrafts which were practically non-existent at the time. Even the children had to forego the rarely available education and be engaged in all sorts of manual labour like collection of firewood, weeding out grass and other growths harmful for crops, and in such seasonal manual works as paddy-transplantation, cutting of sugarcane, winnowing, and other allied works of a similar nature.

The peasant was invariably tied to the land as the latter demanded his constant and fullest attention since he had to bring forth maximum of produce from out of his meagre holdings to sustain his family. Even his crop-production-the—labour of his sweat—depended largely on the bounties of nature, for, quite often blight, frost, hails, pests, floods, of failure of rain and adverse effects on the yield from his fields. These he cast on providence and passively submitted to his fate or '*kismat*'.

The peasant suffered in many other ways as well. While on the one hand there was the constant fear of losing his holdings through ejectment by the *taluqdar* or *zamindar*, he brought upon himself a good many liabilities. These were mainly in the form of marriages and ceremonials, festivals and funerals. A peasant entering matrimony either his or of his children (more specially daughters) had, in ninety cases out of hundred, to incur debts and similar was the case in the performance of customary rituals, of which there is no end in Hinduism, when he had to feed his community or at least his near and dear ones. Then there were festivals and fairs when he had to cater to the needs of his children and other members of the family. Finally, even in death of his own or a member of the family he had to live up to the traditional ways or 'lose face'.

These and many other formalities caused heavy drains on his resources resulting in constant indebtedness. Very often he had to pawn the ornaments or family trinkets to meet the aforesaid eventualities. Usually, the village pawnbroker—the traditional *bania* (merchant or grocer)—the agents of the *taluqdar* or the *taluqdar* himself, took advantage of such opportunities and charge interests varying from 25% to 50% seldom was the vainful hope of the peasant to get back those valuable realised, as the compound interest charged by the usurer-Shylocks often exceeded the value of the ornaments themselves. The net result was further depravity and there was particularly nothing left with him for the future.

There was yet another factor that kept the United Provinces peasant in perpetual debt. The conversion of revenue dues from kind to cash had resulted in selling his crop-produce at rates commensurate with the harvest market-prices which were naturally cheap as there was abundant supply in the market. But in his lean days the cultivator had either to purchase at higher prices the very commodities he had earlier sold, or was compelled to borrow from the hoarder *bania* or even from the master *taluqdar* with the stipulation that he would repay or return 1¼ to 1½ of the amount borrowed, regardless of the fact whether the yield had been normal or scanty (the practice, it is regretted, exists even to this day despite village cooperative societies which also charge the aforesaid minimal amount).

Something about tenant-*talqudar* relations. Very often the *taluqdars* advanced petty loans to tenants of lower castes which went on multiplying with the passage of time. Such practice resulted in the much-abused bonded, system of labour which is well-known to merit description. But the irony is that the tenant, himself so bonded, left it as a legacy to his successor (*s*) as well ; and woe betide the tenant or his son if he tried to run away from such accursed bondage. Further, as noted earlier, taluqdar owned considerable acreage as his *khudkasht*, since he did not have enough teams of oxen to plough all his land, all his tenants were expected to take their pairs of oxen to till his fields at least one day. It hardly mattered whether the tenant's field itself was crying for similar tillage. Even the children of the tenants were hauled up for paddy-transplantation work. The former system—that of tilling the land of the master—was known as *hari* (*har* or *hal* plough-lending) while the latter is known as *begari* (unpaid labour).

But the bitterest cup of sorrow for the tenant was the uncertainty of his tenure of the land under his plough. During the the early phase of the rule of the *Nawabs* (Shujaud-Daula), tenants of the *Huzur* tahsils tilled their fields and paid revenues direct to the treasury. Later this practice had been substituted by the *ijarah* or contract system. The result was that the contractors paid a fixed annual sum to the*Nawab's* treasury and fleeced the tenantry to the maximum for their own gains. Since the pressure on land was too great owing to increasing population, there was competition for cultivable land the contractors found a very convenient method of furthering their grains-through allotting land to the highest rent-paying bidders. Incidentaly, this also led to deterioration in the productivity of land as the tenant was never sure whether the land under his cultivation was going to remain with him in future ; he, therefore, tried to extract maximum of it (land) with less attention on increasing its productivity.

Such was the legal and financial position of the tenantry which, encumbered as it was with a large and growing family, had to subsist in chilling penury, increasing debts and abject servility to his master *taluqdars*.

Taking advantage of the troubled conditions of the times, not only the dispossessed *Rajput* families but also the former *Nawab's* lieutenants, officials and contractors, not to mention the 'faithfuls' of the British during the Revolt, came to be denoted with honorific '*taluqdar*' with very wide powers, as detailed, through devious ways. Some were favoured, some appeased, while many extended their ownership of villages at the expense of their weaker neighbours ; yet others assumed that status through fraudulent means. The British had been quick to realise the hold of many of such influential families over the masses during the days of their adversity and, after the restoration of quietude, adopted the policy of restoring them to their priviledged positions in the areas of their effective control. Though they were not allowed any armed following, yet they were allowed to retain a limited number of arms in view of their privileged positions.

Several factors were responsible for the high position and status a taluqdar enjoyed over the tenants. In the first place, he had the favour of the ruling British on his side and direct access to the officials of the district and the commissioner. Secondly, he enjoyed certain judiciary powers to meet justice in matters already detailed. Thirdly, the village *patwari* (keeper of the village land records) was under his pay and could only be appointed with his concurrence. Lastly, he also maintained a body of musclemen as his *ziladars* who collected the revenues on his behalf.

It has been seen that during the Revolt of 1857, the peasants had rallied round these elements refractory to the British. Their subjugation with the failure of the Revolt and subsequent reinstatement and far-reaching effects on the tenantry of Awadh. The proprietors of the villages who had taken advantage of the situation and grabbed many of the villages of the *taluqdars* had returned them to their former master-*taluqdars*. Now secure under the British Umbrella, the taluqudar virtually considered himself a *raja* (many were honoured with this title as well) with the pomposity of an autocrat specially in relation to his ryots. Since the pressure of the growing population on land was too great, the *taluqdar* in cohort with the *patwari* and even with the *kanungo*, afflicted the tenantry with impunity. He could dispossess a tenant at will and if a tenant tried to seek redress in courts, he was either browbeaten or engaged in such a labyrinthine legal process that he almost became penniless. Further, there was considerable uncultivated land in the villages of his *taluqa* (estate) which could be brought under cultivation by the Inand-hungry villagers. This offered the *taluqdar* a handsome opportunity to make money. Since there were too many candidates to acquire that piece of land, he would grant a *patta* (writ of ownership) to the bidder and payer of the highest amount of *nazrana* (in reality sale money).

Innumerable were the ways in which the *taluqdars* fleeced and tormented their tenant-peasants, some of which have already been detailed earlier. They abhored physical labour, spent their days in frivolous amusements and many a tale, are current about the sordid affairs of their character. But since they had approaches to the higher echelons of officialdom, they generally escaped punishment. Even the power officials of the district, particularly of the revenue department, though it prudent to align with them for fear of complaints, harassment and even transfers.

The *taluqdars* had an association of their own as 'The British India Association' which exists to this day and its admission or membership is generally governed by the right of primogeniture, that only exception being the estate of Maurawan, where every son is entitled to be so. The forum was used to voice their grievances often in cases when the Government tried to enact laws for marginal benefits to tenants. The British Government had favoured this class in many other ways as well ; *taluqdars* were allotted spacious accommodations for ever in the historic buildings of Kaisarbagh for perpetuity (which they still possess) along with the *Baradari* to ensure their loyalty to the British members.

Secure in their position, the *taluqdars* levied numerous types of taxes besides the revenue dues. Even if a tenant died in actual and legal possession of his plots of land, the hereditament by his son or successor had to be confirmed by the taluqdar only after the payment of a suitable *nazrana*. The process, by the way, involved greasing of the palms of many of the *karindas* (agents) also not to mention the *patwari*, the *kanungo*, the *naib* and the senior *tahsildar*, who too demanded their pound of flesh for mutation purposes.

Taluqdars seldom made any serious efforts to help the tenants in improving their agriculture. Even if a tenant wanted to dig a well, he had to seek prior permission from them. Since the village ponds and tanks were his property and sources of income to him through irrigation charges, permission to construct wells was very often withheld as it might cause loss of such revenue to them if the well was to be dug in the vicinity of such irrigational means, howsoever labour-consuming and cumbersome. All that the *taluqdar* was concerned with was the payment of the revenue dues of the Government in time and deal with the tenantry according to his caprices.

Though the government secured the position of the *taluqdars* and *zamindars* in the province of Awadh, it failed in applying the same principles to the actual tillers of the soil, the tenants of the *taluqdars*. The interests of the latter were sorely neglected to the position of being tanants at the mercy of the *taluqdars*. Since the village patwari was on the pay-role of the *taluqdars*, and the *kanungos* turned a blind eyes to such evictions, there was little hope of redressal for the poor tenant. Passively submitting to the atrocities of their masters, a tenant was never sure of tiling the same piece of land which earned him bread and supported his family.

The Mont-Ford Reforms of 1919 did little to alleviate the sufferings of the tenants of Awadh. The provincial legislative Councils were dominated mostly by moneybags and the taluqdars whose vested interests clashed with those of the tenants and as such, there was little hope for their redemption. Further, since pressure on the land was increasing with the growth of population, the taluqdars made immense money by leasing out such fallow land-pieces as were available to those who could bid highest on pattas or writs of ownership under certain conditions. Even in such contracts the *ziladars*, *patwaris* and the *Kanungos* had to be pleased if the deed was to be entered in the revenue-records of the village. It is not surprising, therefore, that quite a good many landless people from Awadh got themselves recruited as labourers and were dispatched by the British to their colonies in Africa, Fiji and the West Indies.

Then came the First World War and the appeal of the British Masters to the loyal sentiments of the *taluqdars* bore fruit in many ways. They not only contributed liberally monetarily but also amulated the princely States by encouraging able—bodied persons to be enlisted in the army. Various types of pressure, incentives and allurements like fear of ejectment, concessions in revenue, lure of land, etc., were offered to them and the test of the loyalty of a taluqdar was the number of recruits he supplied. The various types of additional taxes-rather illegal exactions whose weight had to be borne by the tenantry need not to be repeated here, but those whose enlisted themselves to serve literally as cannon-fodders in foreign lands for the British were exempted from minor harassments.

The patience of the Awadh peasantry was exhausted at last and it could bear no more. Sheer depondency began to breed a sense of rebellion, already the news of the Champaran events had percolated into the United Provinces and they began to dream of redemption from the tyrannies of the *taluqdars*. They found a champion of their cause in Baba Ram Chandra who, along with some like-minded associates, introduced them to the Congress and its ideals. The Kisan Sabha and the Eka Movement were the natural outcome of their remonstrative instincts while political consciousness was also dawning upon them with the historic visit of Jawaharlal Nehru to Pratapgarh. These minor sparks later developed into mass movements.

The Congress Ministry, through a series of enactments removed most of the ills that afflicted the peasantry. The tenants received relief in their rental dues, the ejectment process was overhauled so that the tenants could not be summarily ejected, they could plant trees, dig wells and build houses without seeking permission from the landlord; these and other enactments, it has been seen, infused new life in the peasantry and they could hold their heads high henceforth.

Appendix-A

Land Tenures in Awadh :

Land tenures are usually divided by a section of writers into proprietory and sub-proprietory tenures. A sharp line of distinction is drawn between zamindari and non-zamindari, i.e., between full proprietorship on the one hand and all other subordinate rights on the other. Private rights in land were always recognised both by the Hindu and Muslim rulers.[1] On this vexed question the Indian Taxation Enquiry Committee was unanimously of the opinion that, though the matter was debatable, yet under both Hindu and Muslim rule, the state never claimed absolute or exclusive ownership of land and definitely recognised the existence of private property in it.[2] The British have also recognised proprietory rights in India. The Taxation Committee, after exhaustively examining the subject, was unanimous in its opinion that, in the case of land under the Permanent Settlement, the Government has no proprietory rights. In the case of temporarily settled districts the Committee was divided in opinion, but they were in agreement that the zamindars and the ryots possess certain proprietory rights subject to the payment of land revenue.[3] The zamindars' interest in land, even in the temporarily settled districts of Agra province, has never fallen out of the right of use, if enjoyment of produce, of disposal or alienation, and that of recovery by legal means in

---

1. The problem of ownership of land has been exhaustively dealt with the D.C. Sircar—*Landlordism and Tenancy in Ancient and Medieval India as Revealed by Epigraphical Records.*
2. *The Taxation Enquiry Committee* (1924-25), para 83.
3. *Ibid.*

case of dispossessions.[4] In the case of taluqdars there is no room for doubt on the subject of private proprietory rights. They have their *sanads* in which full proprietory rights have been granted.

Proprietory tenures are divided into three classes :

(a) Taluqdari
(b) Zamindari
(c) Pattidari

Taluqdari :

Before the annexation of Awadh and the grant of *sanads* to the taluqdars by the British there was no legal distinction between the taluqdari tenure and zamindari tenure. Estates lay intermixed with ea ch other. There was no essential difference in the status of the two. After the revolt of Eighteen fifty-seven, the taluqdars received a distinctive superior status which has no parallel in any part of India.[5] According to Act I of 1869, a taluqdar was a person whose name had been entered into the list of taluqdars published by the Government under Section 8 of this Act. He acquired under Section 3 of the Same Act a permanent heritable and transferable right in the estate settled with him at the regular settlement.[6] At settlement, a formal decree was recorded for every village declaring that it was or was not a part of a taluqdari estate.

4. The term zamindari (landlord) is used here in a broad sense, e.g., it includes the various under-proprietors. Ryots is taken to mean actual cultivators.
5. The *Oudh Estates Act* (1 of 1869) defines their privileges. Some of these privileges are not even enjoyed by the zamindars of the Permanent Settlement.
6. Erskine, G.E., *Digest of Circular Relating to the Jurisdiction and Procedure of the Revenue Courts and the Conduct of Settlement Operation in Oudh*, Section V, clause 6, p. 91.

A brief account of the origin and development of the taluqdari system and the various categories of the taluqdari system and the various categories of the taluqdars would not be out of context here. The taluqdars of Awadh[7] were by no means a

7. "The term talookdar means 'holder of a talooqah' or 'Collection of villages' for the payment of the land revenue assessed upon which villages the talookdar or holder was admitted to engage. The single engagement with one person for a number of villages saved the native government trouble, and has long obtained, but it used to convey us right of property to the taluqdar in the villages for which he was engaged. He paid to the state a lesser sum, and realised from the villages somewhat larger one, which constituted his remuneration. If the central authority was weak and the local official his friend, his 'talooqah' would rapidly expand. If a new official arrived unfriendly to him, he would loss many, or all the villages which he acquired. It should be observed that the best native rulers of Oudh were always opposed to the growth of large 'talooqahs'.... Until this system was abused, it no doubt answered well enough, especially where the talookdar was chief in the tribe for whose villages he was engaged. As chief he was the natural medium between his tribe and the Government and received from the spontaneous regards of his people many perquisites and dues. But for nearly half a century the 'talooqdaree system' has been greatly abused and the great aim of the talookdar has been to supplant the villager in the property of the soil and to constitute himself sole proprietor. Where he succeeded, the owner became a tenant and was charged with a rent for the land which he occupied without reference to the Government land tax"—Gubbins, M.R., *An Account of the Mutinies in Oudh*, pp. 61-62.

"These talookdars varied greatly in their origin. Some, and the great number were hereditary heads of Rajput tribes settled in the neighbourhood. Others again were new families, sprung from some Government officials homogeneous body and they may be classed into categories of 'pure' and 'impure' ones. The 'pure' taluqdars emerged out of the conquered *rajas* of small estates which had been reduced by the Mughals. To conciliate such elements the Mughals left them with full powers of internal management of their former estates in return for a fixed revenue or tribute. Thus, they retained control over the collection of revenue, local taxes, and custom dues, and also over administration of justice. The 'impure' taluqdars originated at the time of maladministration of Awadh. As the control of the Mughal Empire relaxed, the *subedars* of Awadh became indolent. Local agents were, therefore, employed or contracted for the realisation of a certain stipulated amount of revenue in the *suba*. Soon such officer and persons became hereditary revenue collectors and in about a hundred or hundred and fifty years, these holders also acquired the character of landlords. A similar process was also noticeable in the case of the *rajas* and chiefs of Awadh.[8]

The opposite theory is explained by Banettin the '*Family History of Chief Clains of the Rai Bareilly District*.' Banett observes, "The division of the class into 'true' and 'false' taluqdars puts the matter in a wrong light. As a matter of fact, all were exactly the same in as for they were taluqdars, middlemen put in by or forced on the Government, Superintendants of arbitrary collection of villages, who as the central power grew weaker, were being gradually and surely transformed into landed proprietors. What has been called a true taluqdar differs from what has been a false taluqdar. Only in the fact that while the former had been for centuries—exercising an *imperium impiore* in on the spot. the latter was an outsider whose fortune, talents or wealth had secured him the position. Both were alike in being taluqdars, though they differed in every other particulars. They included in their ranks representatives of every class of

---

whose local authority had enabled him to acquire a holding of this description."—Gubbins, M.R., *An Account of the Mutinies in the Oudh*, pp. 61-62.

8. Jagdish Raj, *The Mutiny and British Land Policy in North India*, p. 2.

men, powerful but *parvenue nazims*, the descendants of twenty rajas who have successfully ruled with semi-regal powers over tracts as large as an English country, extortionate usurers, the old village revenue officials whose ancestors had been established by Akbar or Ibrahim Sharki, the menials of the King's stable and garden, and the Kayasth, who pillaged his treasury and robbed his subject, all struggled for a place with new aristocracy. It must never be forgotten that the root of their fresh growth was laid in the old Hindu clan organisation, and the whole movement was in fact nothing else than the reaction of the natives against their Mohammedan conquerors. The seeds of the Hindu social system never lost their vitality and asserted it over and again in every part of India on every occasion when Moslem powers showed any trace of weakness."[9]

The former of these views implies that the pure taluqdars are taluqdari tenure is associated with the ideas of chiefship of a clan, acquisition by conquest and possession of an estate for several centuries, the latter on the contrary, lays down that none of these conditions is essential to constitute a talqua. Bannet is of the opinion that they came into existence within the last hundred years. The distinction of taluqas between 'pure' and 'impure' points to the important distinction between estates of recent mushroom growth and old estates.[10] The rise of these impure taluqas corresponds to the foundation of the Nawabi dynasty and forms an epoch in the history of land tenures in this province.

Zamindari :

After the above brief notice of the taluqdari tenure we may pass on to a consideration of the zamindari tenure. The Hindu landlord system and their categories were, according to Sircar,

9. Banett, W.C., *Family History of the Chief Clans of the Rai Bareilly District*, para 87.
10. Misra, B.R., *Land Revenue Policy in the United Provinces*, p. 194.

formed on certain considerations. According to him, there were three types, viz., (a) those who enjoyed complete freedom from tax-payment (b) those who had to pay taxes at concessional rates and (c) those who were not exempt from taxation.[11]

As pointed out earlier, before the occupation of Awadh by the Britishers there was no essential distinction between the two classes of land holders. The internal economy of the estate was originally based on the zamindari type of tenure. The common management of irrigation channels, common management of village functionaries and artisans, common grazing grounds, all testify to the existence of community of property, involved in the zamindari tenure. In Northern India, even today, when the produce is raised from a field, the village functionaries, e.g., the blacksmith, carpenter, potter, sweeper, cobbler and chowkidar (village watchman) receive a share from the common heap besides cash payments which are of recent development.

These functionaries performed free services to the villagers. They are supported from the common fund called '*malba*'. They also received presents in cash and kind on marriages, deaths and festivals. Moreover, wells, tanks, irrigation channels, roads, etc., were all constructed and maintained from the common fund contributed by the villagers.

Zamindari tenures were those in which the entire village land was either owned by a single landlord or a body of co-sharers, who may represent a group of ancestorily connected families. The individual land-lord seldom cultivated the land himself. The agricultural community was divided into two classes —cultivating and non-cultivating, the former representing a tenant older than the land-holding group. The internal economy and the responsibility for the payment of land revenue was different in the villages owned by a body of co-sharers as compared to a single landlord. In the former case, the whole body

11. Sircar, D.C., *Landlordism and Tenancy in Ancient and Medieval India as Revealed by Epigraphical Records*, p. 58.

was jointly and severally responsible for the payment of the Government revenue. The Government revenue and other liabilities were paid out of the rents received from the cultivating classes and the remainder was divided among several partners according to their shares. Where, however, the zamindari tenure consisted of a single individual landlord, there was no division of income. The members of the family received maintenance and the whole income was administered by the head of the family.

Pattidari :

Pattidari tenures were such tenures in which the lands were divided and held in severalty by different proprietors. Each pattidar managed his own land and paid his fixed share of Government revenue. The whole body, however, was jointly responsible in the event of any one sharer being unable to fulfil the engagement. Imperfect pattidari tenures were those in which part of the land was held in common and part in severality, the profits from the land held in common were first appropriated to the payment of the Government revenue and village expenses. The surplus was distributed as profits among different co-sharers and the deficiency was made up by a rate on the several holdings.

But after a certain stage the pattidari form of tenure began to show signs of disruption. The first step towards this dissolution, was perhaps the cultivation and separation of *sir*-land by each individual co-parcener. This ultimately resulted in separation of landed property and ultimately in imperfect pattidari. As the number of co-parceners increased, the aggregate area of *sir*-land increased and the Shamiliat (common) lands failed to suffice for the payment of the revenue. Whatever they paid as rent of *sir*-land they received back as profits. Thus such tenure merged into the imperfect pattidari. A stage arrived later on when each co-parcener even demanded a partition of the *shamiliat* lands in which case imperfect pattidari led to perfect pattidari.[12]

---

12. *Sultanpur Settlement Report* (1873), p. 69.

Under-Proprietory Tenuers :

In Awadh under-proprietory tenures existed not only in unusual varieties and kinds, but also possessing unusual strength. After re-occupation of the state the Government, while granting *sanads* to the taluqdars, announced its intention to "take effectual steps to re-establish and maintain in subordination to them the former rights, as they existed in 1855, of other persons whose connection with the soil in many cases were more intimate and more ancient than theirs." It was further declared that "the only effectual protection which the Government can extend to these inferior holders is to define and record their rights and limit the demand of the taluqdars as against such persons."

The right of a sub-settlement and the right of *sir*- the two important rights—were recognised. Most important was the right of sub-settlement in which an entire village, though included in a taluqa and held in sub-ordination to it, retained distinctive signs of individual proprietory character. The owners of such villages had prevented the destruction of their proprietory rights, and had intercepted a substantial portion of the profits. The few lucky people who were entitled to sub-settlement, were required to pay in no case more than seventy five percent of gross rental to a taluqdar and the only condition imposed upon them was that their payments must be punctual and regular.

Under-proprietory rights differed in different parts of Awadh, the most important being:—

(a) Dihadari or Didari
(b) Nankar
(c) Sir
(d) Birt
(e) Sankalap
(f) Jagir and Mafi (free grant)
(g) Marwat.

Dihadari and Nankar were granted for the support of the out-going proprietors,[13] the former in the form of property, the latter in the shape of annual income, *sir*-land was invariably for the support of petty out-going proprietors as a mark of propreitory position. A zamindar continuously cultivating the same land through his own labour and capital for a period of twelve years acquired the right of *sir*. Birt (crown lands) tenures mostly represent under-proprietory rights created through sale of crown lands. *Sankalp's* grants were always created for religious motives and represent payment in land to Brahmanical classes for the purification of the soul of the grantee.[14] Free grants were created for the personal service of the kinds or their chiefs. Marwat grant was a sub proprietory tenure created for support of the family main slain in battle.

Dihadari :

It was common practice under indigenous rule that when property was transferred by sale or even by voluntary transfer to some neighbouring taluqdar to escape the exactions of a *nazim* (tax-collector), the purchaser assigned a portion of the property (not income) in prepetuity to the former proprietor for his subsistence. Such a grant of land is known as Dihadari or Didari. The assignment was sometimes a fixed proportion of the property. Grants were, at the outset, rent-free. Their rants were below the Government grant.[15]

Nankar :

It originally consisted in the drawback allowance to the zamindar by the revenue authorities from the demand made on the estate, and constituted the main portion of the ostensible profits of the property. It was an object of every *nazim* or

---

13. The former proprietors who lost their property due to various causes, e.g., sale or voluntary transfer.
14. Land, gold and cows even to this day are given to Brahmins to keep the soul of the dead in peace.
15. *Faizabad Settlement Report* (1878), pp. 79-80.

taluqdar, of course, to encourage the old zamindars to stay on and not to abscond from their estates. To effect this, the taluqdar readily granted the *sir* to be held at a low rate. When a fractional share of the rental was assigned as Nankar, it was usually assumed on the rental of that time, and remained a fixed items without being subject to future enhancement or curtailment. The money was either paid over by the taluqdar to the sub-proprietor, or the latter was allowed a remission equal to the amount, in the rents of any lands held as a cultivator.[16]

Sir :

The most common of all sub-proprietory holdings was the *sir*. It was that personal holding, which under any form of common village estate, each co-sharer had for his own special benefit, and which he always cultivated himself or by his personal tenantry. The sir was held at a favourable rate. A person not having been proprietor over the whole village could have proprietary claim to a holding of his own, and this was also considered to be *sir* under the taluqdar. In some places, it was common to assign to the junior branches of a family certain lands for their support (Guzara) instead of giving them the ancestral shares to which they were entitled. Such appanages were also known by the name of *sir*.[17] The *sir* may be said to have consisted of all the land in the immediate occupation of the original proprietors at the time when the village was incorporated in the taluqa.[18]

Birt :

The meaning of the term 'birt' is a cession. It was the purchase of the propriatory rights subordinate to the taluqdar

16. Benett, *Gazetteer of the Province of Oudh*, Vol. I, p. 439.
17. Baden-Powell, *Land Systems of British India*, Vol. I, p. 441; Carnegy, *Notes on Land Tenures and Revenue Assessments of Upper India*, p. 79.
18. *Bahraich Settlement Report* (1873), p. 101.

on certain conditions as to the payment of rent[19] and was always granted for a consideration. Birts were given for the whole village, villages or patches of land in villages. The grant of the zamindari right in a whole village as *birt zamindari* gave more or less of the taluqdari right in that village according to the terms of the deed, but always subordinate right.[20] More precisely, it consisted in the sale of the right to settle a certain plot of waste and to enjoy from that occupation. The birtdar did not, in virtue of this grant, become owner or manager of the plot or the village.[21]

Sankalp :

It denoted land dedicated to religious purposes. In this character it bore a close resemblance to the *waqfs* of Mohammedan Law and the Church-lands of Europe. In later times, the original nature of this tenure was lost. It was bestowed for no consideration but only for the prayers and services of the Brahmins and was irrevocable. Its grant was always hereditary. As a common usage the *sankalp* was granted rent-free. But where rent was stipulated for, it was nominally fixed in perpetuity under the name *barbasti.*

Jagir or Mafi :

These are known by various denominations, *jagir* and *mafi* being the best known. All these forms of tenure were free grants of considerable antiquity, differing only in minor parts. The *jagir* is connected with the performance of some service. It was in a number of cases granted as a fitting reward for distinguished military service either to the man himself or in the case of his death, for the maintenance of his family. The *jagir* was originally a personal grant. *Mafi* (i.e. free grant) was a very wide term

---

19. *Sultanpur Settlement Report* (1873), pp. 77-82.
20. Baden-Powell, *Land Systems of British India,* Vol. II, p. 239.
21. *Bahraich Settlement Report* (1873), pp. 94-95.

and included grants of land given by whomsoever free of rent and revenue.

Marwat :

The taluqdars, when they were also military chiefs, not only paid their soldiers while they served, but acknowledged their liability to maintain the families of those who were killed in a battle. This liability they fulfilled by grant of land called 'marwat' hr '*maroti*' that is, death grant. It usually ran in the name of the deceased, and his children, including his widow. Under the rules, it was held to be "taluqdar's *mafi*" and resuable at will.[22]

Dih :

The word '*dih*' in its primary sense means the deserted site of a village. But in Awadh, for claimants in the courts, it universally meant that portion of a village which, on account of decay or desertion of the buildings, had become open waste and had been taken up for cultivation. The *dih* was always considered the special property of the owner of the village, and the right to hold possession of it, free of all demand whatever, was one which he retained intact long after he was stripped of all other signs of proprietorship.[23]

Daswant or Chacharam :

The words themselves give the clue to the original extent of these sub-ordinate tenures, the former meaning one-tenth, and the latter one-fourth. They may be said to have their origin in *jangal tarashi* or waste-clearing leases where the leare probably stipulated that one-tenth or one-fourth of the village would be considered his own special plot according to the difficulties encountered in the clearance and the expenditure of labour and capital. This was held rent-free.[24]

22. *Sultanpur Settlement Report* (1873), pp. 84-84.
23. *Bahraich Settlement Report* (1879), p. 97.
24. *Ibid.*, p. 100.

Purwa Basna :

It was a grant to encourage a man to found a 'purwa'—outlying hamlet or extension of a village. It gave to the grantee a lease and as long as he could hold it, during that period he received the dues allowed to the zamindar or manager, and if the village was taken under direct management, the grantee retained only the area allotted to him as his *sir* and *nankar* land.[25]

Biswi :

This right was almost confined to Faizabad and Sultanpur districts. When a whole village or entire fractional holding was mortgaged, it was usual for the mortgage to obtain both possession of the land and engagement with government. Occasionally, however, the mortgages obtained possession only, without direct engagements, and in such cases, after deducting his interest from the assumed rental, he paid the estimated difference to the mortgager. Under the native rule, the mortgage was always redeemable, but under the law of limitation after 1856, it ceased to be so. During the settlement where redemption could no longer be allowed, the mortgage was declared to be the proprietor.[26]

Baghat (Groves and Orchards) :

Groves were found to be of four classes :

(a) Belonging to the existing proprietor,
(b) Belonging to the former proprietor,
(c) Belonging to the *sankalpdars* and *birtdars.*
(d) Belonging to ryots.

The first of these was, of course, part and parcel of the owner's property. In the above mentioned three classes, the

25. Baden-Powell, *Land Systems of British India*, Vol. II, pp. 99-100.
26. *Sultanpur Settlement Report*, pp. 84-85.

existing right, superior or subordinate, as the case might be, extended to both-the lands and the trees. In the case of the fourth class, the right of the ryot extended to eating the fruits, gathering wood and cutting down the trees. But the tenure ended on the cultivator leaving the village. He could not replace the trees without special permission of the landlord to that effect.[27]

27. *Revenue Administration Report of the Province of Awadh*, (1878), p. 8.

Appendix-B

V.N. Mehta Report :

(Summary of findings and Recommendations of V.N. Mehta, Deputy Commissioner, Pratapgarh in 1920)

1. His Honour the Lieuteant-Governor's message of assurance that the allegations made by the tenants against their landholders will be inquired into, was received by me on the 18th of September. The lines of inquiry were chalked out on same and I started my work on the 3rd week of October. I finished it about the first week of November.

2. Procedure—I examined in all seventeen hundred witnesses. I toured round about six centres I had selected in the Patti Tahsil.

3. Material—I had received applications of grievances from two bodies; (1) the original Kisan Sabha, Rur-the creation of Ram Chander Sharma—(2) the nucleus of the present Oudh Kisan Sabha, Partapgarh. The former were individual complaints and emphasised the grievance that was felt the keenest. The latter were collective complaints and contained a highly drawn picture of the down-trodden condition of the tenantry but in laying the colours too think no effort was made to separate the truth from falsehood. I also consulted my own record room to enable me to obtain materials that may throw light on the enquiry. Important landholders and protagonists of the kisans also were duly examined.

4. Heads of Inquiry.—For facility of intake of evidence, I have divided the materials under six heads:—

I.—Ejectment, its evils; nazarana—sharp practices connected with its incidence and the evil consequences that follow its percussion on the victims.

II.—Abuses of estate administration.

III.—Raqm siwai excesses.

IV.—New imposts.

V.—Invasion of tenants' easements.

VI.—Miscellaneous.

5. Findings.—After very careful consideration of the evidence before me, I come to following finding :—

The present law is incapable of preventing arbitrary disturbance of tenancy. Ejectment under the law has been systematically mounting up :—

Year.		No. of notices.	Area involved. Acres.
1906—7	...	936	1,791
1911—12	...	1,238	2,864
1916—17	...	1,403	2,474
1919—20	...	2,593	5,815

The proportion of the area actually dispossessed to the area of notice is

{ 1918.19—31 per cent, 1919.20.—29 per cent } for the taluqdari estates and

{ 1918.19—22 per cent, 1919.20—26 per cent } for the mufrid zamindari estates.

This should be compared with the percentage in the Court of Wards Estates which is 83 in 1918-19 and 69 in 1919-20. High and unjustifiable as the figure of actual dispossession appears to the student of Economics, the disparity between a rise in the figure of tenants served with ejectment notice and the real number actually dispossessed is glaring, and I come to one conclusion both on the basis of statistics and oral evidence that ejectments are more freely resorted to create opportunities for extorting nazarana from tenants newly inducted or those already sitting.

6. Land in area is always limited. In the very two parganas where the pressure of population was considerable, the 20 years after settlement have shown an increase of population with a commensurate increase in cultivated area (vide Exh. A). Land hunger is very keen. Tenants have paid up to Rs. 500 per bigha to secure land que mortgagees or permanent lesees in order that they could be called landed men (vide Exh. R). The retired military men; the new soldier and the large number of servitors abroad from this district have rent remitances home to repair their dilapidated fortunes and outbid the stay-at-home cultivator from his cultivation. Exhibit J will show that the amount disbursed by money orders is double the land revenue of a district which is notoriously on agricultural district. Nazarana is generally taken from the incoming tenant about the month of May or June. The tenants, who have not contested the notice of ejectment in the previous November, enjoy under the law *locus penitentiac* up to the end of June next and these are the tenants on whom the utmost pressure is brought to bear to secure a large amount of *nazarana*. There is evidence on record that bogus candidates are put forward. Sometimes land is actually settled with two tenants. The sitting tenant strains every nerve to keep his hold on the ancestral holding in which he feels that by the custom of the country he has indefeasible dominion utile. He may be loaded with *nazarana* debt, but in the words of Tulsi Das—

"Tulsi Ramahin you bhajyo jeon kisan ki riti,
Dam chaugune rin ghano tohun khet se priti."

(Tulsi Das is devoted to his Rama as the kisan to his *kasht*. The rent is fourfold, the deft is heavy and yet he loves his field.) He pays the nazarana arrived at after a great deal of most undignified degrading baggling and is not ousted from his land. Sometimes the holding is divided into two parts and settled with two competitors both of whom having paid substantial *nazarana*. Sometimes the land promised to the sitting tenants after acceptance of *nazarana* is partially or wholly taken away from them because another has made a more tempting offer. Money is then returned but in some case this also is not done. Sometimes the candidate tenant is left in the lurch and being in possession of the *patta* obtained after paying handsome *nazarana*, litigates with the sitting tenant who, too, on his side has been squeezed dry. This process of wholesale milking with all the attendant meannesses and trickeries has increased, is increasing and ought to be put a stop to. It is a serious menance to the economic well-being of the district. Men who have no industries to fall back upon are being evicted from their ancestral buildings and thrown on the road to pick their way as best as they can. Though a victim of the cupidity of the landholder and the land hunger of the nouveaux riches he feels resentment against the Government that allows such a law to remain on the Statute Book. It has demoralized the wielder of the power no less than the victim of its abuse. Several instances have come to light in which this law of arbitrary expropriation of tenancies has lowered the communities living in the district in social scale. They do not get daughters in marriage from across the Jaunpur border with its Dankini *bandobast* and freedom from disturbances. Fathers have sold their daughters for *nazarana* money to husbands of advanced years. This sale of the daughter—Kanya vikraya—is the most heinous sin known to the Hindu *Shastras* but the wretched pater families prefers eternal damnation in the next world to the living hell in this and readily pays up *nazaranas* to prevent ejectment. Brother has been put up against brother and son against father in this mad game of land grab, while all along in strange keeping with this discord *nazarana* papers are clincking into the coffers of the estate.

7. Landholder.—The landholder on his side finds that the prices of staples have gone up from 250 to 300 per cent, during the last 30 years. The cost of living has gone up proportionately and yet his money rents have not risen *pro rata* and the legal

increase is nullified by the falling purchasing power of the rupee. He is being out-distanced in the scheme of social stratifiaction by the enterprising business man or the money-making lawyer and he casts about for a remedy to make good the deficiency that the Statute has created for him in the rule of one-anna-in-the-rupee-increment-every-seven-years.

8. Some of them put forward two alternative proposals: (1) change in the law of enhancement of rent, (2) reversion to rents in kind. As long as the (1) is not done he, so to speak, is bound to his self-interest to make up the difference some way between the economic rent and the statutory rent. While he is in this frame of mind, the temper is nigh ready with hard cash. He succumbs. He undertakes a tour of his estate in the months of May, June and July, less with the object of redressing tenants' grievances than with the desire of ascertaining the riches of his future victims and settling terms with tenants who are to be dispossed from July the 1st next. If one scanes the figures of money order returns, one notices that the figures for the month of May for the three years 1917-18, 1918-19, 1919-20, have been Rs. 2,77,967, Rs. 2,60,692, Rs. 2,71,192, as against an average of Rs. 2,40,150, Rs. 2,32,121, Rs. 25,58,478, the other nine months. This is taken in addition sometimes to the payments made in between the service of notice and the date of tour.

The approximate gross rental being abont three million, the lowest figure of *nazarana* will come to Rs. 4,50,000 a year. But in many cases (vide Exh. 5), it is much more than the annual rent and in some other cases *nazarana* is taken several times during the septennial period and at the interval of every two to three years after that. A superior Government Official of non-gazetted rank described how he paid *nazarana* year after year to keep off ejectment.

9. Rents are kept suspiciously low and 25 to 50 per cent, preference enjoyed by high caste tenant adds to the burden of the low casts tenantry (vide Exh. 6). The nation losses its hare of land assets. The tenants are rack-rented between the rent payment and *nazarana* extortions, while the intermediaries have

become the residuary legatees without any one of the mischances which the recipient of this class is usually subject to.

10. In my opinion the inelastic rule of one-anna-in-the-rupee-increment is at the bottom of this mischief. It renders the honest landholder indigent. It leaves the less scrupulous unscathed. It must give place to some more rational principle of enhancement at periodic intervals.

11. Batai.—The other alternative cannot be thought of for a minute. The evils of the *batai* system have been forcibly brought out by Mr. Boss in his Moradabad settlement and report. I have seen its evils myself in Bahraich. The tenants are dead against it. Here I want to minimize points of friction between kisans and zamindars and not reinforce existing ones by backing an additional one.

12. Recommendations.—The one recommendation put forward is permanent settlement for landholders, occupancy rights for tenants. This is the most empirical way of dealing with a momentous and complex question. Giving a tenant fixity of tenure is one thing; creating a quassi proprietory status for him is the last thing for a country where the inherent weakness is a tendency to live as tenure-earner rather than as cultivating peasant of cultivating proprietor. The position of under tenants with eleven tiers of tenure stratification (as noted in the Backerganj district) between them and the actual recipients of rent will be deplorable indeed with the multiplication of rent charge passed down from tier to tier till its repercussion on the actual cultivator is overwhelming. My object is the creation of a prosperous peasantry that cultivates the soil itself, enjoying a fixity of tenure without rights of sub-letting or transfer and liable to pay enhanced rents at fixed intervals.

13. Permanent settlement of revenue will never be tolerated by the more informed legislators of the country. No body of legislators has a right to foreclose for ever all avenues of future increase in income. The land belongs to the State, that is, to the community whose general will it embodies. No section of the community can barter away the birth rights of the whole,

viz, to share in the increasing value of land brought about by general economic progress. If permanent settlement is a panacea we do not in the words of Burke want it, for we know the consequences of unnecessary physic. If it is a plague the strictest rules of quarantine must be enforced against it.

14. Both these suggestions emanate from that section of the community which fails to realize their bearing on the communal good. The idea of thinking of the whole in terms of a part could not have been carried further.

15. My suggestions are as follows :—

Give tenants fixity of land.

(1) Offer of 14 years leases (in Ireland it is 15 years but as we want to bring in two revisions of rent before the settlement operations at the end of 30 years begin, therefore, I suggest 14 years) to sitting tenants at a rent which may be increased upto 4 annas in the rupee. If the tenant agrees to the offer of rent, he will not be disturbed or his rent enhanced for 14 years more. If he does not agree then he will not benefit by this scheme.

At the end of 14 years, the landholder may make an offer of rent to the tenant by notice. Either he aceepts it or he does not. If he accepts it, he is again safe from disturbance or enhancement for 14 years If he does not, he can appeal to the court to fix a fair rent for him. If he accepts the rent fixed, he is free from ejectment or enhancement for 14 years more. If he does not, he mechanically drops out as a tenant.

The 4 anna in the rupee increment is for this moment only in order to bring up rents to a rational level and it will not be the standard to regulate future increments. In no case will the increments decreed be over 83 per cent of the previous figure without spreading increments out over several years. If any tenant is anxious to have his grain rent converted into cash rent, it may be done now.

(2) Those sitting tenants who do not want to profit by this

14 years offer and any tenants who will become tenants-in-chief in future will mechanically get five years statutory tenancy at the existing rent and the rent agreed upon respectively. They will not be liable to be ejected at the end of five years if they either accept the rent offered by the landholder or the fair rent fixed by the court. Failing either they can be ejected. No squatter can become a tenant-in-chief until he agrees to pay rent. Any tenant can resign his tenancy of this class for the tenancy of class (1).

(3) Tenancies by registered lease can be created for any period at the rent agreed upon. The tenant will be liable to be ejected at the end of the period of lease but if he holds on, then he will be a class (2) tenant.

(4) Landholders can create occupancy rights by registered instrument. They will enjoy fixity of tenure like classes : (1) and (2) tenants but their rents can be enhanced at any time, but once enhanced they cannot be enhanced again for ten years.

(5) All sub-tenants of sir and tenants-in-chief will not be liable to be ejected within five years of their induction, nor is their rent susceptible to enhancement. At the end of the period, they are liable to be ejected by notice. If they are not so ejected, they will get a fresh period of five years.

(6) No sub-tenancies can be created except by a registered instrument (the kanungo's attestation will suffice).

(7) No muafidar can be ejected except he be a chakarana holder. He can be assossed to rent. When once this is done, he will fall in the category of tenants of class (2).

(8) Extinction of tenancies—

(1) Merger, (2) surrender or abandonment, (3) death without statutory heirs,

The heirstaking in order are as follows :—

(1) Son, (2) widow, until remarried, (3) father, (4) mother, unless remarried; (5) brother. Son will include

grandson. Nos. 2, 3, 4 will be tenants for life only; while Nos. 1 and 5 can form fresh stocks of descent.

(9) No transfer of any sort is allowed except transfer for consolidation of holdings, or amongst co-sharers in the tenancy. Surrender to landholder for consideration is allowed.

(10) No tenant can sublet more than half his holding and no plot can be sublet for over ten years.

(11) No division of holding and rent allowed except with landholders's consent. But where individual share comes to less than one acre, further division will not be noted in the village records.

(12) Ejectment—

(1) A tenant can be ejected by notice in execution of a decree for arreares of rent.

(2) If after receiving notice of arrears of half the rent due up to the date of filing of notice, the arrears remain unpaid within three months after amount or contest the validity of the demand. The application of notice will then be converted on payment of necessary fees into a plaint for a suit of arrears of rent.

(3) Expiration of the period of registered lease by notice.

(4) By notice if the tenant fails to pay the rent fixed by court.

(5) By suit on the ground that he has used the land in a manner which renders it unfit for the purposes of this tenancy or has broken a condition consistent with this Act, and on breach of which, he is, under terms of a contract between himself and the landlord, liable to be ejected. It will be statutorily laid down what can be called improvements.

(6) By suit at the end of the statutory period in the highest court of revenue jurisdiction in the district on any of the following grounds :—

(a) for proved libel or defamation of the land-holder, and defiance and denial of his title.

(b) for conviction under a cognizable offence and sentence of rigorous imprisonment to a period over two years.

The district list of assessors will be divided into two parts—tenant assessors and landholder assessors. One of each class will sit as jurors along with the revenue officer. The majority decision will prevail. In decreeing the ejectment, the court may order compensation to be paid for eviction upto the extent of four times the yearly rental.

(13) Improvement.—All tenants (save sub-tenants) can make improvements provided the landholder, does not offer to put through the improvement himself. In that case on service of notice that a tenant wanted to make an improvement the land-holder has either to apply that he will complete it himself within the time agreed upon under the orders of the court or to acquiesce in the tenant's offer. In the latter case, the nature and cost of the improvements will be registered. If the land-holder fails to carry out the work in the time fixed, the tenant's application will be allowed and the nature and value of the improvement will be registered.

Tenants on ejectment will receive compensation for improve-ments.

(14) How rents will be fixed or enhanced—

(1) On the basis of prevailing rentals for lands similarly circumstanced.

(2) Rise of prices during the previous period.

The enhancement shall bear to the previous rent the same proportion as the average prices of the current period bear to the average prices of the preceding period. The average prices of the current period to be reduced by one-third of their excess before applying the rate.

Example,—Rupees 5 rent was fixed in 1905. It is 1919 now, the average price between 1905 and 1891 for the same quantity was 3 while it is 9 between 1905 and 1919. Then X (the unknown factor) :

Rs. 5 present rent

$$: 9 - \frac{(9-3)}{(\ 3\ )} \text{ ., ., } 3 \times X \text{ ---}$$

$$= 11 - 3/8 \text{ Rs.}$$

The deduction of one-third represents the rise in the cost of production. For the five years period the rise will be taken to be a smaller fraction not necessarily proportionately smaller.

(15) In awarding a decree of enhancement due weight is to be given to—

(a) Increase in the productive capacity of the holding caused or likely to be caused by landholder's improvement.

(b) The disutility entailed on the tenant before he was able to profit out of the utility provided.

(c) Increase due to tenant's improvement.

(d) Due to economic or physical causes like fertilizing fluvial action; opening of a new line of communication or markets or starting of some new industry, etc.

In assessing the pecuniary advantages under (d) either partner to the transaction will get half (vide the Bengal and Irish Law).

(16) There must be a provision on the basis of the Bengal Tenancy Act, section 84 for compulsory acquisition of a holding or a part of the holding by a landholder. The applicant will have to produce the certificate of the highest revenue authority of the district that the land is wanted for some reasonable and sufficient purpose, having relation to the good of the holding, for building religious, educational or charitable purpose. Full

compensation will be paid both for compulsory acquisition and for the area parted with.

16. So far as the landholders are concerned, their position must be improved by putting the settlement operations within the bounds of statutory regulations. Improvements will be amply compensated for by reduction in the assets used as basis of assessment. A reduction in the portion for combined revenue and case to the net assets may be made. A reasonable estimate alone should be taken of sayer income. Recorded rentals must be accepted as true unless they appear to be suspiciously low. The country will not be purged easily of the curse of *nazarana* and the State should safeguard itself against any loss of its share of net assets by subterfuges familiar to every District Officer.

17. What I want to bring into being is a tenant with fixity of tenure, a cultivator who is not liable to be disturbed at the caprice of his landholder. He will be paying a fair rent and not the economic or competitive rent. Land is limited and competition between tenants can only and in competition of poverty and not capital. The depth to which a tenant can descend in the scale of life will be the margin up to which economic rents can be screwed up. The report of the Rent Law Commissioners (1880) Bengal, laid down that "such a share should be left with the cultivator as will enable him to carry on cultivation, to live in reasonable comfort and to participate to a reasonable extent in the progress and improving prosperity of his native land." He will be free to make improvements and reap their full benefit. He will not be ejected as long as he pays fair judicial rents. Recusancy will be strictly dealt with and no transfer or prolonged, subletting—the besotting sin of this tenure carving country—will be tolerated.

18. The landholder on his side will mechanically get his share of rising prices. He will be able to put the guillotine through on recusancy. He will be able to enter into free contract of tenancy and will find to his contended and settled tenantry a perennial in place of the present precarious source of

affluence. He will be able to put his revenue on a basis which would not render it susceptible to arbitrary increase. The old order of feudalism is changing. The new era that is being ushered in needs not be without the element of mutuality that was the glory of middle ages. In pouring new wine into old bottles, there is no desire to break the old bottles. The fight between the manor and the farm was a stubborn one in Europe. In England the manor won. In France the victory lay with the farm. I want the contest to be a drawn one for this province and the stakes to be equally divided. The landholder will not be mediatised. He will not be merely a receiver of the rent charge. He will be interested as much in the security of his rent as in the increase of the output. His power to do good has not been curtailed along with his power to do evil. The sixth mode of ejectment is intended to keep up his position in the social economy. It is a replica of the landholder's sanad of good and loyal behaviour to the supreme lioga lord. He will be the man with comparative leisure. He will be the man who is representing volonte generals of the community will be prepared to work without remuneration. Democracy to be pure must be the rule by amateurs with leisure. Land is not workshop where the exploiter puts his money and the exploited his labour to produce agricultural wealth. It is mighty industry of the nation where wealth is produced on a profit sharing basis between the kisan and the zamindar. It is a partnership in rural arts, a partnership in agriculture a partnership in all that make citizenship valuable and a good to be desired. Co-operation instead of mutual exploitation is its moto. Noblesse oblige, instead of assertion of self, its motive power—lest the milkman in the heat of milking forget the calf.

19.II.—*Administrative abuses*—The most glaring that have come to my notice are those in connection with the forcible dispossession, (1) of tenants, (2) abuses about the issue of *pattas* and receipts, (3) fines to tenants, (4) excesses of estate servants, (5) compulsory purchases of grain, ghee and other articles from tenants at lower rates, (6) abuses about planting of trees.

20. The existing law 108 (10) is defective in so far as the

limitation within which relief is available is much too narrow. It may not be advisable to give a wider limit of time to the aggrieved party to proceed against the newly inducted tenant but so far as the evictor is concerned, the time limit should atleast be as long as the one for the recovery of movable article from another. The limitation runs for three years from the date of conversion. Damages will be assessable to the poor dispossessed tenant atleast. One has to read the voluminous evidence on record to be evinced that no need is paid to promise or *patta* if caprice or self-interest dictates dispossession.

21. *Pattas* are not generally issued or renewed after renewal of tenancy or levy of rent at a different rate. Levy of nazarana must mean change in the amount of rent and yet no fresh *patta* is executed from that day. Legislature must fix the standard form of patta and *kabuliat* and delivery of patta be made compulsory.

Receipts are not given as generally as one would desire. I urge that the form should be fixed one and printed receipts with proper foil and counterfoil forms should alone be used. In arrears of rent, suit the receipt book with the counterfoils must by filed. I have heard enough complaints to come to the conclusion that the whole amount preffered is not credited towards rent. This policy is likely to drive tenants to the expedient of dispatching rent by money order; concealed rents do exist but are not common.

22. *Fines.*—I have found that the zamindars who are representatives of the *Rajans*' (leaders of old, the leaders of the *Vaishyas* (inhabitants of the Vish or village) are in the habit of Inflicting fines for misdemeanours or moral deliquencies which according to Shastric injunction really belong under the category of amarcements to the Kind, i.e., the King-Emperor. The instances I have enumerated are sufficient to prove the prevalence of the system. The land-holders informed me that this system should come to end. (vide Exh. 0).

23. *Excesses of estate servants.*—These are inevitable where the tenantry have no right and the landholders are not interested

in the increase of the output of land. The instances enumerated show the existence of the evil. I recommend that landholder will hold daily katchery, bear complaints without let or hindrance, encourage tenants to pay rent at the zamindar's central place and there obtain receipts as well renewal of *pattas*. The collecting staff will not be required in its present strength if tenants are encouraged to go to the landholder and a quicker mode of realizing arrears is brought on the Statute Book. Exhibit T will be interesting as showing high cost of collection compared to cost of collection in Court of Wards estates. Multiplicity of servants on low pay brings about high cost of collection.

24. This evil is considerable. One has to read the instances given by me to be convinced that the system of taking gheee at from 25 to 100 per cent above the market rate, once or several times during the year or whenever wanted are some of the evils that do exist in connection with this valuable commodity. There is no justification for this. Similarly there is no justification in the feudal ratio of compulsory sale of grain to the extent of 10 per cent of the rental at a rate 2 seers above the market rate. It must be stopped.

25. *Trees.*—The grievances are many and as fuel is so scarce, the question intimately touches the daily life of agriculturists.

My findings are :—

(a) Spontaneously growing trees in shamil-jot-parli must be the exclusive property of the tenant. Other trees standing in the *shamil-jot-parti* can be dealt with according to the contract of tenancy.

(b) Tenants must have a right without let or hindrance to replace trees in their groves which have fallen down.

(c) Tenants planting trees in zamindar's *parti* have no right to object to the zamindar's suit for their removal if the suit is brought within six years of their planting or to assessment of a reasonable rent at any time on them. If neither rent is assessed nor suit brought for their removal, the tenant will have exclusive dominion utile over the tree planted by him, and on cutting or sale the landholder will get only his haq-i-chaharum. Consent will be presumed.

(d) The landholder can permit planting of trees after taking reasonable *nazarana*.

(e) Spontaneously growing trees in zamindar's *parti* are his property.

26. III.—*Raqm Siwai or extra rental demands.*—These are found to be of three kinds. Payment in cash-payment, in kind payment, in form of personal service.

I have given innumerable examples of abuse how the original simple system of offering of first fruits has been departed from till it has become oppressive to the tenants. The existing law is clear. No entry in the *wajib-ul-arz* is made unless the levy is well ascertained and definite and a definite proportion of rent or produce and not arbitrary items of payment are enjoyed (vide I, L, R. 35 All, 19). If there is no entry in the *wajib-ul-arz*, section 56, Act III of 1901, will prevent any court or revenue court from taking cognizance of an alleged custom. But as an items of contract of tenancy, rent court can give decree for sums which are the liquidated damages for non-payment of articles or non-performances of services. Section 56 is for the province of Agra only. For Oudh there is little case law.

27. *Attitude of Tenants.*—Tenants are willing to give one jhaos of bhusa per plough—the jhaos being of eight seers capacity. This I have ascertained by general cross—questioning. They are prepared to give one bundle of karbi per tenant, one reasonably sized jar of sugarcane juice and one rupee worth of ghee at double the market rate once a year in Bhadon if their cattle graze on the zamindar's parti free of charge. (Exhibit 64 E).

The leaders of the *Kisan Sabha* movement are changing their ground. Ram Chander Sharma exhorted the tenants to give 15 seers of bhusa, one bundle strau, one bundle of karbi, one jar cane juice. Then they changed their ground. (vide Exh. P) and now the cry is nothing but rent. Exhibit U, which are Pandit Gauri Shanker's demands, may be read.

28. My considered opinion after reading the statements of tenants and zamindars is that the fixed form of patta and kabuliat which landholders must be compelled to us, must not be allowed to contain any reference to raqm siwai items save for a maximum quantity of 12 seers of bhusa per plough—one bundle of karbi of 12 seers in weight or straw bandle of about 12 seers and one rupee as *bhent* for Holi and one rupee as *bhent* for Dasehra. These payments will not offend against the canon of definiteness which renders a contract void under section 29 of the Contract Act.

No reference to delivery of ghee which is not part of agricultural produce or kamal or goat be allowed to be made. These payments offend against the canon of definiteness, are oppressive and vexatious. All imposts on sugarcane growing must be abolished. They take the shape of sugarcane juice one or two jars, one rupee charged for planting a mill, sugarcane for chewing, 10 to 5 maunds of sugarcane for elephants, sugarcane for landholder's gur making. All other imposts levied as raqm siwai must cease. Sir Duncan Baillie has held in 1. Oudh Law Journal, 680, that entries in wajib-ul-arzes are admission in favour of landholders made in their own interests generally behind the backs of those adversely affected by them and are not binding on the latter.

29. I am not in favour of dropping cash nazars for Holi and Desehra but they must not exceed a maximum of one rupee on each occasion. This keeps up the agricultural nexus of landholder and tenant and does not allow the mercenary nexus of exploiter and the exploited to come to the fore. Swearing of allegiance on some fixed day to one's chief has its own utility. It reminds parties of their rights and responsibilities.

30. Service levies.—*Begar* and *hari* are taken in larger numbers than the old time-honoured system of requiring ploughing

in Asarh and ploughing in Katik, helping in transplantation of rice and working at the basket lift for rabi irrigation. The usual form of payment, i.e., parched grain for half day's work and two seers of grain for the whole day's work has been grossly departed from. The number of days tenants have compulsorily to work on certain farms is one day in every eight days. Refusal is resented. Wages paid are admittedly 250 to 300 per cent, below the market rate. Sometimes nothing is paid. I would still leave one hari in the year and one begar in the year as legitimate levels that might form part of the agreement of tenancy but none more. No payment less than the customary one or two seers of grain will be made for the day's work. The sting in begar lies in the fact that one has to work whether one likes it or not. The zamindar resents reluctance to work when he is prepared to pay full wages. Landholders should take to the system of chakrana tenures to ensure a ready flow of menial services required for the various processes of agriculture.

31. In this connection I may note that as Exhibit E will make it clear that the increase in the area of sir has rendered the employment of begar labour very necessary. The statement of witness No. 750 will make it clear that unlimited demand on personal services on full remuneration will not be easily met. The result is great resentment on either side. It will take sometime before rural economy adjusts itself and a class ready to work for adequate hire comes into being.

32. It is said that the present discontent is the protest of the lower classes against what they consider to be unbearable imposts levied on them because of their Shudra class. To a certain extent this is true. Brahmins and Kshattriyas are not expected to render any raqm siwai save the annual bhent. But the contest between landholders and the tenants and as one Brahmin put it they are in some estates shorn equally all round. All the same in patti tahsil, the Shudras alone have to bear the levy. They alone render begar labour and whether paid for or not have willy nilly to remain away from their own cultivation. Exhibit G, will also make it clear that *razil* rents are 25 per cent, to 300 per cent, higher than *sharif* rentals.

33. IV.—An impossible list of imposts was put forward in the doctored applications sent up from the Oudh *Kisan Sabha.* I am glad to note for the good name of the landholders of the district that save in a few cases and those in regard to a few cases the allegations were without foundation. I specifically questioned tenants about these cases and judgement did not go by default because tenants omitted to complain about an impost.

34. It was definitely proved that all impost was levied on tenants of a particular estate when its proprietor got the title of Raja. It was explained that tenants who were invited to the investiture ceremony gave the offering as nazar. Evidence on record disclosed the fact that the offering was not altogether voluntary.

35. In another estate there was evidence of lottery tickets having been freely issued to tenants for a sum double in amount to the admitted value of the article to be disposed of and tenants had to purchase a lottery ticket for a horse willy nilly whether they wanted to have the horse or not. This was a kind of impost neither authorised by old usage not by public opinion.

36. In other estate money was raised from tenants in order to enable the landholder's manager to have a motor car. The evidence on record fully convinces me of this illegal levy. In the same estate a levy was started to replace an elephant that had died but it remained without response.

37. Money was levied in one estate for the purchase of an elephant. Tenants have clearly deposed of it. The landholder alleged that he borrowed the money for the purchase of the elephant. I am inclined to think that the amount borrowed was to supplement the amount raised by the cess or it may be that a cess was levied to pay off the elephant debt.

38. Money was taken under the name of War subscriptions or reorbiting subscriptions, but the sums were really nazaranas made to mosquerade under the name which rendered realization in those days of storm and stress easy. This mode of rising ordinary nazarana was highly blameworthy.

39. Fixity of tenure and improvement in public opinion will put an end to this abuse.

40. There was complaint that a certain lavy of 10 per cent was made for *nachna* or a marriage of son, or daughter. Naved money is taken in a girl's marriage but not in a boy's. It is kind a kind of "aid" levied from one's tenants. When tenants come into their own, they will willingly offer this aid, provided that it is not of the nature of a cess but a reasonably small fixed sum. I see nothing vexatious or unreasonable in this levy for a daughter's marriage. To help in giving away a daughter in a marriage is an act of merit both amongst the Hindus and Musalmans.

41. V.—Tenants enjoy a right of irrigation from existing tanks, but this right has been encroached upon by the wanton way in which landholders have appropriated these tanks to individual use of tenants who have cut the ramparts of the tank, let out the water and sown the land with crops. The tenants of the village complained bitterly against this invasion of their easement. They were prepared to pay for the exercise of this right of taking water but they objected to being shut out.

42. Similarly tenants objected to the enclosure of the common parti by the landholder. Their cattle used to graze on this parti. Now the zamindar has converted it into arable land or put plantlings in the area, so that it may be converted into a grove. Some zamindars prevent the cattle of tenants from grazing on the parti which they reserved for their own cattle only. Tenant's cattle have enjoyed the common of grazing and this right, if invaded upon, will be bitterly resented. The zamindar can levy a small fee to regulate grazing but the tenants cattle cannot be shut out unless some parti is seprately reserved for them. Some zamindars maintained that one fourth the arable area must be under pasture by Statute. The Government must do something to have fodder preserves for cattle because the landholders are short-sighted and the tenants in the satisfaction of their land hanger are no less conspiring with them in the fast conversion of parti into arable land.

43. Village tracts are being encroached upon and right of way are being seriously interfered with. The village Panchayat Act can go a long way to regulate the evil.

44. Lastly I would strongly recommend the appointment of a development officer for each district to direct all the rural activities of agriculturists in proper channels—co-ordinate in himself co-operative and agricultural propagands and remould the life of the country faster and more systematically then a Central Officer can do.

Glossary

Amani	Held in trust or deposit; revenue remitted when amount is based on actual collection without any previously stipulated terms.
Amil	Officer of the Government, especially a collector of revenue or a farmer of the revenue; contracter for revenue invested with supreme authority both civil and military.
Amin	Surveyor, auditor, subordinate officer.
Asami	Cultivator, tenant, one who tills the soil.
Badhni	Loan for meeting revenue payments made on the security of the crop.
Basta	Bundle; file of papers tied together.
Bedakhli	Eviction of tenant from holding.
Bhaiacharya	Tenure in which lands of a village held jointly by co-sharers are apportioned among holders on an equal basis.
Bigha	Measures of land, in upper India (Awadh) usually standardised at 3,025 squares yards or 2/3 to 5/8 of an *acre*.
Birt	Maintenance grant awarded by a land-holder.
Birtia	Holder of a *birt*.
Biswadar	Holder of a share or shares in a coparcenery village, especially under a superior taluqdar.

Chakladar	Superintendent or collector of the revenue of a *Chakla*, i.e., a large division of country comprehending a number of *parganas*.
Chaudhari	Headman, usually of a village.
Dastak	Passport, permit; warrant, especially for revenue default.
Dastur-ul-amal	Rules, regulations, manual of management.
Diwan	Chief Officer of state, especially head financial minister charged with the collection of the revenue.
Durbar	Court, hall of royal audience; the holding of a court.
Girdawar	Patrol, watch; on officer who goes on circuit to supervise the work of subordinate officials.
Guzara	Living, subsisting; tenure for providing and individual's subsistence.
Halqa	Circle, group of villages.
Haq	A right.
Huzur tahsil	System of revenue collection in which head of village proprietory body pays revenue directly to government treasury.
Ijara	Price, profit, especially to denote the forming or lease of revenue of an area on a contract basis.
Ilaqa	Area of land; estate, division of territory.
Inam	Gift from a superior to an inferior; land free of either rent or revenue.
Jagir	Land of which the revenue was made over to an individual, usually as payment for service.
Jama	Sum, total, total rent or revenue payable by cultivators to a landlolder; total government revenue assessed on land.

Kachcha	Unripe, crude, built of unbaked bricks; below standard, uncertain, ineomplete.
Kankut	A method of crop appraisement when a standing crop is surveyed and an estimate is made by the landlord's agent of the likely yield.
Khalisa	Lands not given out as *inam* or *jagir* or held by an intermediary; land for which government dues are paid directly by officers of the government.
Kham	Raw, unripe, settlement made with cultivators without the intervention of a *zamindar*, hence an estate managed directly by officers of the government.
Kharif	Autumn, the fall harvest, fall crops.
Khudkhasht	Resident, as contrasted with non-resident (*paikasht*); settled, permanent.
Kisan	Peasant, cultivator.
Lakhiraj	Land free from revenue payment.
Lakhirajdar	Holder of *lakhiraj* land.
Mahal	Revenue paying unit; palace.
Malguzar	One who pays revenue; landholder.
Malik	Landholder, owner.
Malikana	Allowance, usually a percentage of government revenue paid to a zamindar or *malquzar*. under the British awarded also to those excluded from settlement in recognition of a former title.
Muafi	Land held free of rent or revenue.
Muafidar	Holder of *muafi* land.
Muhafizdafter	Record Keeper.
Mukhtar	Agent, representative, attorney; but not empowered to plead in court.

Muqaddam Chief, leader, headman of a village or caste.

Mushtarka Shared or a form of join zamindari.

Mustajir One who hold lands under a proprietor at a stipulated rent, revenue farmer collecting on behalf of a zamindar on payment of a fixed sum.

Nankar Allowance or payment in land or money, usually in return for service to the government.

Nazim Administrator, governor, superior officer of a province in charge of police and criminal law.

Nazr Gift or offering from an inferior to a superior.

Nazarana Tribute, present, gift.

Nikasi Total net proceeds or income, assessed valuation.

Nizamat Office of nazim; government, administration.

Nuzul Property that falls to state as escheat on failure of heirs; crown or government land.

Pakka Ripe, mature; of baked brick, solid, permanent; land held at a fixed rent.

Pargana Revenue sub-division of a district group of villages of which several go to make a *chakla* or a *tahsil.*

Patta Deed of lease; document given to the tenant by the landlord as proof of the former's right to cultivate lease land.

Patti Part or portion of a village; division of land; in N.W.P. and Awadh, a share in a coparcenary village or estate.

Pattidar Holder of a *patti* (share).

Patwari One who keeps the revenue accounts for one or more villages, village account.

Peshkar	Assistant; manager, deputy, agent, one exercising delegated authority in revenue and customs affairs.
Pukhtadar	Holder of land on fixed rental; under proprietor with whom a sub-settlement was made.
Qabuliyat	Written agreement, especially signifying assent or acceptance.
Qabz	System of payment in which soldiers porcure their own pay from a given area; seizure confiscation.
Qanungo	*Pargana* accountant or registrar.
Quist	Portion, instalment, usually of revenue.
Qistbandi	Settlement or payment by instalment.
Rabi	Spring, spring harvest, spring crops.
Royat	Agriculturist, subject, especially a cultivator.
Royatwari	Settlement directly with the cultivator for revenue payment.
Srdr	As a noun: headquarters, seat of government. As an adjective; main, chief, principal.
Sanad	Grant, diploma, charter, patent, document conveying to an individual title, privileges or rights to revenue.
Sarkar	The Government, a district.
Sarishtadar	Record keeper, especially head Indian Officer of a court of justice or of a Collector's office.
Shankalapdar	Holder of a charitable land grant (*sankalpa*); holder of rent free land.
Shikmi	Subordinate cultivator, sub-tenant.
Sir	Lands cultivated by a landholder or village zamindar directly or with hired labour; home farm.
Suba	Province of a state or kingdom.

Subadar	Governor of a province.
Tahsil	Sub-division of a district, or an estate, under the charge of a tahsildar. In British administration intermediate in size between district and *pargana.*
Tahsildar	Officer in charge of a *tahsil*; collector of revenue or rent from a *tahsil.*
Taluqa	Dependence upon, or connection with a superior; a collection of villages formed into an estate.
Taluqdar	Holder of an estate, or taluqa; in Awadh after 1858 only those so designated by the British.
Taqavi	Advance of money to cultivators at sowing time, in bad season or for capital investment.
Theka	Contract, usually entitling the holder in return for the payment of a specified sum to collect rent or other produce on an estate.
Thekadar	Holder of a *Theka*; contractor.
Ugahmi	A leavy on cultivators.
Waj-i-bularz	Village paper or document regarding local rights, duties and obligations of agrarian population.
Zamindar	Landholder; one who controls land and is responsible for the payment of the assessed revenue to the government, under the British a landowner.
Zila	District, tract under jurisdiction of a British collector or Deputy Commissioner.
Ziladar	District Superintendent; Collector of rent for an estate.

Bibliography

Uttar Pradesh State Archives WCK now (UPSA)

The bulk of research for this work was carried out in the Uttar Pradesh State Archives, Lucknow, U.P.; Office of the Uttar Pradesh Board of Revenue, Lucknow and the Regional Centre of U.P. State Archives, Allahabad. The series of records that proved most useful were :

(a) The *Oudh Revenue District Records* of Faizabad, Pratapgarh, Bahraich, Sitapur, Sultanpur, Unnao and Rae-Bareli. The *Oudh District Files* are indexed in individual printed volumes.

(b) *The Board of Revenue Oudh General Series*, bound together by subject, for the period under study. This is the most comprehensive set of documents for the development of revenue policy in Awadh.

(c) The *Proceedings* of the Government of North-Western Provinces and Oudh, 1860-1900—United Provinces of Agra and Oudh 1900-1921 and United Provinces. The *Revenue Proceedings*, printed, bound and indexed annually, are a necessary supplement to the Board of Revenue Records for the period under study, and are particularly full for the Oudh settlement revision during the second summary settlements in the province.

(d) The Commissioner's Records for Lucknow and Faizabad Divisions valuminous but poorly indexed, these files duplicate much available elsewhere.

(e) *Butler Collections* (Microfilm).

(1) IOR MSS EURF. 116/63, *Harcourt Butler Collection.* Two pamphlets by Harcourt Butler on Oudh Policy (1896, 1906) with letters and reviews on the second, memorandum on the Oudh Rent Act.

(2) IOR MSS EURF. 116/80, *Butler Collection*, Memoranda, accounts of meetings with the taluqdars and correspondence on the amendment of the Oudh Rent Act, correspondence with some of the taluqdars 1921-1922.

(3) IOR MSS EURF. 116/104, *Butler Collection*, Report on the administration of the United Provinces of Agra and Oudh by Harcourt Butler.

(f) *Hailey Papers.*
(g) *Haig Papers.*

National Archives, New Delhi (NAI)

The Foreign, Political and Secret Consultations contain the fullest account of British relations with the Nawabs of Awadh, the annexation of that province under the course of the Revolt of 1857-58, restoration of taluqdari system in Awadh and subsequently the Land Revenue Policy of the Government of India with special reference to Awadh.

Nehru Memorial Museum and Library (NMML), New Delhi.

(a) The proceedings of the 'British India Association of Oudh' (BIA) and personal papers of few taluqdars are preserved here. They provide a detailed account of working of the taluqdars' Association and its dealings with the Government. These papers throw light on the informal distribution of powers within the association or on the activities of individual taluqdars during the period under study.

(b) Ram Chandra's Manuscript Diary (This was secured by Shrimati Jaggi, the widow of Baba Ram Chandra of village Dandpur, Tahsil Patti, District Pratapgarh).

Unpublished thesis in the Tagore Library, University of Lucknow, Lucknow.

(a) *Nasir-ud-din Haider, King of Oudh*, 1827-1837 by Mohammad Ahmad Taqi.

(b) *Two Kings of Awadh: Muhammad Ali Shah and Amjad Ali Shah* by Safi Ahmad.

(c) *Awadh undar Saadat Ali Khan,* 1808-1914 by Nafees Ahmad Siddiqi.

(d) *History of Revenue Administration in the Ceded and conquered Provinces,* 1801-1803 by R.N. Nagar.

(e) *The Role of the Taluqdars of Awadh during the Revolt of 1857-58 in Awadh* by Virendra Deo Pandey.

(f) *Uttar Prudesh in Transition: Changes in its Agrarian Structure* by Prashant Mishra.

(g) *Growth and Development of Agrarian Legislation in U.P.* by S.M.S. Sinha.

(h) *The Administration of the United Provinces of Agra and Oudh under Sir William Malcolm Hailey* (1928-1934) by A.K. Mishra.

(i) *Land Revenne Administration of Awadh* Dr. Virendra Deo Pandey.

News Papers :

The Abhyudaya, 1917-22 & 1945, NAI.

The Aaj, 1920, Benaras.

The Independent, 1919-22 (micro-film) NMML.

The Leader, 1917-22 (micro-film) NMML.

The Pioneer, 1920-22, Lucknow.

The U.P. Native Press Report, 1918-22, NAI.

Gazetteers and Settlement Reports :

Bannett, W.C. (ed.), *Oudh Gazetteers,* Vol. I. Lucknow, 1887.

Nevill, H.R. (ed.), *District Gazetteer,* Vol. XXII, Allahabad.

Nevill, H.R. (ed.), *District Gazetteer—Rae Bareli,* Vol. XXXIX, Allahabad, 1905.

Nevill, H.R. (ed), *District Gazetteer—Pratapgarh*, Vol. XLVII, Allahabad, 1904.

Nevill, H.R. (ed.), *District Gazetteer—Sultanpur*, Vol. XLVI, Allahabad, 1903.

Nevill, H.R. (ed.), *District Gazetteer—Bahraich*, Vol. XLV, Allahabad, 1903.

Nevill, H.R. (ed.), *District Gazetteer—Gonda*, Vol. XLIV, Allahabad, 1908.

Nevill, H.R. (ed.), *Distvict Gazetteer—Barabanki*, Vol. XLVIII, Allahabad, 1905.

Nevill, H.R. (ed.), *District Gazetteer*—Unnao, Vol. XX-XVIII, Nainital, 1907.

Nevill, H.R. (ed.), *District Gazetteer—Hardoi*, Vol. XLI, Lucknow, 1908.

Nevill, H.R. (ed.), *District Gazetteer—Sitapur*, Vol. XL, Nainital, 1904.

Government of India, *Imperial Gazetteer*, Vol. III & IV, Oxford, 1907.

Bradford, E.O., Harrington, A.H., & Blennerhassett, W., *Hardoi Settlement Report*, Lucknow, 1880.

Browning, F.W., *Sultanpur Settlement Report*, Allahabad, 1898.

Clarks, E.G., *Bahraich Settlement Report*, Lucknow, 1873.

Forbes, W.E., *Pratapgarh Settlement Report*, Lucknow, 1877.

Saunders, J., *Pratapgarh Settlement Report*, Lucknow, 1896.

Butt, M.N., *Lucknow Settlement Report*, Lucknow, 1898.

Frementle, S.H., *Rae Bereli Settlement Report*, Allahabad, 1898.

House, H.F., *Fyzabad Settlement Report*, Lucknow, 1900.

Macandrew, J.F., *Rae Bareli Settlement Report*, Lucknow, 1872.

Millett, A.F., *Fyzabad Settlement Report*, Lucknow, 1880.

Millett, A.F., *Sultanpur Settlement Report*, Lucknow, 1873.

Ferrar, M.L., *Sitapur Settlement Report*, Lucknow, 1875.

Benett, W.C., *Gonda Settlement Report*, Lucknow, 1878.

ACTS :

Act XIX of 1868 (*The Oudh Sub-Settlement Act*).

Act XXXII of 1871 (*The Oudh Civil Law Courts Act*).

Act XVII of 1876 (*The Oudh Land Revenue Act*).

Act XVIII of 1876 (*The Oudh Laws Act*).

Act X of 1869, 1873, 1885. (*The Oudh Estate Act*).

Act XXII of 1886 (*The Oudh Rent Act*).

Act III of 1901 (*The Oudh Land Revenue Act*).

Act IV of 1901 (*The Oudh Rent Amendment Act*).

Act VII of 1921 (*The Oudh Rent Amendment Act*).

Act III of 1921 (*The U.P. Tenancy Act*).

Government Reports and other Publications :

Agrarian Distress in the United Provinces (*Being the* Report of the Committee appointed by the Council of the U.P. Provincial Congress Committee of enquire into the Agrarian situation in the Province), Allahabad, 1931.

Annual Report on the Administration of the Provinces of N.W.P. and Oudh, 1856-1920.

Digest of Chief Commissioner's Circular order upto 31st December, 1874, Lucknow, 1875.

Digest of Circulars Relating to the Jurisdiction and Procedure of the Revenue Courts and the Conduct of Settlement Operations in Oudh, compiled by G.E. Erskins, Luknow, 1871.

Land Revenue Policy of the Indian Government (Resolution recorded by the Governor-General of India in Council on the 16th January, 1902), Calcutta, 1920.

Alphabetical Index to Old Oudh Records for the years 1858 to 90 (Oudh General), Allahabad, 1942.

Alphabetical Index to Old Oudh Records, Bahraich district, Allahabad, 1941.

Alphabetical Index to Old Oudh Records, Gonda District. Allahabad, 1941.

Alphabetical Index to Old Oudh Records, Lucknow District, Allahabad, 1942.

Alphabetical Index to Old Oudh Records, Bahraich District, Allahabad, 1941.

Alphabetical Index to Old Oudh Records, Sultanpur District, Allahabad, 1942.

Alphabetical Index to Old Oudh Records, Unao district, Allahabad, 1942.

Alphabetical Index to Old Oudh Records, Kheri district, Allahabad, 1941.

Alphabetical Index to Old Oudh Records, Rae Bareli district, Allahabad, 1941.

Alphabetical Index to Old Oudh Records, Hardoi district, Allahabad, 1941.

Alphabetical Index to Old Oudh Records, Fyzabad district, Allahabad, 1941.

Alpabetical Index to Old Oudh Records, Pratapgarh district, Allahabad, 1922.

Alphabetical Index to Old Oudh Records, Sitapur district, Allahabad, 1921.

Papers Relating to the Administration of Oude, 1861-1864.

Papers Relating to the Administration of Oude, 1865.

Review of the Revenue Administration of the Province of Oudh, 1865-77.

Revenue Administration Report, 1930.

Report of Rent Law Commission, 1880 (Bengal).

Report of Royal Commission on Agriculture in India, 1928.

Report on Agriculture in United Provinces, prepared for the Royal Commision on Indian Agriculture, 1926.

Report of Irrigation Commission, 1901-03.

Report, Annual, Irrigation Department, U.P., 1921, 26.

Report, on the Administration of the Department of Agriculture, 1928.

Report of the Board of Revenue on the Revenue Administration of U.P., and Oudh, 1905-07.

Report on Imprervement of India Agriculture by Dr. J.A. Voelc-kar, U.P., 1893.

Report (annual) Agriculture Department, 1870 to 1900 and 1921-1926, U.P.

Report on Revenue Administration. 1918-1926.

Reoport on enquiry regarding cesses in Oudh, 1922, by D.M. Stewart, 1923.

Report of Revenue Administration, United Provinces, 1883-1884.

Report of Revenue Administration, 1907-08.

Report of Administration in United Provinces, 1900-1901.

Report of Adminisration in United Provinces, 1921.

Reports of a Royal Commission on Agriculture in India, 1928.

Revenue Administration in United Provinces of Agra and Oudh, by W.H. Moreland, Allahabad, 1911.

Report of the United Provinces Provincial Banking Enquiry Committee, 1929-30, Vol. I & II.

Report on the condition of Tenantry in Oudh, Vol. I & II, 1933.

Report on Agriculture in the United Provinces, Prepared for Royal Commission on Indian Agriculture, 1926.

Report on the Agrarian situation in United Provinces, 1931.

Report of the United Provinces Zamindari Abolition Committe, Vol. I, Allahabad, 1948.

The Settlement Circulars on the Rise and Progress of Revenue Law in Oudh, 1904.

Rent and Revenue Policy in the United Provinces Prepared in 1931 by A.A. Waugh.

Selections from Revenue Records, Oudh, Government Press, Allahabad.

Proceedings of the Legislative Council of the United Provinces, 1981 to 1923, U.P. Government Press, Allahabad.

History of Services of Gazetted Officers (Civil Department) Attached to the United Provinces-corrected upto 1st July, 1919, Part I, U.P. Government Press, Allahabad, 1919.

Census of India, Vol. II, United Provinces, Report I.A. Report, Superintendent, Printing and Stationery, U.P., India, 1952.

Unrepealed Circulars of the Judicial Commissioner and of the Financial Commissioner of Oudh, Luknow, 1875.

Circulars of the Board of Revenue of the United Provinces, Volumes, I & II, Allahabad, 1907.

BOOKS :

Anstey V., *The Economic Development of India*, London, 1931.

Arathoon, J.H.W., *Oudh Tennures or the Laws Relating to Land Tennures in Force in Oudh*, Lucknow, 1885.

Ahmad, Shaikh Siddiqi, *Tarikh-i-Anjuman-e-Hind, Awadh*, Vols. I to III, Lucknow, 1927.

Aitchison, C.U., *A Collection of Treaties, Engagements and Sanads, Relating to India and Negihbouring countries*, Vol. II, Delhi, 1930.

Arnold, E., *The Marquis of Dalhousie's: Administration of British India*, London, 1865.

Ascoli, F.D., *Early Revenue History of Bengal and Fifth Report*, London, (n.d.)

Awasthi, D., *Administrative History of Modern India*, (Sir Spencer Harcourt Butler's Ideas, Policies and Activities in the United Provinces of Agra and Awadh, 1918-22), Delhi, 1973.

Baden-Powell, B.H., *Land System of British India*, 3 Volumes, London, 1972.

Baden-Powell, B.H., *Short Account of the Land Revenue*, Oxford, 1907.

Ball, C., *The History of the Indian Mutiny*, 2 Volumes, London, 1858-59.

Banerjee, D.N., *Early Land Revenue System in Bengal and Bihar*, Vol. I and II, Calcutta, 1949.

Basu, Purendra, *Oudh and the East India Company*, 1785-1801, Lucknow, 1943.

Basu, D.M., *The Transferability of Occupany Rights*, Calcutta, 1912.

Banett, W.C., *A Report on the Family History of the Chief Clans of Roy Barelly* District, Lucknow, 1870.

Bhatnagar, G.D., *Awadh Under Wajid Ali Shah*, Varanasi, 1968.

Bhargava, G.S., *The Criminal Tribes : Social and Economic Study of the Principal Criminal Tribes and Castes in Northern India*, Lucknow, 1945.

Bhargava, B.K., *Indian Peasant Proprietorship*, Bombay, 1936.

Butler, Donald, *Outlines of the Topography and Statistics of the Southern Districts of Oudh*, Calcutta, 1859.

Campbell, C., *Memories of My Indian Career*, Volumes I, II, London, 1893.

Carnegy, P., *Notes on the Land Tenures and Revenue Assessment of Upper India*, London, 1874.

Chaudhari, S.B., *Civil Rebellion in the Indian Mutinies* (1857-59), Calcutta, 1957.

Chand, T.P., *The Administration of Awadh* (1858-1877), Varanasi, 1971.

Chandra, Bipan, *The Rise and Growth of Economic Nationalism in India,* (Economic Policies of Indian National Leadership, 1880-1905), New Delhi, 1969.

Chesney, George, *Indian Polity*, London, 1894.

Crooke, W., *Natives of Northern India,* London, 1907.

Das, M.N., *Studies in the Economic and Social Development of Modern India* : 1848-56, Calcutta, 1959.

Datta, Davijadas, *Landlordism in India*, Bombay, 1931.

Datta, B.N., *Dialectics of Land-Economics of India*, Calcutta, 1952.

Driver, P.N., *Problems of Zamindari and Land Tenure Reconstruction in India,* Bombay, 1949.

Dhanagre, D.N. *Agrarian Movement and Gandhian Politics*, Agra, 1975.

Dutt, Romesh, *The Economic History of India*, Volumes I & II, New Delhi, 1960.

Edwardes, M., *The Orchid House*, London, 1960.

Elliot, C.A., *The Chronicles of Unnao*, Allahabad, 1862.

Erskine, G.E., *Digest of Circular Relating to the Jurisdiction and Procedure of the*

Revenue Courts and the conduct of Settlement Operations in Oudh, Lucknow, 1871.

Field, C.D., *Landholding and the Relation of Landlord and Tenant in various Countries*, Calcutta, 1883.

Frykenberg, R.E., (ed.), *Land Control and Social Structure in Indian History*, wisconsin, 1969.

Ghani, Najmul, *Tarikh-i-Awadh*, Volumes I to V, Lucknow.

Ghoshal, B.C., *Some Notes on Raja Nanpara or the Tragic Story of the Premier Muhammedan Estate in Oudh*, Lucknow, 1918.

Gopal, S., (ed.), *Selected Works of Jawaharlal Nehru*, Volume I, New Delhi, 1972.

Guha, R., *A Rule of Property for Bengal*, La-Haye, 1963.

Gupta, S.C., *Agrarian Relations and Early British Rule in India*, London, 1963.

Habib, Irfan, *Agrarian System of the Mughal Empire*, London, 1963.

Heber, Bishop, *Heber's Journal or Narrative of a Journey Through the Upper Provinces of India from Culcutta to Bombay*, 1924-25, London, 1828.

Husain, I., *British Land Revenue Policy in North India*, 1801-33, Calcutta, 1967.

Hussani, Kamaluddin Haider, *Qaisar-ut-Tawarikh*, Lucknow, 1897.

Irwin, H.C., *The Garden of India or Chapters on Oudh History and Affairs*, London, 1880.

Jafri, S.N., *History and Status of Landlords in the United Provinces*, Allahabad, 1932.

Jagdish Raj, *The Mutiny and British Land Policy in North India*, 1856-1868, Bombay, 1965.

Joshi, G.N., *Indian Administration*, London, 1938.

K-nighton, W., *The Private Life of an Eastern King*, Oxford, 1921.

Lucas, Samuel, *Dacoitee in Excelsis or the spoliation of Oude by the East India Company*, New Edition, Lucknow, 1971.

Maine, H.S., *Village Communities in the East and West*, New York, 1876.

Mac Andrew, I.F., *Some Revenue Matters chiefly in the Province of Oudh*, Calcutta, 1876.

Maurya, R.R., *Uttar Pradesh Land Laws*, Allahabad, 1978.

Masihuddin, Maulvi Mohd., *Oudh : Its Princess, and its Government Vindicated*, London, 1857.

Malaviya, H.D., *Land Reforms in India*, Bombay, 1956.

Misra, B.R., *Land Revenue Policy in the United Provinces under British Rule*, Benares, 1942.

Mookerjee, R.R., *Occupancy Rights*, Calcutta, 1919.

Mookerjee, R.K., *Land Problems of India*, London, 1933.

Mookerjee, Radha Rumud, *Indian Land System, Ancient, Medieval and Modern with special reference to Bengal*, Calcutta, 1936.

Moreland, W.H., *The Revenue Administration of the United Provinces*, Allahabad, 1911.

Moreland, W.H., *The Agrarian System of Moslem India*, Cambridge, 1929.

Metcalf, T.R., *The Aftermath of Revolt : India, 1857-70*, Princeton, 1965.

Metcalf, T.R., *Land, Landlords and the British Raj*, Oxford, 1978.

Nanda, B.R., *The Nehrus : Motilal and Jawaharlal*, London, 1962.

Nehru, Jawaharlal, *An Autobiography*, London, 1936.

Narain, D., *The Impact of price Movements on Areas under selected crops in India*, 1900-39, Cambridge, 1965.

Patel, G.D., *The Indian Land Problem and Legislation*, Bombay, 1934.

Paton, J., *The British Government and the Kingdom of Oudh*, 1764-1835, Edited by Bisheshwar Prasad, Allahabad, 1944.

Pemble, John, *The Raj, the Indian Mutiny and the Kingdom of Oudh* (1801-1859), Sussex, 1977.

Phillips, A., *The Law Relating to Land Tenures in Lower Bengal,* (Tagore Law Lectures) Calcutta, 1876.

Probyn, J.W., *Systems of Land Tenure in Various Countries,* London, 1876.

Pande, M.B., *Oudh Ke Kisanon Ki Durdasha,* Allahabad, 1921.

Pande, M.B., *Kisanon Ki Phansi,* Allahabad, 1921.

Pandey, G., *The Indian National Congress and Political Mobilisation in the United Provinces,* 1926-34, Oxford University, 1975.

Pandey, V.D., *Man Singh of Shahganj and the Revolt of 1857,* Lucknow, 1972.

Pandey, V.D., *The Taluqdars of Awadh and Eighteen Fifty-seven,* Lucknow, 1978.

Prichard, I.T., *The Administration of India,* 1858-1868, London, 1869.

Raikes, Charles, *Notes on the North Western Provinces of India,* London, 1852.

Ray, S.C., *Land Revenue Administration in India,* Calcutta, 1952.

Rousseau, S., *A Dictionary of Mohammendan Law, Bengal Revenue Terms, Shanscrit, Hindoo, and other words used in East Indies,* London, 1802.

Sarvadhikari, R.K., *The Taluqdari Settlement in Oudh,* Calcutta, 1882.

Saksena, M.P., *A Commentary on the Oudh Rent Act* (Act XXII of 1886), Hardoi, 1925.

Sen, S.K., *Agrarian Struggle in Bengal*, 1946-47, New Delhi, 1972.

Shamin, T., (ed.), *Peasants and Peasant Societies*, London, 1971.

Siddique, A., *Tarikh Anjuman Hind Oudh*, Volumes I, II & III, Lucknow, 1937.

Siddiqui, Majid Hayat, *Agrarian Unrest in Northern India United Provinces* (1918-1922), Bombay, 1965.

Singh, V.B., (ed.), *Economic History of India* (1857-1956), Bombay, 1965.

Sitaramayya, Pattabhi, *History of the Indian National Congress*, Volumes I & II, Bombay, 1969.

Singh, Baljit and Misra, Shridhar, *A Study of Land Reforms in U.P.* Lucknow, 1958.

Strachey, J., *India, Its Administration and Progress*, London, 1911.

Sykes, J.G.W., *Compendium of Oudh Taluqdari Law*, Calcutta, 1885.

Sleeman, W.H., *A Journey through the Kingdom of Oude*, (1849-1850), London, 1858.

Srivastava, A.L., *The First Two Nawabs of Awadh*, Agra, 1954.

Srivastava, A.L., *Shuja-ud-Daulah*, Agra, 1956.

Whitecombe, E., *Agrarian Conditions in Northern India*, Volume I, New York, 1971.

Wolf, E., *Peasant, Wars of the Twentieth Century*, London, 1971.

Articles :

Bahaduri, A., Agriculture Backwardness Under Semi-Feudalism, *The Economic Journal*. 1973.

Cohn, B.S., Comments on Papers on Land Tenure, *The Indian Economic Social History Review*, Volume I, No. 2.

Crawley, W.F.. Kisan Sabhas and Agrarian Revolt in United Provinces, 1920-21, *Modern Asian Studies*, Volume 5, 1971.

Crane, Robert, The Indian National Congress and the Indian Agrarian Problem, *Indian Economic and Social History Review*, Volume I, No. 1, July—September, 1963.

Dhanagre, D.N., Peasant Protests and Politics—The Tebhaga Movement in Bengal (India) 1946-47, *The Journal of Peasant Studies*, Volume 3, No. 3, April, 1976.

Dhangre, D.N., Congress and Agrarian Legislation in Oudh, 1920-22 and 1930-32, *South Asian Studies*, No. 5, December, 1975.

Gough, Kathleen, Indian Peasant Uprisings, *Economic and Political Weekly*, Annual Number August, 1974.

Joshi, P.C., The Pre-Independence Thinking on Agrarian Policy, *Economic and Political Weekly*, Volume, 12, No. 8, 1867.

Kelkar, Govind, Kisan Unrest and the Congress in U.P., 1920-22, *Economic and Political Weekly*, Volume 52, December, 1975.

Metcalf, T.R., The Social Effects of British Land Policy in Oudh, in R. Frykenbery (ed.), *Land Control and Social Structure in Indian History*, Volume X, 1957.

Mital, S.K., Baba Ram Chandra and Peasant Upsurge in Oudh, 1920-21, *Social Scientist*, No. 71, 1978.

Pandey, G., Mobilisation in a Mass Movement : Congress Propaganda in the United Province (1930-34), *Modern Asian Studies*, Volume 9, No. 2, 1975.

Reevees, Peter, Agrarian Legislation and Rural Society in Uttar Pradesh, India : A Historical Study, *Modern Asian Studies*, Volume 8, No. 1974.

Reevees, Peter, Landlords Party Politics in the United Province, 1934-37, in Low (ed.) *Soundings in Modern South Asian History*, London, 1968.

Siddiqui, Majid, A note on Some Sources for the Study of Peasant Movements—*Proceedings of Indian History Congress*, 33rd Session, Muzaffarpur, 1972.

Siddiqui, Majid, The Peasant Movement in Pratapgarh, 1920, *Indian Economic and Social History Review*, Volume 9, No. 3, 1972.

Stoke, Eric, The Structure of Landholding in U.P. 1869-1948, *Indian Economic and Social History Review*, Volume 12, No. 2, April—June, 1973.

Tripathi, Amlesh, Land Revenue Policy, 1818-1905, Majumdar, R.C. (ed.), *British Paramountcy and Indian Renaissance*, Part IX, Bombay, 1965.

Index